THE
MAGYARS IN THE NINTH CENTURY

THE MAGYARS

in the

NINTH CENTURY

By

C. A. MACARTNEY

*Sometime Scholar of Trinity College
Cambridge*

CAMBRIDGE
AT THE UNIVERSITY PRESS
1930
REPRINTED
1968

Published by the Syndics of the Cambridge University Press
Bentley House, 200 Euston Road, London, N.W. 1
American Branch: 32 East 57th Street, New York, N.Y. 10022

PUBLISHER'S NOTE

Cambridge University Press Library Editions are re-issues of out-of-print standard works from the Cambridge catalogue. The texts are unrevised and, apart from minor corrections, reproduce the latest published edition.

Standard Book Number: 521 07391 x
Library of Congress Catalogue Card Number: 31-19298

First published 1930
Reprinted 1968

First printed in Great Britain at the University Press, Cambridge
Reprinted in Great Britain by John Dickens & Co. Ltd, Northampton

AUTHOR'S NOTE FOR CUPLE REPRINT

ONE new, and one pseudo-new, source have come to light since this book was first published. A fuller text of Ibn Fozlān has been discovered. The best of the many editions and translations is M. Canard, "La Relation du Voyage d'Ibn Fadlān chez les Bulgares de la Volga", *Annales de l'Institut d'Études Orientales*, XVI, Algiers, 1958, pp. 41–146. It contains nothing calculated to alter my analysis. In 1931 Professor V. Minorski discovered an "Universal Geography", compiled in Afghanistan in 982. He published the chapters of interest for this work in the *Nouvelle Revue de Hongrie* in April, 1937, and the whole in his volume, *Sharaf al-Zamān Ṭāhir Marvazī on China, the Turks and India*, London, 1942. The chapters of interest to us, at least, are simply another version of al-Dzaihāni. There are, it is true, a couple of variants in Report B: Mirvāt for M.rdāt and V.n.nd.r for N.nd.r. Minorski identifies the former with the Moravians and the latter with the Onoghundur or Onogurs. He regards my Reports B and C'', between which he does not distinguish, as locating the Magyars on "the North-Western corner of the Black Sea."

On the Western side, the outstanding development is the new edition of Constantine's *D.A.I.*, Vol. I, text, ed. G. Moravcsik, Vol. II, commentary, ed. R. J. H. Jenkins, with notes by six contributors, those on cc. 37–42 by Moravcsik, London, 1962. A considerable number of Hungarians have tried their hands at re-interpreting the material, in conjunction with the traditions reflected (with considerable distortion) in the Hungarian national Chronicles, and with archaeological, etc. data. Nearly all of this is in Magyar, but there is an excellent summary of their conclusions in two articles by T. Bogyay in the *Hungarian Quarterly*, N.Y., vol. 3, 1962 (the first on pre-history, the second on our period). Work published up to 1961 is listed also in a bibliography to the notes of the edition of Constantine (*op. cit.*, II. 142), and Moravcsik refers to some of them in his notes. None of these efforts, ingenious as many of them are, have moved me to abjure my main conclusions, nor, despite my enormous respect for his learning, does Moravcsik's refusal to accept them wring my withers.

I have myself seen the light on one point. Taking too easily the word of others, I assumed (p. 94) that Jordanes, c. 50, said that "Var" was the Huns' name for the Dnieper, and that the Βαρούχ of the *D.A.I.* c. 38 must be that river. I have shown the falsity of this in my article on "The End of the Huns", *Byzantinisch-Neugriechische Jahrbücher*, 1934. Var simply means "fortress", as it does in Magyar today, and refers in Jordanes to the natural fortress of the confluence of the Danube and the Tisza. There is no reason to connect it with the Dnieper, and the obvious transliteration of Βαρούχ is the Zbrucz, the other river-names referring respectively to the *head-waters* of the Pruth, Sereth, Dniester, and the *Polish* Bug. In other words, the place in which the Magyars spent the last years before crossing the Carpathians, which, again, Constantine does *not* say that they called Etelköz, was in East Galicia. This accords with their national tradition, properly interpreted (which it never is).

There was much dissent from my suggestion (p. 107) that the Κάγγαρ who drove the Magyars across the Don were the Circassians, and I would not go to the stake for it; but I have a point in what I write about the name, and I wish someone could find a better explanation than mine.

I also wish heartily that I had been a better proof-reader in 1930; above all, that I had corrected "Magyars" to "Bulgars" on p. 108, para. 3, 1.7, and emended the date given in the map for the Magyars' sojourn in Etelköz (Levedia) to 835, which is what I meant.

I still cannot see why anyone should want to emend the "three" years given by Constantine (c. 38) in connection with the Khazar-Magyar association. It seems to me completely obvious that the figure does not relate to the total length of the association, but only to the period which elapsed between its commencement and the Khazar Khagan's decision to reinforce it by a dynastic marriage.

Oxford, 1968   C. A. MACARTNEY

PREFACE

THIS work is an attempt to throw a little more light upon one of the darkest of historical riddles. Where so much has to be constructed by deduction and interpretation out of so little, no man can claim to have said the last word, or to have attained absolute certainty. I hope, however, to have made some contribution here to a subject which has occupied many pens in Central Europe, but hardly any in England. Many friends have given me much kind help and advice, and, if it does not seem ungracious to single out some rather than others, I should like here to express my especial gratitude to three persons: to Miss M. Smith, Ph.D., who very kindly made me the translations which I required from Arabic and Persian authors; to Professor Norman Baynes, who in the most selfless fashion read my manuscript in three several stages, and gave me advice, both as regards the matter and the manner, of inestimable value; and to Professor Németh, of Budapest University, to whom I am also most deeply indebted. I feel also that there is one book to which any worker in this field ought to express his peculiar indebtedness, more especially as the author of it is now no more: Professor Marquart's *Osteuropäische und ostasiatische Streifzüge*. Professor Marquart's writing is always difficult, and in many points of interpretation I have differed from his conclusions; but there is no more stimulating work than his, and in its field it is epoch-making.

1930   C. A. MACARTNEY

CONTENTS

Appendix; translated texts (cont.)

ABBREVIATIONS USED

D.A.I. = Constantine Porphyrogenetos, *De Administrando Imperio*, ed. Bonn.

U.J. = *Ungarische Jahrbücher.*

K.C.A. = *Körösi Csoma Archivum.*

Marquart, *Streifzüge* = J. Marquart, *Osteuropäische und ostasiatische Streifzüge* (Leipzig, 1903).

Marquart, "Komanen" = J. Marquart, "Ueber das Volkstum der Komanen" (*Abhandlungen der k. Gesellschaft der Wissenschaften zu Göttingen*, 1922).

Fehér, "Beziehungen" = G. Fehér, "Bulgarisch-Ungarische Beziehungen in den V–Xen Jahrhunderten" (*Keleti Szemle*, xix, No. 2, Pécs, 1921).

Fehér, "Gebietsgrenzen" = G. Fehér, "Ungarns Gebietsgrenzen in der Mitte des Xen Jahrhundertes" (*U.J.* Bd. ii, Heft 1, April, 1922).

B.Z. = *Byzantinische Zeitschrift.*

Migne, *P.G.* = *Patrologia Graeca*, ed. Migne.

Migne, *P.L* = *Patrologia Latina*, ed. Migne.

THE
MAGYARS IN THE NINTH CENTURY

INTRODUCTORY

THE problem of the origin and early wanderings of the Magyars has long perplexed scholars. It will be unnecessary to enter here into a history of this question; but it may be said, broadly speaking, to have passed through two main phases.

In the first, the Hungarian national tradition in its various forms, and the Byzantine and other written sources were taken as the main basis for investigation. Unfortunately, those sources proved to be so confused and mutually inconsistent, and the analysis of them was undertaken on so summary lines, that the results proved to be more than unsatisfactory. Hungarian scholars then attacked the problem from a different angle, and have achieved, especially within the last two decades, remarkable results from the application of painstaking methods of linguistic research. These results I naturally shall not question; but I am bound to state that the conclusions are neither so exhaustive nor in all respects so certain, as they are claimed to be. The linguistic results are necessarily intermingled with a considerable number of deductions based on the historical sources, or even on pure hypothesis. These latter conclusions I shall take leave to question, and hope to show here that a re-examination and closer analysis of the written sources is still able to throw a considerably new light on the riddle of early Magyar history, confirming the linguistic conclusions reached by Gombocz, Szinnyei, Zichy and others, but showing reason to abandon certain of the historical hypotheses which at present hold the field.

The certainties to which I refer seem to be the following:

(1) The Magyar nation belongs to the so-called Finnish-Ugrian group, its nearest neighbours within this group being the Voguls and Ostjaks. Its origin must therefore be sought in

the home of that linguistic group, viz. on the eastern slopes of the Ural mountains.[1]

(2) In their first home the Magyars were a nation of nomadic hunters and fishers, acquainted, however, with the use of metals; mounting at need on horseback, and living in tents.[2]

(3) At some period unknown they moved southward, and were in contact with Alanic and other Caucasian elements.

(4) At some period before the division of the Bulgarian race into its eastern and western halves, the Magyars were in close contact with, and probably dominated by a Bulgar race. Under Bulgarian influence, which probably extended from the fifth to the seventh centuries A.D., the Magyars became a semi-sedentary pastoral and agricultural nation. It would appear, also, that their religious convictions, and in part, their military tactics were transformed during this period.[3]

Almost all other conclusions regarding the early history of the Magyars are drawn from the written accounts, and susceptible of modification, if these are shown to be untrustworthy, or to be understood in a different light from that hitherto accepted.

Of the written sources, two far transcend all the others in importance. These are the *De Administrando Imperio* of Constantine Porphyrogenetos, and one Arabic account. The two are very different; Constantine's work purports to be a brief history, while the Arabic document is a geographical description, and therefore (apparently) static as regards time. This geographical description is, however, written at such a date that it ought to cover part at least of the period described by Constantine. Thus our two main accounts ought to be mutually confirmatory.

Unfortunately, as at present read, these two stories are not only mutually inconsistent, but also contradict themselves in many places. No reasonable interpretation can be given to

1 See B. Hóman, "Les récentes études sur l'origine des Hongrois", in the *Revue des études finno-ougriennes*, 1924, pp. 156 ff.

2 Count Stephen Zichy, *ibid.* 1923, p. 7.

3 Gombocz, "Die Bulgarische Frage und die Ungarische Hunnensage", *U.J.* 1922, pp. 194 ff., puts the date at fifth to seventh centuries; Fehér, *Beziehungen*, p. 37, at fourth to sixth centuries; but in the table of contents to the same volume, at A.D. 461/5–578.

either of them, much less to the two combined, which does not involve interpreting large parts of them in a very arbitrary fashion, or even ignoring much of them altogether. I propose, therefore, in the present essay, to submit each of these two documents to an entirely new analysis, from which it will, I hope, emerge that each of them is not homogeneous, but composite. The Arabic document consists, not of one, but of three descriptions of the Magyars, each clear enough in itself and each susceptible of corroboration from outside sources. These refer, however, to three different districts, and to two different periods of time. The Greek account, on the other hand, consists of two parallel versions, from different sources, of one story, which have been erroneously joined together. Each of these versions is sensible and consistent, and each agrees with the results yielded both by the Arabic source, as re-analysed, by subsidiary sources, and by linguistic and archaeological research; the whole forming a brief but coherent picture of the history of the Magyars during the ninth century after Christ.

I shall begin with consideration of the Oriental source.

4

<table>
<tr><td>

α

Khwārism merchant; wrote on the countries on and east of the Volga, early ninth century, and on the Magyars of the Cuban; to this was added

γ

further details on the Cuban Magyars and their neighbours in the Caucasus.

</td><td>

β

Probably a Slav prisoner of war in Constantinople. Wrote on Slavs, Rūs and Magyars on the Don. Rather later than α or γ.

</td></tr>
</table>

X

"The archetype." Added β to α, made one or two corrections to fit the new situation arising out of the move of the Petchenegs and Magyars. Perhaps added some fresh information. Wrote early tenth century A.D., and may be identical with al-Džaihānī.

Ibn Rusta. Early tenth century. Further emended X by omitting report on Petchenegs, and γ, and by other minor alterations; added some information from other sources.	Al-Džaihānī. If not identical with X, took him over with few variations, but may have made certain small changes and additions. Early tenth century.

Gardēzī. Wrote 1050–2. Reproduced Džaihānī in corrupt form, but with few conscious alterations. Also drew on Ibn Khordādbeh.	Al-Bekrī. ob. 1094. Summarised Džaihānī, introducing other information from Ibn Fozlān (about 925), Masʿūdī (about 940), and Ibn Jāqʿūb (late tenth century). Omitted all parts of Džaihānī which he thought superseded by his later sources. This involved omitting all of β.

PART I

The Oldest Report on the Countries of the North

VERSIONS AND SOURCES

AT some early period or periods, an Arabic or Persian report on the countries lying on each side of the Volga, from the Aral Sea in the East to somewhere near the Carpathians in the West, was compiled by an unknown hand or hands. The original of this report has been lost; but a great number of versions, at second, third or fourth hand, often differing widely from each other, have been preserved. The later the date of these versions, the more corrupt and distorted they usually are; thus that given by the Persian Šukrullah b. Sāhīb (who wrote in 1456),[1] the first known to Western scholars, and therefore the first basis for their investigations, is now known to be completely misleading.

There are, however, three versions of comparative purity and respectable antiquity.[2] None of them represents the original; but all are near enough to it to make it possible, by careful comparison of the three, to form some idea of how the original must have run.

These three versions are the following:

(1) An extract from the *Book of Precious Jewels*, written apparently in the early tenth century by the Arab Abū 'Alī Ahmad b. 'Omar ibn Rusta.[3]

---

1 This work was issued with French translation by Baron J. von Hammer-Purgstall in his *Sur les Origines Russes* (St Petersburg, Imprimerie de l'Acad. Imp. des Sciences, 1827). Comparison of Hammer-Purgstall's translations of Šukrullah, Ahmed of Tous, etc., with the earlier versions of the same reports given in the Appendices to this essay will show the hair-raising corruptions which the old descriptions underwent in course of transmission.

2 There are said to be two other versions of comparative purity; one in Muhammed-i-'Aufī's *Collection of Anecdotes*, the other the work of a Persian geographer discovered by the Russian traveller Tumanskij and reported on by him in the *Zapiski* of the Russian Archaeological Society, vol. 1 (St Petersburg, 1897); cf. Marquart, *Streifzüge*, p. xxx. As, however, neither of these works is available in Western Europe, I have had to confine my analysis to the three versions described below, which are also the three generally accepted as worth close attention.

3 The Arabic text, with Russian translation, was issued by Chvolson in his *Izvestija o Cosarach*, etc. (St Petersburg, 1889). The text was edited by de

(2) An extract from the chronicle of the Persian Abū Sa'id 'Ab al-Hajj b. ad. Daḥḥak b. Mahmud Gardēzī, who wrote 1050–2.[1]

(3) An extract from the *Book of Kingdoms and Roads* by the Spanish Arab Abū 'Ubaid 'Abdallāh b. 'Abd al-Azīz al-Bekrī, who died 1094.[2]

I append these three extracts, in parallel columns, at the end of this work, in a translation most kindly made for me by Miss M. Smith, Ph.D., of the London School of Oriental Studies. I believe this to be the first complete translation in English, at any rate in one volume.

It is generally assumed that these three extracts comprise three versions of a single, and homogeneous, earlier report; and it is further almost universally assumed that the common origin of all three was the work of al-Džaihānī, Vezir of the Samanides from 301 H. (913–14) and author of a *Book of Roads and Kingdoms*.[3]

This explanation, however, errs on the side of simplicity. The inter-relations between the three reports are more complicated. I hope to prove in this section that they are rather as shown in the table facing p. 5. Džaihānī is certainly the common source for al-Bekrī and Gardēzī; but these two writers have used their material very differently. Gardēzī has reproduced it with small change, except for his very considerable corruptions and mistranslations; al-Bekrī has done no more than summarise Džaihānī, adding or substituting further information from the later writers, Ibn Fozlān, Ibn Jāq'ūb and Mas'ūdī. Ibn Rusta's work may represent a third version of Džaihānī, in which case it is probably the nearest to the original of the three. None the

---

Goeje in his *Bibliotheca Geographica Arabicorum*, vol. VII (Leyden, 1892). The MS is in the British Museum (MS Add. 23,378). A recent translation, from Chvolson's Russian version, appeared in the *Slavonic Review*, vol. VIII, no. 22, July 1929.

1 Arabic text with Russian translation issued by W. Barthold in the *Zapiski* of the Académie Impériale des Sciences, série VIII, vol I, no. 4 (St Petersburg, 1897).

2 Arabic text with French translation issued by Défrémery in the *Journal Asiatique*, 1849. Al-Bekrī is known to us only through the extracts from his work preserved in Jāqūt's *Geographical Dictionary*.

3 Cf. Marquart, *Streifzüge*, p. xxxi *et passim*.

less, there are important additions, changes and omissions, in which Ibn Rusta varies from Džaihānī. It is also possible that Ibn Rusta and Džaihānī alike drew on a slightly older archetype, compiled in the early tenth century, but based on two main sources, each of which dates from the ninth century.

As our object is to discover (a) what were the contents of these two primary sources, which I have named α and β; and (b) what were the additions made by Džaihānī to the archetype; and as this can only be achieved by a process of elimination it will be necessary to begin with our latest version (that of al-Bekrī), and our first step must be to analyse the sources used by him.

Composition of al-Bekrī's report. If the parallel columns in the Appendix be consulted, it will be seen that al-Bekrī's main source for the countries in which we are interested is one common also to Ibn Rusta and to Gardēzī. In a passage which he has in common with Ibn Rusta, al-Bekrī explicitly names Džaihānī as his source;[1] and as Gardēzī's source for the passages which he has in common with al-Bekrī is almost undoubtedly Džaihānī,[2] one may take it with some certainty that al-Bekrī's source, where he corresponds with Ibn Rusta and Gardēzī, is Džaihānī.

Al-Bekrī, however, has not treated his material in the same way as his colleagues. Where he corresponds with them, he is invariably much more laconic than either of them; on the other hand, he has added a considerable amount of information not common to the other two.

The fact appears to be that al-Bekrī, a comparatively intelligent man, realised that Džaihānī was not the only, nor, in his day, the latest source of information for the countries of the north. He therefore took only what seemed to him still worth taking, adding or substituting later information from other writers.

The differences between al-Bekrī and Gardēzī are, briefly, these:

The reports on the Petchenegs, Khazars, Volga Bulgars and

---

1 Marquart, *Streifzüge*, p. 26.
2 See below, pp. 7–8.

Burtās are summarised. In the case of the two first-named considerable additions are made from other sources.

The report on the Magyars "A"[1] is summarised, a single sentence being added from another source. That on Magyars "B" is omitted altogether, but what appears to be an entirely new section is inserted in its place.

The reports on Magyars "C", the Slavs and the Rūs are omitted altogether. In their place is given a report on the Slavs by Ibrāhīm ibn Jāq'ūb, a Jewish traveller of the late tenth century,[2] with some additions from Mas'ūdī.

A report on the Burğān (the Danube Bulgars) is inserted.

The sources used by al-Bekrī, apart from Džaihānī, appear to be three in number; and failing proof to the contrary, only three.

The report on the Slavs is taken in the main from Ibn Jāq'ūb, who is quoted by name.

The report on the Khazars is taken very largely from the work, either of Istachrī, or, more probably, of Ibn Fozlān,[3] and

---

1 These divisions are adopted by me in the Appendix, and I try in this essay to justify them.

2 A recent translation of this report, with notes, is that by G. Jacob, *Arabische Berichte von Gesandten an Germanische Fürstenhöfe aus den IX und Xen Jahrhunderten* (Berlin, 1927). A still more recent English translation, by M. Semen Rapoport, is in the *Slavonic Review*, vol. VIII, no. 23 (Dec. 1929).

3 Ibn Fozlān and Istachrī give identical reports on the Khazars; clearly, therefore, one is copying from the other. Ibn Fozlān says that he took his famous journey in 921/2; Istachrī wrote only some thirty or forty years after that event. It would therefore seem, on the face of it, obvious that the later writer borrowed from the earlier. Of late, however, Ibn Fozlān's credit, which once stood so high, has been much blown upon. Professor Marquart (Markwart) proved that several anecdotes which Ibn Fozlān represents as happening to himself in Bolgar are more than suspicious ("Ein arabischer Bericht, etc.", *U.J.* Dec. 1924, Bd. IV, Heft 3/4; see especially Marquart's conclusion, p. 319). M. Kmosko has attempted to prove that both Istachrī and Ibn Fozlān drew on an older source, and that the latter never visited the Khazars at all ("Die Quellen Istachrīs in seinem Bericht über die Chazaren", *K.C.A.* I Köt. 2 Szám, 1921). I may, perhaps, be permitted to say that I do not think that M. Kmosko at all proves his case. Istachrī's report reads to me very clearly like a reproduction of Ibn Fozlān's, with a rather clumsy interpolation of extraneous matter. In any case, Ibn Fozlān was certainly utilised by Mas'ūdī, the latter part of whose account of Bolgar (*Meadows of Gold*, pp. 420 ff.) is simply a very brief summary of Ibn Fozlān's account of Bolgar and the Baškirs. The fact that writers so near Ibn Fozlān in date used him seems to prove that his journey was actually undertaken; it was, moreover, a famous event, which it would be difficult to forge altogether. Undoubtedly there are incredible travellers' tales in it; on the other hand, it must be remembered that

a sentence in the report on the Magyars "A" comes from Ibn Fozlān.

The report on the Slavs also contains certain information from Mas'ūdī, who, in this instance, is named as a source. It is probable that the lost works of Mas'ūdī are also the basis of all the remaining material in al-Bekrī's report, the sources for which have not hitherto been identified with certainty: viz. parts of the reports on the Petchenegs and Khazars, the whole of al-Bekrī's version of the Magyars " B "; and the report on the Burğān.

Ibn Jāq'ūb never travelled to the Caucasus, much less to the Volga. Istachrī wrote on those countries; but we possess his work, and it bears no resemblance to al-Bekrī's, except for the passage on the Khazars. We appear also to have all of Ibn Fozlān's report, which covers only the Baškirs, the Volga Bulgars, the Khazars and the Russian colony in Ītīl. Mas'ūdī, on the other hand, who was the most voluminous of all his kind, and was very frequently quoted, often without acknowledgment, by others, wrote copiously on the countries in question, and although most of his writings have been lost, those which survive contain strong indications in support of my conclusion.

In his report on the Khazars, al-Bekrī gives a long account of the conversion of the Khazar Khagan to Judaism; Mas'ūdī expressly tells us that one of his lost works contained an account of this event.[1]

Al-Bekrī's account of the Petchenegs contains a story of the conversion of part of them to Islam. This story is almost entirely unsupported. All our later evidence concerning the Petchenegs, which becomes fairly copious when they come into contact with Greek, Russian, Hungarian and Western writers, shows them

the portion of the report which contains the tallest of these (the section on Bolgar) has been preserved only in Jāqūt's very late version, which undoubtedly contains some extraneous matter. Probably legends crystallised round this journey. Some of the details are extraordinarily convincing. With regard to al-Bekrī he does not anywhere else, to my knowledge, utilise Istachrī, although that writer dealt with countries which should have interested him; on the other hand, I believe myself to have identified a further sentence in al-Bekrī's report on the Magyars as coming straight from Ibn Fozlān (see below, pp. 38–9).

1 *Meadows of Gold*, tr. Springer (Oriental Translation Fund, London, 1852), I, 407: "As we cannot insert in this book the history of the conversion of the King of the Khazars to Judaism, we refer the reader to our former works".

as complete heathens, except for two partial and temporary conversions to Christianity.[1] Only Mas'ūdī, in his very strange story of the "Valandar hordes", talks of Moslem Petchenegs, and his whole story seems vaguely to echo what we find here in al-Bekrī.[2]

Al-Bekrī's note on the Burǧān is an abbreviated version of a longer account found in a certain work known as the *Abrégé des Merveilles*.[3] This work is of disputed origin; and it seems impossible to ascribe it *tel quel* to Mas'ūdī; but he is undoubtedly a main source for it, and particularly the chapter containing the account of the Burǧān is certainly very largely based on Mas'ūdī's work.[4]

There remains to be considered only al-Bekrī's version of the Magyars "B"; and it is necessary to postpone examination of this passage until we reach it in our analysis of the archetype. I shall then show that here, too, al-Bekrī was in all probability drawing on one of Mas'ūdī's lost works. I must anticipate my proof to insist on the important point that al-Bekrī here describes the same country as Gardēzī; only he has taken a later and verbally different description of that country.

We have thus arrived at our analysis of al-Bekrī; viz. a summary of Džaihānī, supplemented by further information drawn from Ibn Jāq'ūb, Ibn Fozlān and Mas'ūdī.

Gardēzī's version. Gardēzī's work consists of an account of the Turkish nations and of a section on the peoples of the north, comprising sections on the Petchenegs, Khazars, Burtās, Volga Bulgars, Serīr, Alans, Magyars "A","B" and "C", Slavs and Rūs.

Gardēzī quotes as his two sources, Džaihānī and Ibn Khordādbeh. We possess the works of the latter writer, and they do not contain any passages corresponding to those which we are considering. It is possible that what we have is only an abbreviated

1 I shall go into this question in detail in an essay on the Petchenegs which I hope to publish shortly.

2 The whole of this complicated story will be discussed in my essay on the Petchenegs; it is not essential for the purposes of this essay. The passage in Mas'ūdī mentioning the Moslem Petchenegs occurs in the *Meadows of Gold*, pp. 446 ff. See also the *Livre d'Avertissement* (tr. B. Carra de Vaux, Paris, 1896), pp. 244–5.

3 *L'Abrégé des Merveilles*; Ouvrage attribué à Mas'ūdī, traduit par B. Carra de Vaux, Paris, 1898.

4 See Excursus I.

version;[1] nevertheless, it is difficult to suppose that this great section should have vanished wholesale, more especially as Mas'ūdī, who used Ibn Khordādbeh, also has no traces of the report, so far as we can judge from his extant works. Moreover, Mas'ūdī, while commending Ibn Khordādbeh as "the best writer", says of him expressly that "he has no account of the kings and kingdoms."[2] It is, therefore, only logical to suppose that Gardēzī's source for the section on the North was the other author quoted by him, viz. Džaihānī.

It would seem, therefore, that in Gardēzī we had preserved to us the work of Džaihānī. It must, however, be asked, how far Gardēzī's transcription is accurate, and whether he has himself made any changes or additions. This is no easy task, since we have not got Džaihānī's work.

Nevertheless, it is clear that anything in Gardēzī which is also in al-Bekrī must have been in the original Džaihānī; and any material common to Gardēzī and Ibn Rusta must, *a fortiori*, be at least equally old. Thus the passage (γ) in Magyars "B" to which I referred above (the description of the two rivers and of the Magyars' neighbours) must be at least as old as Džaihānī, since al-Bekrī must have had it before him in his original. The same is true of the section on the Petchenegs.

1 See M. de Goeje's introduction to his edition of Ibn Khordādbeh (with French translation) in the *Bib. Geog. Arab.* vol. 1. Ibn Khordādbeh, who was Director of Posts under the Chalif Mut'ammid Billah, wrote a geography which subsequently attained great fame, but is, from the descriptive point of view, a singularly jejune work, consisting almost wholly of a list of posting stations within the Chalifate, together with the distances between them. When he comes to touch on countries outside his own, he becomes more interesting, but also notably less critical. He has a brief note on the Russian trade with Khazaria, via "the Tanais, the river of the Slavs", and also a description of the voyage of "Sallam the Interpreter" to Alexander's wall and the countries of Gog and Magog. This latter part of his work has been borrowed also by Ibn Rusta, who quotes Ibn Khordādbeh as his source for it. (For a recent discussion of this voyage, see Count Stephen Zichy in *K.C.A.* 1 Köt. 3 Szám, June 1922; an ingenious discussion, but vitiated by too implicit belief in the reliability of this fairy-story.) On the true Turks, far away to the east of the countries in which we are interested, Ibn Khordādbeh is well-informed. It will be of interest to note, in passing, that the section in question, which appears to have been compiled from fresh information, and is dated by Marquart (*Streifzüge*, p. 390) at A.D. 885/6, contains a reference to the Petchenegs, among the other Turkish tribes of the north-east, unaccompanied by any suggestion that that nation had already crossed the Volga.

2 *Meadows of Gold*, c. 1.

There are also, at the ends of Gardēzī's sections on the Burtās, the Khazars, the Magyars "C" and the Slavs, and perhaps also the Volga Bulgars, additions not found in Ibn Rusta's text. Owing to al-Bekrī's method of working, we cannot tell whether these passages were in his original or not. If, then, Ibn Rusta copied Džaihānī, these passages must be additions by Gardēzī to Džaihānī. If Ibn Rusta and Džaihānī alike drew on an older source, the additions may have been made, either by Gardēzī to Džaihānī, or by Džaihānī to his own source. Similarly, the responsibility for various textual corruptions and mistranslations must be left undecided until the relations between Džaihānī and Ibn Rusta have been settled.

Džaihānī, as we said, became Vezir of the Samanides in 913–14, and probably wrote his work not long after that date. Ibn Rusta states in one passage of his work that he visited Medina in 290 H., i.e. A.D. 903. He therefore wrote after, but not very long after that date, and is nearly contemporary with Džaihānī.

Ibn Rusta quotes his authorities fairly fully. Those whom he mentions are: Ibn al-Tayyib, al-Farghānī, Abū Ma'shār, M. b. Mūsa, Abū 'Ubayd, Hāran b. Yahya, Ibn Ishāq, Ibn Khordādbeh and M. b. Ludda. The name of Džaihānī is not, as will be seen, in this list.[1] For this reason I find it difficult to assume with the *a priori* certainty of some other investigators that Ibn Rusta copied from Džaihānī.

The converse—that Džaihānī should have copied from Ibn Rusta—is hardly possible. There are certain passages, the most obvious of which is the report on the Petchenegs, which very clearly form an integral part of the original report, and are reproduced by both al-Bekrī and Gardēzī (and therefore by Džaihānī), but omitted by Ibn Rusta. If, then, Džaihānī copied from Ibn Rusta, he must also have had before him the archetype from which Ibn Rusta himself copied; which comes to the same

---

1 See M. Rieu's analysis of the MS in the British Museum Catalogue. Ibn Khordādbeh's contribution has been mentioned above (note 1, p. 11). That of b. Yahya consists of a report of a journey to Constantinople and Rome. It is analysed by Marquart, *Streifzüge*, pp. 206 ff. Muhammed b. Mūsa was an astronomer, who was sent on a mission to Khazaria under al-Vāthek (*ibid.* xxxii). The other names are unknown to me.

thing as if we suppose that the two of them made versions, independently, from the same archetype.

This last view is that which I have adopted in my scheme, and shall treat throughout as though it were the correct view. I may, however, say at once that it makes not one iota of difference to our general conclusions whether we take Ibn Rusta as copying from Džaihānī, or both as copying from a single archetype; for we are concerned, not with Džaihānī's literary reputation, but with the facts concerning which he writes. It is open, therefore, for any person who so prefers, to erase any mention of the "archetype X" in the following pages, and substitute for it the name of al-Džaihānī.

Ibn Rusta, then, represents one version of an archetype, which we may agree to call "X", while Gardēzī represents a second version, which was in any case derived from Džaihānī. By comparison of the two (with the assistance of al-Bekrī in the passages in which that writer drew upon the same source), it should be possible to arrive at some idea of the contents of this original X.

The Archetype. There can be little doubt that, of the two versions, that of Ibn Rusta is by far the purer. Gardēzī's is nearly 150 years later; it has probably passed through more hands, and it is a translation from the Arabic into the Persian. Corruptions and mistranslations in Gardēzī's version often give rise to considerable divergencies, affecting not only single words, but often whole paragraphs. It will not be necessary to point these out in detail here, as those which affect our present enquiry will be considered as they arise.[1] It may, however, safely be said that in cases of divergency, Ibn Rusta's version

1 In some cases we get mistranslations of a single word, where Gardēzī can definitely be said to be wrong, since al-Bekrī agrees with Ibn Rusta; e.g. in the report on the Serīr, where Gardēzī has "they worship a lion", the other two having "a withered head". Sometimes these confusions are important, e.g. the beginning of the section on the Magyars "A", where Gardēzī has written "Bulkar" twice, for "Bulkar" and "Petchenegs". Cases where he has embellished, in more or less harmless fashion, are very numerous; the section on the Serīr is full of them. Often his version is rather a paraphrase than a translation, especially where he has misunderstood the original. An excellent example will be found in Ibn Rusta's account of the baths enjoyed by the Slavs in winter. Here Gardēzī seems to have been beaten by the passage altogether, except that he gleaned the idea of the Slavs shutting themselves up in a confined place in the winter. Out of this he makes another reference to the Magyars raiding the Slavs.

should, on principle, be preferred, and will generally be found
to be more correct. There remains, however, the possibility that
a few variations in Gardēzī may be due to deliberate correction;
but as he wrote a long time after his primary sources, such
corrections are likely, at the best, to represent an attempt to
harmonise the situation as depicted in the original with conditions in the writer's own day, which may not at all have been the
conditions which were true when the original was written. I
believe such deliberate corrections, however, to be comparatively
few in Gardēzī's report; they are actually more numerous, and
more important, in Ibn Rusta's.

There are, further, a certain number of passages at the ends of
various sections, notably those on the Burtās, Khazars, Magyars
"C" and Slavs, which are given by Gardēzī and not by Ibn Rusta.
These I take to be additions, not found in the archetype, but
added by Džaihānī (if not himself identical with the archetype),
or by Gardēzī himself. Conversely, Ibn Rusta has a passage at
the end of his section on the Alans which seems to have been
added from one of his other sources; and the same may be true of
one or two passages in the report on the Slavs, and one in the
section on the Magyars, which are not reproduced by Gardēzī.

More important is one particular set of variations, in which it
seems as though Gardēzī or rather, his source, had made a
half-hearted attempt to bring his material up to date, while
Ibn Rusta, having these emendations before him, had gone
farther, introducing a second set of amendments. Thus neither
of our two versions represents the original X in its purity.

To explain this statement, we must turn for a moment to
examine the date of X.

In the section on the Volga Bulgars, there occurs the statement (in all three versions) that the king of that nation is called
Almuš, and is "an adherent of Islam". The nation is represented as mainly, but not entirely Mahomedan, and as possessing
a certain organisation, with "mosques and boys' schools and
muezzins and imams".

Now, we possess an extraordinarily interesting report from a
certain Aḥmed ben Fozlān,[1] who tells us that:

1 This report (in Miss Smith's translation) is reproduced in the Appendix.

There arrived a letter from Almuš ben Shilki Blatawār, king of the Slavs [sic], to the commander of the Faithful, Muqtadir b'Illāh, in which he asked him to send him someone who would instruct him in the sacred law of Islam, and build a mosque for him and erect a pulpit for him, that from it the call to religion might be proclaimed throughout his kingdom. He asked him for a builder [who could build him] a fortress in which he could fortify himself against hostile kings.

The Chalif agreed, and a mission was sent, which arrived at Bolgar on May 11th, 922.

On the strength of this passage, Jāqūt, who quotes it, tells us that "the king of Bolgar and his subjects had Islamised in the reign of Muqtadir b'Illāh" (who ruled A.D. 908–32). Mas'ūdī, who also knew Ibn Fozlān's report, and summarises it very briefly, goes even further by saying: "The king of Burgār ruling in our day is a Moslem, who received Islam in the time of al-Muqtadir b'Illāh after the year 310 (922/23) on account of a dream which he had."

Both Jāqūt's and Mas'ūdī's statements are, however, founded solely on Ibn Fozlān's report, and if we read the latter carefully, we do not find that it fully authorises either statement. On the contrary, the king and some of his nation were certainly already Moslems by the time Ibn Fozlān arrived, and a muezzin is represented already as functioning on his arrival. Moreover, there are other passages in the Oriental writers which seem to indicate an even earlier date for the conversion of the nation.[1]

It is not, therefore, necessary to suppose that the archetype, to contain the sentence to which we referred, must have been

---

1 Mas'ūdī's own second reference to the subject is inconclusive. In his account in the *Meadows of Gold* (pp. 297 ff.) of the Russian invasion of the Caspian in 913/14, he says: "Some of them were slain by the Burtās, while others reached the land of the Burgār, the Moslems, who slew them". This mention may have historical value, or it may be merely a gloss.

On the other hand, the later Risālat al-intisāb, quoted by Frähn ("Drei Münzen der Wolga Bulgaren", *Mém. de l'Ac. Imp. de St Pétersbourg*, VI sér. t. I, p. 186, 1830), writes: "The land of Bulgar is the land of the Moslim Turks. They adopted the faith under the Chalifate of al-Ma'mūn and of al-Vāthek, and again under the Chalifate of Qāïm bi'amri'llah 30,000 tents accepted Islam". This would put the conversion of part of the nation at about A.D. 840.

Marquart (*Streifzüge*, p. 476) imagines this to be a mistake for the Khazars, but I cannot follow his reasoning; however, the point may be left open.

written after Ibn Fozlān's mission. Indeed, from the fact that Ibn Rusta's and Gardēzī's reports make no further use of Ibn Fozlān's narrative, outside this single sentence, I am strongly inclined to think that the archetype was composed *without* knowledge of Ibn Fozlān's report, and perhaps even before his journey. The bare fact that the king of Bolgar was called Almuš and was a Mahomedan could well have been known from other sources.

On the other hand, although it seems quite possible that Almuš was not a name, but a hereditary title, the king's explicit statement that his father was an unbeliever forbids us to date the sentence in question very many years before A.D. 922, and forces us to place the composition of X in the early years of the tenth century—about the time when Džaihānī and Ibn Rusta were both writing.

The Petchenegs in the ninth century lived on the Volga and the Ural, and about the year A.D. 885 moved westward to the right bank of the Don, expelling the Magyars thence. Closer consideration of this historical event will occupy a large part of the present essay; but the event itself is agreed, and the date is agreed to within twenty or thirty years. But the original reports on which X was founded were written before the move; the section on the Petchenegs describes them, as we shall see, in their old feeding-grounds. But the editor-compiler of X wrote after the event, and he was aware of it. Consequently, we find a certain amount of editing in both versions of the report, to bring it into line with the new situation. This editing is, of course, grossly insufficient; but it is there, and it accounts for several puzzling touches in both versions, and for several discrepancies between the two, due to the fact that Ibn Rusta has made further independent alterations of his own. Most of these take the form of omissions of information which no longer fits the new situation, while Gardēzī (Džaihānī) quite unconcernedly leaves the old and the new in together.[1]

These passages (to which I shall return when I come to each of them in my consideration of the text) are the following:

Changes by X. In the report on the Petchenegs: substitution

---

[1] I believe one sentence at least—the reference to the ditch of Perekop—to be an addition by Ibn Rusta; see below, p. 68.

of the name Saqlāb (Slav) for that of the Burtās as the Petche-negs' western neighbours.

In the opening of the section on the Slavs: substitution of the word "Petchenegs" for the original "Magyars" in the sentence "between the country of the ... and that of the Slavs is a ten days' journey".[1]

Gardēzī actually keeps the original sentence at the end of his section on the Magyars.

Further Changes by Ibn Rusta. The omission of the section on the Petchenegs.

The omission, in the report on the Magyars, of the sentence referred to above: "From the Magyars to the Slavs is a ten days' journey".

The further important omission, in the section on the Magyars, of the sentences which I describe as γ, being the description of the Magyars' neighbours, at the time when they were living on the river Cuban. These sentences were themselves an addition to the original report α, and Ibn Rusta's piece of editing has thus had the effect of restoring the original report. It did not, however, succeed in bringing it up to date, even for the author's day; but perhaps it was near enough for his purposes. It left the Magyars living "between two rivers", which are not more closely defined; and that was true, even when the rivers were the Danube and the Theiss. It is not, however, to be supposed that Ibn Rusta knew this.

To recover the text of the archetype, then, in these cases, we must work back, not from Ibn Rusta, but from Gardēzī. Besides this, we must slough off a few additions, mostly at the ends of the various sections, made by one or the other writer from his private information, in exactly the same way as we have sloughed off the far more important and extensive additions made by al-Bekrī.

But it is not enough to discover only what was the text of X. We must also examine the further sources of that report.

---

1 I am deeply suspicious of the whole opening sentence, which is suspiciously reminiscent of the sentence giving the route from the Petchenegs to their western neighbours before their move, the Khazars. If the original form has been preserved by Gardēzī in the Magyars "C" ("they constantly plunder the Slavs and from the Magyars to the Slavs is a ten days' journey"), then the whole of this sentence must be an interpolation.

Sources of X. It has generally been assumed, on what grounds I know not, that Ibn Rusta's report, at least, is broadly homogeneous, or at any rate, describes a single historical situation, all sections of it being contemporary. I propose to show that this is not the case; that, on the contrary, X is composed, apart from the small editorial alterations referred to above, of two clearly distinguishable original sources, from different hands, and composed at different times. I shall refer to these as α and β respectively. α, in addition, contains a small section (γ) which was added to it by another hand, but was contemporary with it, and thus describes the same historical and geographical situation.

The methods of the old Oriental geographers were, as a rule, simple. They commonly composed their works in the form of a series of sections, divided by nations or "climates". A geographer who had in his hands a work of this sort, and subsequently came into possession of later information on the same headings, would not, as a rule, undertake more than the roughest work of editorship, but would simply append his new information at the end of each appropriate section (or not infrequently, to the confusion of the twentieth century, under the wrong section). One would thus get, in such a combined work, a series of sections, each of which began with the information from the older source, and ended with that from the later. Very commonly there would be no transition to mark the division between the two sources.

Any page of any mediaeval Oriental geographer will exemplify this.

This is what has been done in the present case.

α consists of the sections on the Petchenegs, Khazars, Burtās, Volga Bulgars, Serīr, Alans, and Magyars "A" and " B "; β of the sections on the Magyars " C ", Slavs and Rūs. The two sources only overlapped, at least to any important extent,[1] in the case of the Magyars; thus while each of the other sections is wholly or practically homogeneous, that on the Magyars contains informa-

---

[1] It is quite possible that the section on the Khazars, and even that on the Volga Bulgars, may contain some sentences contributed by β. In the main, however, they assuredly come from α.

tion from two different sources, and of two different dates. The clue to this otherwise incomprehensible report will be found in the fact that the two sections describe different localities, and different historical periods.

The distinction between α and β is very marked. The writer of α would seem, from internal evidence, to have been a merchant, who had himself travelled in the countries which he describes. He presents himself as a simple and straightforward soul, interested mainly in straight business: in the roads, the opportunities for watering on the way, distances and trade openings. So far as his report goes, it is a model of its kind; the more satisfactory, in that it is based on a sort of skeleton of directions and distances, the whole forming a description of a trade route from Khwārism.[1]

The route is given first to the Petchenegs, thence to the Khazars, Burtās, Bulgars, Magyars "A", and from the Khazars to the Serīr and Alans. All these sections are closely linked together by their opening sentences. The Petcheneg section refers back to Khwārism, on to the Khazars; the note that the neighbours of the Petchenegs (Khazars and Burtās, the word Slav having been substituted by the compiler of X for the latter name) raid them and take them prisoners, is echoed when we reach the sections on those nations.

The section on the Khazars gives the distance from the Petchenegs (i.e. the route from Khwārism), and repeats the remark about the Khazar-Petcheneg wars.

The sections on the Serīr and the Alans give the route to those nations from the country of the Khazars, and not from across the Caucasus, as one would expect.

The section on the Burtās gives the route with reference only to the Khazars and the Volga Bulgars, and its remarks on the political relations of the nation cover only the Khazars, Bulgars and Petchenegs. Here we find another reference to annual hostilities with the Petchenegs, as in the Khazar section; and as in that section, the local religion is described as "resembling

---

1 Marquart's dating (*Streifzüge*, xxxi, xxxii) seems based on the assumption that the information came from a colleague of Sallam the Interpreter or from that traveller himself.

the religion of the Ghuzzīyyā"—a natural comparison for a native of Khwārism, which was one of the chief Guz markets.

The section on the Bulgars links up with that on the Burtās; the section on the Magyars "A" begins by placing them with reference to the Petchenegs and the Bulgarian Ašgil, who are mentioned in the Bulgar section.

Genuine references, in this report, to the Slavs and the Rūs are confined to the report on the Volga Bulgars, and even there they are quite incidental.

When we come to β, the situation is quite other. Here we have a block of reports covering countries on or near the Black Sea, and comprising the Magyars "C", Slavs and Rūs. The inter-connection between the three sections is exceedingly close, while the centre of the stage is held by the Slavs. It would, indeed, hardly be unfair to describe the Magyar section as a brief essay on Magyaro-Slav relations. The Russian section, too, contains many references to the Slavs; of the other nations, however, who fill the stage of α, we only get one or two quite incidental mentions.

The difference is even more marked if the first sentence on the Slavs be omitted, as I feel convinced that it ought to be, as spurious. The careful skeleton of α, with its record of distances and neighbours, all inter-related and leading back to Khwārism, has now, in β, vanished altogether. β is conceived on quite a different plan; it is much more philosophical in tone, con-sisting essentially of a description of the manners and customs of the nations with which it deals; these manners being looked at mainly from the point of view of the Slav.

Two other points may be mentioned in favour of the division which I advocate. Firstly, there is no trace in al-Bekrī of *any* of the reports which I group together as β. He omits them all *en bloc*, substituting for them a single report on the Slavs, as though seeing in β, essentially, an account of the Slavs only.

Secondly, reference to the list which I gave above of the passages preserved by Gardēzī but not found in Ibn Rusta—these constituting the additions made by Džaihānī to the archetype—will show that in every single instance except one, such additions come at the end of a section. This, as has been remarked, is the normal place for an Oriental geographer to add later information on to an earlier report. The single exception is the addition γ in Magyars "B"; and if we adopt the division which I propose, we shall find the rule coming true as before; here, again, the addition will be found to be at the end of a section.

Finally, I hope to show in the course of this essay that the situation described in Magyars " C " is different in time and place from that described in Magyars " A " and " B ".

To sum up my conclusions:

On a report describing the countries on and east of the Volga (α) has been superimposed a second describing the countries north of the Black Sea (β). The person who combined these two reports himself made a few changes and additions; thus producing an archetype X.

Ibn Rusta copied X closely, but with certain further changes, consisting largely of omissions. Džaihānī, if not himself identical with X, copied X closely; but may have made some further additions. Gardēzī's work is practically a copy of Džaihānī's with certain additional corruptions and mistranslations. Al-Bekrī's work is a summary of Džaihānī, with further information from other sources, notably Mas'ūdī's lost *Book of Different Sorts of Knowledge*. Of the section on the Magyars, which is the particular subject of the present essay, "A" and " B " belong to α, " C " belongs to β.

I shall now consider these reports in detail, and hope to show that much may be learned from them on the history of the Magyars in the ninth century after Christ.

THE REPORT ON THE MAGYARS "A"

(α)

General situation in α. The route in report α takes us from Khwārism to the Petchenegs, and from the Petchenegs to the Khazars. The route to the Burtās is given from the Khazars, and to the Volga Bulgars from the Burtās; the "first frontier of the Magyars", in the same way, is located by references to the Petchenegs on the one hand, the Bulgars on the other. The whole report therefore hangs together, being linked up by the sentences giving direction and distance at the beginning of each section. While the possibility that the end of each section might contain later matter is not to be excluded, the beginning sentences in each case certainly belong to the original.

It is not possible to date the report from internal evidence.

The Petchenegs. The traveller starts from "Korkanj", or Džordžania, in Khwārism; a famous mediaeval trading centre, the site of which is known exactly.[1] We thus have our starting-point fixed. The road to the Petchenegs seems to pass up the western side of the Aral Sea, crossing or passing along the edge of the vast Ust Urt plateau, to this day one of the most arid and little-known quarters of the world. The springs to which the traveller refers cannot be identified with certainty. Since his route ends by bringing him to within no great distance from the Khazars, he must eventually have turned north-west; he thus places the Petchenegs in precisely the same region which they were occupying, according to Constantine, before their

1 For details of this city, see Le Strange, *The Lands of the Eastern Caliphate* (Cambridge, 1905) and Bretschneider, *Mediaeval Researches*, 1, 23. According to Dimašqi (*Cosmographie*, tr. Mehren, p. 314), it rose to the rank of city, and became capital of Khwārism, after Mansur, the first capital, had been submerged beneath the waters of the Oxus. It derived its name from the fact that it was the terminus of the caravans from the country of Džordžania. In Ouseley's version of Istachrī (p. 240) we read that "Džordžan is a smaller town than Khwārism; but it is the pass into various parts; from it the caravans set out for Khorasan and Gurhan and the Guz and Khazar and other places". Mas'ūdī (*Meadows of Gold*, p. 413) tells us that in his day caravans went regularly between Džordžania and Bolgar on the Kama, although "several wandering hordes of Turkish origin, who are distinct from the Bolgars," lived on the route and made it unsafe. Here he is summarising Ibn Fozlān's report. It was from this city that Ibn Fozlān started for Bolgar in A.D. 921, covering the journey in seventy days. The town, in Ibn Hauqal's day, was situated on the extreme frontier of the province.

It was known to the Mongols (who destroyed it in 1221) as Urghendj. In the days of Chinghiz Khan it stood, according to Rešid-ed-din, on both banks of the Oxus, which were connected by a bridge, and Ye-tu Ch'u ts'ai described it as "still more rich and prosperous than Bokhara". After its destruction it recovered, but the change in the flow of the Oxus ruined its prosperity. A new city, called Yeni Urghendj, took its place as the commercial capital of the Khiva district, while the old city was called Kunia Urghendj, a name which it still bears. It lies ninety miles north-west of Yeni Urghendj, and twenty-seven miles west of the present channel of the Amu-Daria (Oxus). According to Pascal of Vittoria, the body of Job was buried there (see Yule, *Cathay and the Way Thither*, 3rd ed. vol. III, p. 85).

expulsion by the Uz, viz. on the Ural and Volga rivers.[1]
Probably their feeding-grounds extended as far east as the Emba.
Constantine gives as the Petchenegs' neighbours the "Mazars"
and the Uz; but as he makes the Uz combine with the Khazars
to expel the Petchenegs, we see from his narrative also that the
Khazars must have been the south-western neighbours of the
Petchenegs, just as the present report tells us.

Our report gives as the neighbours of the Petchenegs: north,
the Qypčaq; south, the Khazars; west, the Slavs. There seems
to be an error of about half a quadrant here, according to our
reckoning, as, judging from the map, we should place the
Khazars due west, the Turkish tribes north-east or east, and
the Burtās (whose name must have figured in place of the Slavs
in the original report)[2] north-west. The error is an interesting
one, since we find a precisely similar case recurring in a description of Hungary by a Turkish tribe in the *D.A.I.*;[3] but it need
not detain us here.

Neither is it necessary to go into great detail regarding the
Petchenegs' eastern neighbours, described here as the Qypčaq,
but by Mas'ūdī as the "Guz, the Kharlūkh and the Kimäk",[4]
while the Petchenegs themselves, when telling their story to
Constantine, mention the Guz alone.[5] A passage from Muham-
med-i-'Aufī, which seems to contain an account of the expulsion
of the Petchenegs from the feeding-grounds in which they are
found here, also shows that the Guz were the Petchenegs'
eastern neighbours.[6]

1 *D.A.I.* c. 37: Ἰστέον ὅτι Πατζινακῖται τὸ ἀπ' ἀρχῆς εἰς τὸν ποταμὸν Ἀτὴλ
τὴν αὐτῶν εἶχον κατοίκησιν, ὁμοίως δὲ καὶ εἰς τὸν ποταμὸν Γεήχ, ἔχοντες τούς
τε Μαζάρους συνοροῦντας καὶ τοὺς ἐπονομαζομένους Οὔζ.

2 See below, p. 26.

3 *D.A.I.* c. 40; see below, p. 141.

4 *Livre d'Avertissement*, p. 244. It would be a mistake to attribute too much
weight to Mas'ūdī's words; the fact that he had read or heard that all these
three nations (Guz, Kimäk and Kharlūkh) lived somewhere north of the
Aral Sea would be quite enough for him to bring them all into the Petcheneg
wars, just as, on the other side, he places four nations (Pačna, Pačnāk, Baġğird
and Unkarda), whereas actually only one migrated on the occasion to which he
refers.

5 *D.A.I.* c. 37.

6 Cit. Marquart, *Komanen*, pp. 40–1: "To (the Turks)· belong also the
Marqa, called Qūn. They issued out of the land Qytā and left their own

The Qypčaq are given in Gardēzī's report on the Turkish
nations as one of the seven hordes of the Kimäk, who are
shown as living on the Irtisch.[1] Istachrī gives the Kimäk as
neighbours of the Guz, and separated from them by a river
which would appear from the description to be the Kama; but
a confusion with the Irtisch seems probable.[2] Without going
into much detail here, we may say with sufficient accuracy for
our purposes that the Qypčaq in the ninth century were living
as the westernmost of the Siberian Turks, their western frontier
probably reaching almost as far as the Ural mountains.[3] The
Guz, who are far better known, were living at this time on
the Aral Sea and the Sir Daria. Afterwards they took the
place of the Petchenegs as far westward as the Volga and the
Caspian.

The Khazars. Our report places the Khazars ten days south-
west of the Petchenegs. Their capital, Ītīl, of which we have
several descriptions, was situated near the mouth of the Volga,
and on both sides of the river, which was commonly known as
"the river of the Khazars". We have no information how far
east of the Volga the Khazar empire extended, but it would
seem probable that the river itself was the frontier. In the
south, Khazaria seems to have extended as far as the Caucasus;

headquarters, because of the narrowness of the feeding-grounds....Then a
horde named Qajy attacked them, and being superior to them in numbers and
armaments, hunted them out of their own feeding-grounds. They moved
then into the land Sārī, and the inhabitants of Sārī moved into the land of
the Turcmāns. The Guz moved into the land of the Petchenegs near the coast
of the sea of Armenia (= the Caspian)". Marquart, who discusses this
passage at great length, seems in his text to attribute the first part of it to the
eleventh century; but there seems to me no reason not to suppose it homogeneous. See also Marquart's own note, *op. cit.* p. 202.

1 This report is edited and translated (into Russian) with the rest of Gardēzī's
work by Barthold, *op. cit.*

2 The passage (given in full in the Appendix) runs: "The land of the Guz
lies between the land of the Khazars, the Kimäk and the Bulgars. The land
of the Kimäk lies beyond the Kharlūkh in the north, and the latter between
the Guz, the Kirghiz and the Slavs....The river Atel rises near the Kirghiz,
and flows between the Kimäk and the Guz, forming the boundary between
them. Then it turns west, towards the Bulgars, but again flows east to near
the Rūs, passes by the Bulgars, then by Burtās, till it flows into the Caspian".
The situation described here is, of course, that after the Petcheneg move,
and is tolerably clear except for the mention of the Slavs near the Kirghiz,
which can only be due to a bad confusion in Istachrī's mind.

3 See Marquart, *Komanen, passim.*

south-west, to the frontiers of Alania;[1] westward, at one time over the Slavonic tribes as far as Kiev itself[2] and into the Crimea; but in the tenth century, the western frontier was formed by the Don.[3]

Our only information about the northern limit of Khazaria is that contained in the present report.

The Burtās. Our report puts the Burtās on the Volga, fifteen days' journey from the Khazars. They formed one of the string of three Volga nations: the Khazars, the Burtās and the Volga Bulgars, and undoubtedly occupied the whole country between their two neighbours. Istachrī tells us definitely that "the Burtās are a people bordering immediately on the Khazars. They live scattered in villages along the Volga... the inhabitants have wooden houses, and live scattered (i.e. not in large communities)." Mas'ūdī has a remark to the same effect.[4] At the period of our report, they were tributary to the Khazars—another proof that the two countries were contiguous; while additional proof is to be found in the fact that no writer mentions any other nation on the middle Volga until a much later date, although references to the Burtās are not infrequent.[5] The

1 *D.A.I.* cc. 10, 11. 2 "Nestor", I, 19, 21.

3 *D.A.I.* c. 42.

4 *Livre d'Avertissement*, p. 93: "The Burtās are a great nation of Turks living between the country of Khwārism and the country of al-Khazar, but they are adjoining al-Khazar". In the *Meadows of Gold*, p. 412, this statement is repeated almost word for word, with the important difference of "Burgar" for "Khwārism". "Burgar" is unquestionably the right reading, because it happens to make sense. When Mas'ūdī writes, "The river of al-Khazar passes by the city of Ītīl...and towards it flows the river of Burtās....In this river great ships ply with merchandise and all kinds of goods from Khwārism (*recte* Bolgar) and elsewhere", he is only the victim of an obvious confusion, which may have arisen out of his own earlier story of the Russians who, after their defeat by the Khazars at Ītīl, "sailed along the bank of the river on which Burtās is situated. Some of them were slain by the inhabitants of Burtās, and others came into the country of the Burgar (the Moslems)" (*Meadows of Gold*, pp. 419–20). The river on which Burtās is situated was none other than the Volga, and so is the "river of Burtās" which Mas'ūdī's receptive mind thought to have found. It need not therefore be painfully sought in the Oka, the rivulet today called Burtas, or the Irgiz; and all arguments as to the ethnographical character of the Burtās, or to the extent of their territory, which have been based on the supposition that any other river than the Volga is referred to in these passages of Mas'ūdī, or by his copyists, ought to be rejected.

5 Besides our own report, Istachrī and Mas'ūdī, Ibn Hauqal mentions the Burtās in connection with the destruction of al-Khazar by the Russians, and

Burtās must have been even nearer to the Bulgars, if our report is correct in placing the distance at only three days; and the mention of hostilities between them and the Petchenegs shows that they were neighbours of that nation, and forces us to suppose that the name "Slavs" in the list of the Petchenegs' neighbours is a correction by the later editor for the original text "Burtās". In this case, their main homes were probably on the left bank of the Volga, although they appear to have extended also to the right bank and to the forests in which their kinsmen, the Mordvinians,[1] were living.

The Volga Bulgars. The famous trading city of Bolgar lay near the junction of the Kama and the Volga (its ruins have many times been described by travellers), and was the capital of an empire which, although its exact limits are uncertain, must have extended for a considerable distance to the east and south-east; perhaps also to the west, if Ibn Fozlān is not altogether arbitrary in referring to the king of Bolgar as "the king of the Slavs".

As one of the principal centres of the important luxury-trade in furs which brought the Arab traders northward in quest of satisfaction for the beauties of Baghdad, and as the most remote Islamic state, Bolgar was an exceedingly familiar name to the old Arabs. All of the old geographers and historians have something to say about it, and all, without exception, understand under the name of Bolgar, only the city on the Kama.

they recur in nearly all the later copyists and geographers. They did a considerable trade in furs, including the black foxes which the Arabs called after their name.

1 Smirnov, *Les Populations Finnoises*, I, 266 ff. quotes very remarkable documents which show that at a later date, at least, the Burtās were very explicitly distinguished from the Mordvinians. In one such document, Mordvinians are described as having settled in country formerly inhabited by Burtās. By this time the Burtās, who were looked on as a kind of Tatars, had crossed to the right bank of the Volga; but they had probably been driven thither by the Tatar invasion. Mas'ūdī's story certainly reads as though the Burtās, in his day, lived mainly on the left bank; but in spite of their camels, which Smirnov adduces, they cannot have been, as he suggests, solely "nomad shepherds issued from Central Asia", and pure steppe-dwellers. They lived in forests, inhabited scattered wooden houses, and were trappers and hunters— all indications that they inhabited also the wooded right bank. The natural conclusion to be drawn from such few authorities as we possess is undoubtedly that they were distinct from the Mordvinians, although in all probability closely related to them.

The Bulgars of the Danube, so familiar to us, were hardly known to the Arabs. The single detailed report on them (that of al-Garmī) describes them under the name, not of Bulgar, but of "Burğān", under which name Mas'ūdī and Ibn Khordādbeh know them;[1] and the few references to them which occur in Istachrī etc. are tacked without understanding on to the name of Volga Bulgar.

Thus it can be said with absolute certainty that the present report refers to the Volga state, and not to the state on the Danube. The names of the three tribes or "classes" who made up the nation are not particularly easy to interpret,[2] but in view of the quite explicit statement by both Ibn Rusta and Gardēzī that "all three live in one place", it is entirely out of the question to take any one of them as living in Transylvania, on the Cuban, or in any other outlandish district in which commentators who

1 See below, Excursus 1.

2 The Barsūl seem to have had an old connection with the Bulgars. John of Ephesus (who wrote 585/6) makes the Khazars and Bulgars "come into the land of the Alans, which is called Barsalia" (*Chron. de Michel le Syrien*, ed. Chabot, c. 13). The geography of Ps.-Moses Chorenaci, which is based in part on very old sources, speaks of an island in the Volga "to which the people of Basilk' repairs and fortifies itself against the mighty nation of the Khazars and the Bulgars" (ed. Soukry, p. 26). The same source tells us that the wife of the Khazar Khagan was of the race of Barsilk' (*ibid.* p. 27; cf. Marquart, *Streifzüge*, p. 59). Both Theophanes (p. 358, ed. de Boor) and Nicephorus (p. 34, ed. de Boor) in their accounts of the wanderings of the Bulgars, make them come from "Barzilia" (Nic. Βερ⟨ζ⟩υλία) in First "Sarmatia". Theophylactus (VIII, 8) gives the Βαρσήλτ, or Σαρσήλτ, among the Hunnish tribes who, with the Unuguri and the Savirs, fled in confusion on the arrival of the Pseudo-Avars. Menander (Frag. 5; *Excerpta de Leg.* ed. de Boor, p. 443) has substantially the same story, with the variant Ζαλοί. It thus looks as though the Barsūl were a tribe, perhaps of Turkish origin, which first inhabited the country at the north-east of the Caucasus, combined with the Bulgars, and eventually shared their migration northward.

A name closely resembling the Ašgil is found in the Orkhon Inscriptions, which have the following passage: "As the Empire of my uncle the Khagan had become rebellious, and the people were filled with hatred against him, we fought against the Izgil people.... The Izgil people were destroyed" (see Thomsen, "Alttürkische Inschriften", *Zeitschrift der deutschen morgenländischen Gesellschaft*, LXXVIII, 1924, p. 154). This looks as though the Ašgil might have been a Turkish people who were driven north-westward and coalesced with the Bulgars on the Volga. On the other hand, since the etymology of the word "Székler" is still unexplained, and it seems possible to believe, with Hunfalvy (*Die Rumänen und ihre Ansprüche*, Vienna and Teschen, 1883, p. 47), that its meaning is "frontier guards", it is not at all impossible that our Ašgil might be connected *etymologically* with the Széklers of Transylvania, although any geographical connection is emphatically to be repudiated.

prefer their own theories to the plain reading of the text may prefer to place them.[1]

The report seems, however, mistaken in calling the Bulgars a small nation. Al-Bekrī's figure of 500 families seems in any case to be due to a corruption. It is possible, however, that the Bulgars proper formed a comparatively small ruling caste, who had imposed themselves on more numerous and more peaceable subjects. At all events, they were a very considerable power throughout the Middle Ages. The "Outer Baškirs" of the Ural mountains were tributary to them, as we shall see presently. They were strong enough for Constantine Porphyrogenetos to advise their employment to keep the Khazars in check;[2] they gave the early Russian principalities considerable trouble up to the thirteenth century, and even soundly trounced the Mongols themselves when they first attacked them, being defeated only in a second campaign fourteen years after the first.[3]

General Summary. We thus get the following picture: the Kimäk and/or Qypčaq on the Irtisch; the Guz on and east of the Aral Sea; the Petchenegs between the Emba and the Volga; the Khazars on the lower Volga, and west of that river; the Burtās astride the Volga above the Khazars; the Bulgars on the Volga and the Kama. By elimination, then, we should be able to find the position of the Magyars, which is given with reference, direct or indirect, to most of these nations; but here, for the first time, we shall encounter difficulties.

---

1 Chvolson, *op. cit.* p. 159, followed by Kuun, *Relatio*, etc. I, 129, identifies the Ašgil with the Széklers of Transylvania, with disastrous results. Fehér (*Beziehungen*, pp. 98 ff.) is, if possible, even less happy when he prefers to Ibn Rusta the text of Gardēzī, with its slip "between the Bulgars and the Bulgars", and goes looking for a race of Bulgars on the Black Sea. Our report is most explicit on the fact that all three classes of Bulgars *live in one place.*

2 *D.A.I.* c. 12.

3 See below, Excursus II, p. 160.

THE REPORT ON THE MAGYARS

It will readily be seen that the report on the Magyars falls far short of the others in lucidity. In fact, if it be taken as it stands, it is impossible to fit in all indications contained in it without hopeless contradictions being involved. If, for example, the dry steppe of the opening sentences be accepted, what is to be done about the moist ground, many trees and much water of the latter part? If the Magyars are neighbours of the Petchenegs and the Bulgars, how can they be at the same time living on the Cuban, their backs to the Caucasus? And what truck can they be having with the Slavs and the Russians?

The more the report is considered as a whole, the greater will the difficulties be found to be. Nor will such difficulties even be confined to the subject-matter. They will extend also to the form; for the great divergencies between the three versions of the report ought to be explained somehow.

If, however, the three versions be set side by side, the report will be seen to fall into three clearly marked divisions.

("A") A portion common to all three versions alike.

("B") A portion in which Gardēzī agrees in part with Ibn Rusta, while adding certain supplementary information; whereas al-Bekrī has what appears to be a totally different description.

("C") A portion in which Ibn Rusta and Gardēzī practically agree, while al-Bekrī drops out altogether.

The key to the interpretation of the whole report is the understanding that this division is not a meaningless one. Each of the three, in fact, describes a different situation. Two of them are contemporary, and belong to the original report which I term α (or rather, to be quite accurate, $\alpha + \gamma$); but they describe two different localities, the Magyar nation having been, at that time, divided into two parts, whose frontiers were not contiguous. The third (portion "C") comes from a different source (β) and describes a later situation, which again differs from both of the others. The inconsistencies now vanish, and three separate pictures emerge, each consistent and sensible in itself, and each supported by external evidence.

REPORT "A"

Ibn Rusta	*Al-Bekri*	*Gardēzī*
Between the country of the Bajanakiyya and the country of the Aškal, who belong to the Balkariyya, is the first of the Magyar boundaries.	The Muhaffiyya are between the country of the Bajanakiyya and the country of the Aškal, who also belong to the [Balk]ariyya.	Between the country of the Balkar and the country of Aškal, which is also part of Bulkar,[1] is the boundary of the Magariyāns.
	The Magyars are idolaters, and	
The Magyars are a race of Turks, and their chieftain rides with horsemen to the number of 10,000, and their chieftain is called Kanda (and this name denotes their king, for the man who is king over them is called Jula, and all the Magyars accept the orders of their king Jula, in the matter of war and defence and the like).	The name of their king is Kanda.	And these Magyars are a Turkish race and their leader rides out with 20,000 horsemen, and they call this king Kanda (and this is the name of their greater king, and that chief who superintends their affairs is called Jula, and the Magyars do whatever Jula commands).
They possess leather tents, and they travel about in search of herbage and abundant pasture.	They live in tents and they go in search of the place where rain falls and places where there is pasturage.	They have a plain which is all dry herbage.
Their country is extensive, and one frontier extends to the sea of Rūm.	The extent of their country is 100 parasangs in breadth. One boundary of their country adjoins the region of Rūm.	[They have] a wide territory, and their country has an extent of 100 × 100 parasangs and it adjoins the sea of Rūm.

1 So Gardēzī's text; but not only the sense, but also the consensus of the other two versions proves that this word is a slip for "Petchenegs".

Another, and abbreviated version of the same passage (in al-Bekrī's rendering) is given by Abulfēdā,[1] as follows:

Almadjagarya.
According to the Athoual, 78° 44′ longitude, 51° 44′ latitude. Madjgarya is the capital of the country of the Madjgers, in the north of the seventh climate. The Madjgars are a people of Turkish race. Some authors say that their land is situated between the Petchenegs and the Aškal, who belong to the Bulgars. The Magyars are fire-worshippers; they dwell in tents and pavilions, and seek for places irrigated by water and covered by pasturage. Their country is 100 parasangs in length and as much in breadth; one of its ends touches the Empire of Rūm, which bounds it on the desert end.

Unfortunately this passage has only been available to me in Reinaud's French translation, and I am unable to say how far the variations from my version of al-Bekrī correspond to variations in the original text. It is, however, at least very significant that this passage should be standing alone in Abulfēdā's version, which contains no trace of the later portion of our report; and this alone would be strong support for the correctness of the division which I have made. I will return later to the individual phrases. Meanwhile, it is necessary to locate the district referred to.

Let it once be understood that these sentences (portion "A") form part of that coherent and homogeneous report which we have described as α, and the conclusion follows automatically. The Petchenegs were living between the Emba and the Volga; the Bulgars on the middle Volga and the Kama. Therefore the "first frontier of the Magyars" must be placed somewhere on the line between these two, i.e. somewhere on the southern slopes of the Ural mountains.

There is strong independent support for this conclusion.

Constantine's Μάζαροι.

Firstly, we have practically contemporary evidence to the same effect—an extremely valuable testimony for which we are indebted, unexpectedly enough, to the Petchenegs. In c. 37 of the *D.A.I.* (a chapter ultimately derived, beyond any doubt, from a Petcheneg source), we find the following words:

---

[1] Aboulfēdā, *Géographie*, tr. Reinaud, II, 324.

"Petchenegs lived originally (ἀπ' ἀρχῆς) on the river Volga, and likewise on the river Ural, having as neighbours the Mazars and the so-called Uz".[1]

The emendation, which many editors have made, of this enigmatic name of Μαζάρους to Χαζάρους is purely arbitrary. Μαζάρους is the only reading of the text, and no reason can be given why the original and apparently much easier X, if it had been the original, should have been changed. The error could only have been due to a pure slip of the pen, almost unparalleled in Constantine's text.

Nor, again, is it sound to advance the argument that a different transliteration of the Magyar name—Μεγέρη—occurs elsewhere in Constantine's work. For in the passage in question, which occurs in c. 40 of the *D.A.I.*, Constantine is deriving his information from a different source—apparently Magyar or Kavar.[2] The name in c. 37, on the other hand, comes ultimately from a Petcheneg source. It may even be true that the name is not correctly transliterated according to Petcheneg rules—although as our entire knowledge of the Petcheneg tongue amounts to twenty or thirty names, transmitted through Greek, Slavonic, Hungarian or dog-Latin sources, this is hard to judge with apodictic accuracy. Yet granted this, strict philological rules cannot be applied in the case of a single name, not even understood by the person who heard it, but written down blindly—for had Constantine realised the identity of those "Mazars", he would probably have changed the name to Τοῦρκοι. Who knows how this name actually entered Constantine's pages? Perhaps the Petcheneg who transmitted it had his mouth full at the time; perhaps he, or the man who took it down, was drunk. Perhaps it was not a Petcheneg at all, but a slave speaking one of the seventy-two languages of the Caucasus.

There appears, therefore, to be no justification for rejecting the reading Μαζάρους, which affords striking confirmation of Džaihānī's statement.

It may be asked, why of all their neighbours, the Petchenegs should have chosen to mention these two: the Uz and the

1 *D.A.I.* c. 37.　　　　2 See below, pp. 112 ff.

Magyars. And I believe that even to this reasonable question an answer can be found. The Uz and the Magyars must have been neighbours of the Petchenegs in a sense very different from the sedentary Khazars, behind the river-barrier of the lower Volga, or the Burtās, in the forests further north. These two nations were, like the Petchenegs, nomad herdsmen; they must have shared and often disputed the feeding-grounds with them, and impressed their proximity upon them in a peculiar way.

Survival of the name of Magyar. Furthermore, the name "Magyar" is found in or near the district in question, many centuries later, reappearing, mingled with the name of Baškir, both in later Russian documents, and also in place-names.[1] The majority of these are on the right bank of the Volga; but it is natural to suppose that the Magyars, like many other races of the Volga basin, were driven some distance westward by the Mongol invasion.

No less important is the archaeological evidence. Buttons and other products bearing specifically Magyar design, and dating, apparently, from about the ninth to the thirteenth centuries, have been found in considerable quantities in the same districts. Certain investigators would be prepared to recognise the existence of Magyars in the precise district where our report places them, and in a larger area north-east of it, on this archaeological evidence alone.[2]

Magyars and Baškirs. A point which deserves rather more detailed consideration is that of the affinity between the Magyars and the Baškirs.

The question whether the Magyars were, in point of ethno-graphical fact, identical with the Baškirs, is, I understand, still disputed among specialists. Professor Homán, in the essay quoted at the beginning of this work, writes that "Professor Gombocz' discoveries have put an end once and for all to the

1 Smirnov, *op. cit.* quotes a large number of names compounded with Mažar or Možar in the Governments of Kazan, Simbush, Tambov and Saratov, which prove that a people bearing the name must at one time have constituted a large element in the population.

2 For this information I am indebted to Dr N. Fettich, of the Budapest National Museum.

imagined identity of the Magyars with the Baškirs ";[1] but
Professor Németh's even more recent article on "Magna
Hungaria" concludes that "the Baškirs are originally a part of
the Magyar people, which probably migrated northward from
the Caucasus together with the Volga Bulgars".[2]

Whatever be the ethnographical facts of the case, it is not in
dispute that the Oriental geographers and historians believed
the Magyars and the Baškirs to be identical. Indeed, the name
of Magyar was hardly, if at all, known to them, except in the
passage which we are now discussing, and the later passages
derived from it. Mas'ūdī, in his various references to the
Valandar hordes, which undoubtedly contain, amongst other
ingredients, a reminiscence of the Magyar raid on Constantinople in 934, includes a nation of "Baģģird" which can be none
other than the Magyars; the same writer, where he tells us that
the kingdom of al-Firāg (Prague) makes war on the Rūm, the
Franks and the Bažkarda, is once again describing the Magyars
under the name of Baškirs.

In later writers the identification is even clearer. Thus Jāqūt,
after giving a story of "Baškirs" in Hungary, goes straight on to
quote Ibn Fozlān's report of the "Baškirs" whom he encountered on his journey from Khwārism to Bolgar. In other
writers, to whom information from Western sources was also
available, a very curious confusion arises. The "Hungarians"
(Unkār) are represented as living side by side with "Baškirs"
in the present Hungary—the identity of the single nation not
being realised under the two names.[3] The practice was so wide-

1 The quotation is from memory, as I have not now the work by me; but I
believe it not to misrepresent the sense.

2 J. Németh, *Magna Hungaria*, Separatabdruck aus *Beiträge zur historischen
Geographie, Kulturgeographie, Ethnographie und Kartographie, vornehmlich
des Orients*, Leipzig and Vienna, 1929.

3 A convenient list of references is given in Németh, *op. cit.* Failure to
realise the cause of the confusion has led an earlier generation of Hungarian
historians into deep waters on many occasions, e.g. Vambéry's suggestion that
Kazvīnī and Jāqūt are speaking with knowledge of events of their own time, and
describe the Cumans under the name of Baškirs, is untenable. Abulfēdā (ed.
Reinaud, I, 294) makes the Baškird Moslem Turks (a reminiscence of Jāqūt's
story) "established in the neighbourhood of the Germans, with whom they
live in constant harmony", while the "Hungarians, the brothers of the
Baškird", live next them to the east, but are Christians. Dimašqi (*Cosmographie*, pp. 255–6) makes Baškird and Ankāradah live together on the shores

spread and so deep-rooted that the Ural Cossacks who entered Hungary in 1849 are said to have addressed the Magyars there as Baškirs.

It is thus certain that the term was one in common use, and this can have been due only to one of two causes: either that the Magyars were actually identical with the Baškirs, or else that those Magyars with whom the Oriental geographers first came into contact were so mixed with and assimilated to the Baškirs as to be indistinguishable from them. The result, for our purposes, is precisely the same; for such conditions could not have occurred in any place except in the country south of the Urals (where the Baškirs are living today)—that district where the Petchenegs placed the Μάζαροι and our own writer the "first frontier of the Magyars".[1]

We are therefore justified in asking whether there do not exist some descriptions of the Baškirs under that name, in the same locality, which might confirm our result regarding the "first frontier of the Magyars". The passage which immediately leaps to the mind is, of course, Ibn Fozlān's description of the Baškirs whom he met on his journey;[2] and I think that there is an exceedingly strong case for believing this description actually to have been one of the Magyars. At all events, it was so taken, not only by Jāqūt, but also, as I shall show below, by al-Bekrī.

More interesting still is a very old merchant's itinerary, also dating from before the Petcheneg migration, and preserved in various versions, of which we may quote:

of the Black Sea (this last is derived directly from Mas'ūdī's "Valandar hordes", and might have put commentators right on his text, which the Paris edition, with perverse ingenuity, reads Nūkarda = Nūkobarda, Lombards).

[1] The geographers were familiar enough with the countries lying on the road to Bolgar, but exceedingly ill acquainted, until a much later date, with the lands lying immediately north of the Caucasus—a region shut off from civilisation by the great wall fabled to have been built by the great Iskander to shut in the detestable peoples of Gog and Magog. So well did the wall do its work (even though none of Alexander's handiwork) that on one of the rare occasions when an Arab force did venture past it, they were able to persuade the inhabitants of the steppe that they were angels, and consequently invulnerable. The deception went swimmingly, until one pragmatical sceptic put it to the test, with disastrous results for the subject of his experiments. See Tabarī, O.T.F. edition, III, 499.

[2] See Appendix.

Istachrī (tr. Mordtmann):[1]

From Atel to the first frontier of Burtās, 20 days' journey. From one end of Burtās to the other, about 15 days. From the first frontier of the Burtās to the Bedjnāk (Petchenegs), 10 merhileh; from Atel to the Bedjnāk, one month. From Atel to Bolgar by the steppe, about one month; by water, two months going up, one month down. From Bolgar to the first frontier of the Rūm,[2] about ten days; from Bulgar to Kiev, about 20 days; from the Baškird to the inner Bulgars, 25 days.

Istachrī (tr. Ouseley)[3] has:

Itil-Burtās, 20 days; Burtās-Petchenegs, 10 days; Itil-Petchenegs, one month; Itil-Bolgar, one month by land, two by water; Bolgar-Rūm, 10 merhileh; Bolgar-Kiev, 20 merhileh; Petchenegs-Baškirs, 10 days; Baškirs-Bolgar, 20 merhileh.

Idrīsī has the variant: "Petchenegs-Inner-Baškirt, 10 merhileh; Inner-Baškirt-Bolgar, 25 merhileh".[4]

While it is difficult to be dogmatic regarding the original text of which these three versions are variations, it seems probable that Idrīsī has preserved the true text. Istachrī (tr. Mordtmann) has been misled into transferring the epithet "inner" from the Baškirs, to which it properly belongs, to the Bulgars by his acquaintanceship with the "inner Bulgars", or Bulgars of the Danube, to which he devotes a note immediately preceding that quoted above.[5] This impression is confirmed by comparison with a parallel descriptive passage, also originally dating from

1 See Appendix.

2 This is a difficult phrase, which undoubtedly contains some corruption. The most reasonable explanation seems to be that the original in the itinerary had "Rūs", but a change was made, either by accident or on purpose, to suit later information to hand about the Danube Bulgars, the wide separation between the two nations not being realised. See below, note 5. Mas'ūdī also makes the Volga Bulgars attack Constantinople, and even further afield, and nis words have been taken *au pied de la lettre* even by such scholars as Rambaud in his *Empire Grec*. So much confusion may arise out of a single letter!

3 *The Geography of Ibn Hauqal*, p. 190 (this is not, however, Ibn Hauqal's work, but a MS of Istachrī, containing considerable variations from the MS used by Mordtmann).

4 Edrisi, tr. Jaubert, II, 463.

5 Artha (= the Ersa Mordvinians) lies between the Khazars and the Great Bulgaria which borders on the Rūm to the north. These Bulgars are very numerous, and so powerful that they impose tribute on the Rūm, who are their neighbours. The Inner Bulgars are Christians.

the time before the Petcheneg move (although brought up to
date in the Oriental fashion), and first found in al-Balḥī (although the original text must have been older).[1]

Al-Balḥī's version runs as follows:

There are two kinds of Bašǧirt. The one lives hard on the frontiers
of Guz, behind the Bulgars. It is said that their numbers amount to
2000 men, who are so protected by forests that no man can subdue
them. They are subject to the Bulgars. The other Bašǧirt are neighbours of the Petchenegs. They and the Petchenegs are Turks, and
neighbours of Rūm.[2]

This description is repeated by Istachrī, Ibn Hauqal (with
the variant "the greater part of the Bašǧirt are neighbours of
the Petchenegs"), Idrīsī and Abulfēdā.

Idrīsī, in the same passage, has a detailed description of the
countries of Inner and Outer Baškirt, from which it may be
clearly seen that the Magyars of Hungary are not meant under
either name.[3] On the contrary, the "Outer Baškirt" are shown
as living at the southern extremity of the Ural mountains, the
"Inner Baškirt" eleven days west of the others, approximately
between the Kama and the Emba.

This description of the Baškirs agrees, it may be added, with
that of Gardēzī, who places the Baškirs between the Khazars
and the Kimäk.[4]

Putting together the descriptive passage and the itinerary,
we get the impression that the nation described as the "Outer
Baškirs", in the Urals, are the Baškirs of today. The "Inner
Baškirs", on the other hand, are placed in exactly the same

1 Al-Balḥī died in A.D. 934, but the original text certainly refers to nations
east of the Volga only, and Németh, *op. cit.* seems mistaken in supposing that
the homes of the Guz referred to here are their new feeding-grounds (the
old Petcheneg territory).

2 The last words are confusing, but explicable if taken as referring to the
Petchenegs alone, and inserted, as a late addition, after the Petcheneg move;
cf. Istachrī's own account: "One Turkish people has separated from the
rest, and gone to dwell between the Khazars and Rūm; they are called
Bedjnāk". This passage does not, it will be observed, mention the Magyars.

3 See Appendix.

4 Gardēzī, in his section on the Turks, tells us that a certain Slav noble, after
staying with the Khagan of the Khazars, "went to Bašǧirt, who was one of
the nobles of the Khazars, and dwelt between the Khazars and the Kimäk
with 2000 horsemen". The coincidence of the number 2000 in both accounts
is very striking.

locality as our report's "first frontier of the Magyars", with whom they should be identified. Both are identical with Ibn Fozlān's Baškirs; for this is the country through which his journey from Khwārism to Bolgar must have brought him.

These Baškir-Magyars make a sudden and most interesting reappearance in history in the thirteenth century, when emissaries were sent from Hungary to get into touch with them. The discoveries of these missionaries go to confirm our conclusions still further; but the subject is too long to be dealt with in the course of our argument, and I have therefore relegated it to another place.[1]

Detail of the report "A". I hope that the identification of the district in which our author gives the "first frontier of the Magyars" has now been placed beyond doubt. It remains to remark on a few points of detail in this section of our report.

The division between the section now under discussion and the next one is clearly enough marked, at least in the purer texts of Ibn Rusta and al-Bekrī, both of whom make the proper distinction between the first and second "frontiers". On the whole, the report, though brief, is clear and sensible, and presents few points of difficulty.

The chief difficulty is undoubtedly al-Bekrī's statement to the effect that "the Magyars are idolaters". Neither of the other two versions has anything corresponding to this sentence, this being the only sentence in the section where al-Bekrī has any independent information. Further, the statement is incompatible with what both Ibn Rusta and Gardēzī say of the Magyars in the later portion of the report (C).

The discrepancy has perplexed various writers,[2] but the difficulty disappears when al-Bekrī's system of working is understood. We have shown above that he habitually epitomised Džaihānī, and also that he added information from other sources, where available. We have also shown that he was acquainted with Ibn Fozlān's report on the Khazars. Our difficulties therefore vanish if we can assume that he also knew

---

1 Excursus II.

2 So Szinnyei, *Die Herkunft der Ungarn*, p. 47, says that "it is incomprehensible where al-Bekrī got his idol-worship from".

of the same writer's report on the Baškirs, and inserted this sentence from that source, which has a very drastic description of the Baškirs' idolatry.

The statement, common to all three writers, that "the Magyars are a race of Turks" cannot be taken as first-class ethnographical evidence, although Ibn Fozlān, and after him Mas'ūdī, have the same statement. The early Oriental writers used the term "Turk" in a very loose sense. It is, however, worth noting that al-Kašgarī, in his eleventh-century Turkish grammar, reckons the Baškirs as Turks and groups their speech with that of the Kimäk.[1]

When it is understood that this branch of the Magyars is not the same as those of whom Constantine writes that "they had no king, but there were certain voivodes among them",[2] the contradiction of evidence disappears. Whether Kanda be a name or a title, I cannot say. It is tempting to compare the Χανδίχ mentioned by Menander as the Avar ambassador to Justinian in A.D. 568.[3]

Although al-Bekrī omits the passage on the Jula, its appearance in both the other texts proves that it must have been in the archetype. It is interesting to find the same institution as we know to have been flourishing among the Magyars of Hungary in the tenth century[4] also existing among their cousins of the East. The institution of a *roi fainéant* is, of course, typically Turkish. It must have been current among the Magyars since an early date, and was perhaps a relic of the Bulgar domination.

The description of the Magyars' way of living (which al-Bekrī repeats in almost identical terms of the Petchenegs in the steppes south of the Magyars) is another proof for our identification of the locality described. The description is not at all

---

1 See Brockelmann, "Mahmud al-Kašgharī", *K.C.A.* 1 Köt. 1 Szám, April 1921, p. 36: "I give a list of the chief Turkish tribes. The tribe nearest the Rūm are the Päcänäg, then Qyfčaq, then Jämäk, Bašgirt, Bašmil, etc....The Qyrgiz, Qifčaq, Oguz, Tuxsi, Jagma, Čigil, Igraq and Čaruq have one single, pure Turkish speech. That of the Jämäk and the Bašgirt resembles it".

2 *D.A.I.* c. 38.

3 *Excerpta de Legationibus*, ed. de Boor, p. 470.

4 *D.A.I.* c. 41, and below, pp. 117–21.

applicable even to the plains of South Russia, which have, at least, large rivers; much less to the well-watered plains of the Caucasus. It is definitely characteristic of an arid steppe region, such as lies north of the Caspian.

In view of Abulfēdā's support, Gardēzī's reading, 100 × 100 parasangs may be accepted.

The last sentence forms a connecting link with the second section of the report, in which connection it will be considered.

THE REPORT ON THE MAGYARS "B"

(See pages 41 and 42)

Section "B" of our report is given shortly by Ibn Rusta, at greater length by Gardēzī, and in an almost entirely different form by al-Bekrī. This portion is easily the most difficult, but also the most interesting of the three to elucidate.

Ibn Rusta's version. The first point to be noted here is that the report in Ibn Rusta's version appears to form a homogeneous whole with report "A". Ibn Rusta's report is, indeed, perfectly clear, and presents no difficulties, except that it is couched in such general terms that the two rivers might be any two running into the "Sea of Rūm"—a phrase by which we must certainly understand, in this instance, the Black Sea.[1]

Ibn Rusta, like al-Bekrī, makes a clear distinction: the "first frontier" in the Urals, while "one frontier" extends to the Black Sea. His information on the latter "frontier" is, however, more scanty than on the former, as is only natural, when it is remembered that this report forms part of α and probably is the work of a merchant from Khwārism, who can never have penetrated to the Black Sea coast.

[1] The later Arabic writers regularly use the name Nītōs (Pontus) for the Black Sea, while the "Sea of Rūm" properly denotes the Mediterranean; but among the earlier writers, great confusion prevails between these two seas, and also the Palus Maiotis. It is obvious that the Mediterranean is out of the question here.

REPORT "B"

Ibn Rusta

Their country is extensive, and one frontier extends to the sea of Rūm,

and two rivers flow into that sea, one of them greater than Džaihūn,[1] and their dwellings are between these two rivers, and in the winter they go to whichever river is nearest to them, and settle there for the winter. They catch fish from it, and their abode for the winter is reserved to them here.

Al-Bekri

The extent of their country is 100 parasangs in breadth. One boundary of their country adjoins the region of Rūm.

At the other boundary, where it touches the steppe, is a mountain, and the people who dwell there are called Ayin. They have horses and flocks and cultivated land.

[1] = the Oxus.

Gardēzī

(They have)...a wide territory and their country has an extent of 100 × 100 parasangs and it adjoins the sea of Rūm,

since the river Džaihūn flows into that sea. They dwell between (sic) that river and when winter comes any person who is far from the Džaihūn comes near it again and in winter remains there and they catch fish and subsist thereby. That is the Džaihūn which is on their left hand. Beside Saqlāb there is a people of Rūm who are all Christians and they are called Nandar, and they are more numerous than the Magyars, but they are weaker.

They call these two rivers, the one Ītil and the other Dūbā. When the Magyars are on the bank of the river they see these Nandarin there.

Above the bank of the river is a great mountain, and water flows out on to the side of the mountain,

42

REPORT " B " (continued)

Ibn Rusta

Al-Bekri

Below this mountain on the shore of the sea are a people called Awghūna, and they are Christians, and adjoin the country of those Moslems connected with the country of Tiflis and it is the beginning of the country of Armenia. This mountain extends as far as the land of Bāb-el-Abwāb and adjoins the country of the Khazars.

Gardēzi

and behind that mountain are a people of Christians called Mirdāt;

between them and the Nandar is a ten days' journey. They are a numerous people, and their dress resembles that of the Arabs (consisting) of skirt and turban and overcoat. They have cultivated land and seed and vineyards for with them the water runs over the surface of the land and has no canals for irrigation. They state that their number is greater than that of the Rūm and that they are a separate nation. The greater part of their trade is with Arabia. The river which is to the right of the Magyars goes to Saqlāb and from there dwindles away in the district of Khazar, and that river is greater than these two rivers (*sic*).

The other two versions are more extensive, and at once introduce difficulties, and enable us to locate the "two rivers".

Gardēzī's version. Gardēzī's version consists of a rendering of Ibn Rusta's, plus an explanatory addition (γ) describing the two rivers and the Magyars' neighbours. Whether this addition is contemporary with α, or later, will be discussed shortly. For the moment, we will confine ourselves to elucidating it.

The addition has been made in a remarkably clumsy fashion. Out of five consecutive sentences, the first, third and fifth are concerned with the river alone; the second (which has got itself mixed up grammatically with the first) refers to a people, the "Nandarin", alone; the fourth to the Nandarin and the river. A descriptive passage follows, ending with another reference to the rivers. The river on the side of Saqlāb (the Slavs) appears both on the left and the right of the Magyars. We are left with two rivers, the Ītīl and the Dūbā, and two nations, the Mirdāt and the Nandarin, to identify.

The Dūbā. For Dūbā a very slight emendation[1] would give us Kūbā=the Cuban. This interpretation is *a priori* so satisfactory that we shall keep it unless we find later reason to believe ourselves wrong.

The Nandarin. Beyond the Cuban, looking across it at the Magyars, are the "Nandarin". The *name* is unintelligible; at least, no satisfactory explanation of it has, to my knowledge, ever been given.[2] On the other hand, once given the identification of the river, the identification of the nation follows as a matter of geography, since the district in question has been occupied since time immemorial, and, indeed, is still occupied today, only by the nation of the Circassians. Our ninth-century sources, which should be contemporary with the report which we are discussing, are, unfortunately, almost non-existent; but tenth-century sources are abundant enough, and Constantine

---

1 دوبا for کوبا.

2 If, as seems likely, this information was derived ultimately from a Magyar source, one would expect the name to be a Magyar one; but Hungarian scholars are not agreed on its interpretation, nor on that of the only other Magyar name resembling it: Nandorfehérvár, the mediaeval Magyar name for Belgrade (fehérvár = White Fortress). A colony of "Nandarin" prisoners of war seems difficult to suppose.

Porphyrogenetos,[1] Istachrī,[2] Masʿūdī[3] and the Russian Chronicle[4] all attest the presence of this numerous race in the haunts where both older and younger writers find them.

The description of the Circassians as a people of Rūm may present some difficulty; I have been unable to find any reliable information as to the exact extent of Byzantine influence in the Western Caucasus in the ninth century.[5] The description of them as Christians does, however, appear to be correct, or at all events, near enough accuracy for an Oriental geographer. "Zichia", as the sea-board of Circassia was commonly known to the Greeks, has behind it a record of Christianity dating at least from the sixth century,[6] while from the ninth or tenth century onward, it may even have been a centre of missionary work for surrounding countries.[7] In any case, at a time when

---

1 *D.A.I.* c. 42 *fin.*: ἀπὸ τὸ Ταμάταρχά ἐστι ποταμὸς ἀπὸ μιλίων ιη´ ἢ καὶ κ´, λεγόμενος Οὐκρούχ (the Cuban), ὁ διαχωρίζων τὴν Ζιχίαν καὶ τὸ Ταμάταρχα. ἀπὸ δὲ τοῦ Οὐκρούχ μέχρι τοῦ Νικόψεως ποταμοῦ, ἐν ᾧ καὶ κάστρον ἐστὶν ὁμώνυμον τῷ ποταμῷ, ἔστιν ἡ χώρα τῆς Ζιχίας τὸ δὲ διάστημά ἐστι μίλια τ´· ἄνωθεν τῆς Ζιχίας ἐστὶν ἡ χώρα ἡ λεγομένη Παπαγία καὶ ἄνωθεν τῆς Παπαγίας χώρας ἐστὶν ἡ χώρα ἡ λεγομένη Κασαχία (again two names—Ζιχία and Κασαχία —for Circassia)· ἄνωθεν δὲ τῆς Κασαχίας ὄρη τὰ Καυκάσιά ἐστι, καὶ τῶν ὀρέων ἄνωθέν ἐστιν ἡ χώρα τῆς Ἀλανίας.

2 Istachrī has the phrase "the mountains of Kasākīa" for the western end of the Caucasus.

3 Masʿūdī, *Livre d'Avertissement*, p. 249, gives the Kašāk and Kāšah (inaccurately dividing them into two nations) as among the peoples inhabiting the Caucasus. In the *Meadows of Gold* he has a long description of the nation, to which I shall return below.

4 "Iasi" (= Alans) and "Kassogues" (= Circassians) occur frequently in that part of the Russian Chronicle which relates to the annals of Taman, e.g. "Nestor", I, 90, 171–2.

5 It is worth noting that in the *De Ceremoniis* the Emperor issues "orders" (κελεύσεις) to the petty princes of the Caucasus.

6 A Bishop John of Phanagoria was present at the Synod of Constantinople in 518, and a Bishop Domitianus of Zichia signed the condemnation of the Patriarch at the Council of Constantinople in 536 (J. Zeiller, *Les origines chrétiennes dans les provinces danubiennes*, Paris, 1918, pp. 384, 496).

7 The Παλαιὰ τακτικά have an Ἐπαρχία Ζιχίας with three autocephalic churches at Bosporus, Cherson and Nicopsis (Constantine, *De Ceremoniis*, pp. 792–3). A letter by Nicholas Mysticus in the early tenth century (Migne, *P.G.* cxi, letter 58) invites the unknown addressee (who may well have been the Archbishop of Taman) to give all assistance to the Archbishop-designate of Cherson, who had been sent to ordain bishops and propagate the gospel in the course of attempts then on foot to convert "Khazaria". In the syntagma compiled under Alexius Comnenus, Taman appears as a metropolitan bishopric, under Constantinople; under Andronicus Palaeologos, the Arch-

Christianity was being propagated all about it—in Khazaria under the Iconoclasts, through St Cyril, and in the tenth century;[1] in Abasgia from an early date; in Alania in the tenth century at the latest;[2] and even among the distant Serīrī, it is unthinkable that the sea-board population, which was in such close touch with Taman, Cherson, and Constantinople itself, should have remained unaffected.[3] The evidence on the other side is confined to the Georgian Chronicle[4] and a single passage in Mas'ūdī,[5] and it is easy to imagine that these might both refer rather to the mountainous inland districts, which would naturally cling longer to their old pagan beliefs. The Circassians, it must be remembered, were never a united people; and in any case, the nations of the Caucasus never minded having several religions, consecutively or even simultaneously.[6]

Mas'ūdī has a detailed description of the Circassians,[7] which

bishop of Taman appears as titular Archbishop of Zichia (ὁ Ματράχων, ὃς καὶ Ζηκχίας λέγεται), and is raised to the rank of Metropolitan. See, for these points, especially J. Gelzer, "Ungedruckte und wenig bekannte Bistumsver-hältnisse", *B.Z.* I, 245 ff. and II, 22 ff. Some authorities believe that the bishopric of Taman was revived by the patriarch Photius; but this seems to be no more than a conjecture, however plausible. Cf. Dvornik, *Slaves, Byzance et Rome au IXième Siècle*, Paris, 1926, p. 146.

1 Dvornik, *op. cit.* pp. 137 ff.

2 The letters of Nicholas Mysticus show the Abasgians already Christians, and the missionaries hard at work in Alania. Mas'ūdī tells us that the Alans were originally heathens, adopted Christianity under the Abbaside dynasty, and repudiated it after the year 320 H. (A.D. 922), expelling the bishops and priests whom the Greeks had sent to them. Our own old report *a* (see Appendix) makes the king of the Alans a Christian, but the mass of his people idolaters.

3 The letter from Photius (Migne, *P.G.* CII, col. 828) is interesting in this respect, as where he expresses to the Bishop of Bosporus his gratification that the shores of the Black Sea, formerly so inhospitable (ἄξεινος), were now becoming, not only hospitable (εὔξεινος), but also pious (εὐσεβής).

4 Tr. Brosset, I, 68. The Blessed St Andrew "went to Djiketh, whose inhabitants were fierce, given over to vice, unbelieving and without religion. Not only did they refuse to receive him, but they planned to kill him. But Divine protection saved him. Seeing their hardness of heart and their beastly minds, he left them and departed; this is why today they still persevere in unbelief".

5 *Meadows of Gold*, p. 437.

6 Cf. in the Appendix the cases of the Alans, the Serīrī, the Khazars, and most notable of all, the district of Jandan, near Serīrī, where Islam, Christianity and a private heathen cult were all practised simultaneously.

7 *Meadows of Gold*, pp. 436 ff. The translation which I give is by Miss Smith.

I consider interesting enough to quote in full. It will be seen that, just as our own report describes the Magyars facing another nation (the Nandarin) across the Cuban, so Mas'ūdī describes the Circassians facing across the same river an unnamed nation. I believe that in all probability that nation is none other than the Magyars, and that our own report and Mas'ūdī's are mutually confirmatory.

Adjacent to the country of the Alans are a people called Kašaks who [dwell] between the Caucasus and the Sea of Rūm.

They are a clean-living people, following the religion of the Magians. Among the nations whom we have mentioned [as living] in this district, there is none in which [is found] a more pleasing appearance, a clearer complexion [or fresher colour], more handsome men, more comely women; nor [are any] more upright in bearing, more slender in the waist, with more prominent hips and buttocks, and with finer figures than this people.

Their women are celebrated for the charm of their favours and for the white garments they wear, and their dresses of Greek brocade and scarlet cloth and other kinds of brocade embroidered in gold. In their country different kinds of cloth are manufactured from flax: one kind is called "Tala",[1] finer than "Dibaqi"[2] and more durable. One length of it costs 10 dinars, and it is exported to the neighbouring Islamic countries. These kinds of cloth are exported also from those peoples who live near to them [i.e. the Kašaks], but the most celebrated [or the best] comes from them.

The Alans have shown themselves stronger than these people, and the latter could not maintain themselves against the Alans unless they were protected against the Alans by means of their fortresses on the sea-shore.[3] There has been some controversy as to the sea on which they live; some people consider it to be the Sea of Rūm, and some think that it is the Sea of Nītās [Pontus]. At any rate they keep up an intercourse by sea with Trebizond, and merchandise comes to them by ship from there, and they, in their turn, send supplies thither.

The reason for their weakness as regards the Alans is that they have ceased to be ruled by one king, who could unite them [lit.

1 O.T.F. edition, "Tati".
2 Damask cloth.
3 Compare with this the closely parallel passage in Constantine, *D.A.I.* c. 42:
ἡ δὲ τῆς Ζιχίας παράλιος ἔχει νησία, τὸ μέγα νησίον καὶ τὰ τρία νησία· ἔνδοθεν δὲ τούτων ἐστὶ καὶ ἕτερα νησία τὰ ἐπινοηθέντα καὶ παρὰ τῶν Ζιχῶν κτισθέντα, τό τε Τουργανανῆρχ καὶ τὸ Τζαρβαγάνι καὶ ἕτερον νησίον, καὶ εἰς τὸν τοῦ ποταμοῦ λιμένα ἕτερον νῆσον, καὶ εἰς τὰς Πτελίας ἕτερον, ἐν ᾧ ἐν ταῖς τῶν Ἀλανῶν ἐπιδρομαῖς οἱ Ζιχοὶ καταφεύγουσι.

make them agree in their speech], and if they were united, neither the Alans nor any other people would get the better of them.

The meaning of their name, which is Persian, is "pride" and "arrogance" and in fact the Persians, if a man is proud or arrogant, call him "Kaš".

Adjoining this people on this sea, is another people whose country is called "The Seven Lands". They are a great nation, able to protect themselves, whose jurisdiction extends to a great distance. I do not know [anything of] their people [or rites] nor has any information reached me concerning their religious faith.

Next to them dwells a numerous people, between whose country and that of the Kašaks is a river as great as the Euphrates, which flows into the Sea of Nītās, on which Trebizond is built. These people are called Irem; they are possessed of unusual character and are given up to paganism.

In connection with this country on this sea there is a strange account of fish which come to them [i.e. these people] every year, and they take a portion from the fish, which afterwards return a second time and present to them the other side [of their body] and those people supply themselves from that [side] and [meanwhile] the flesh has been renewed on the place whence it was taken the first time. [This] story about this people is well known among the unbelievers of that country.[1]

Here we find a clear and most interesting account of the Circassians, living on the sea-shore, with the Alans at their backs (a situation similar to that described by Constantine); but who are their neighbours, the "Seven Lands" and the "Irem"?

Both of these are certainly conceived as living north of the Circassians. The southern neighbours of the Circassians were the Abasgians, with whom Mas'ūdī was acquainted, and to whom the descriptions are inapplicable in every respect. Moreover, Mas'ūdī goes on to wander into the realms of semi-legend, showing that he is describing an unknown and distant country, which can only lie in the north. The "river greater than the Euphrates" can be none other than the Cuban, which Constantine also gives as the northern frontier of the Circassians. The "Seven Lands" are also north of the Circassians; for

---

1 This story appears to be a reference to the simple habit of the fisherman, on catching the sturgeon, of slitting open its belly, taking out the eggs, and throwing the fish back into the water. It would be equally applicable to any nation of fishermen in the Cuban, which from earliest times was renowned for its sturgeon.

reading "next to them" as meaning "next to the Seven Lands", we get the "Seven Lands" neighbours of the Irem, north of the Cuban; or if, as I think more likely (arguments follow below), the paragraph beginning "next to them" is a second version of that beginning "adjoining this people on this sea", we have the Seven Lands identical with the Irem, and again immediately north of the Cuban.

Now, the difficulty is to identify any "great and powerful nation", unknown to Mas'ūdī, in this place. In the tenth century, when Mas'ūdī wrote, we are able to judge fairly well of the ethnographical conditions in this locality. The point has been discussed at some length by Westberg,[1] whose purpose it was to show that Black Bulgars could not exist in this region, precisely because it was fully occupied by other nations. His arguments hold equally good for any other nation.

It is certainly true that the whole of the hinterland here appears to have been divided, in the tenth century, between the Khazars and the Alans. Precisely where the frontier ran, we do not know; but the Alan power seems to have extended far down into the plains. The Georgian Chronicle, indeed, makes them originally inhabitants of the plains, and says that they were first driven into the mountains by the Mongols in the thirteenth century, when they intermarried with the Circassians.[2] The Emperor Constantine speaks of the Alans with respect in the De Ceremoniis,[3] and in the D.A.I. he represents them as neighbours of the Khazars, and in a position to attack the wealthy corn-bearing districts of Khazaria, known as the "Nine Climates",[4] as well as to raid the sea-board of Circassia at will.[5] The same impression may be drawn from the letters of Nicholas Mysticus, who actually threatens Symeon of Bulgaria with a combined attack from the Alans, Petchenegs and other races.[6]

---

1 Westberg, "Die Fragmente des Toparcha Gothicus", *Mémoires de l'Ac. Imp. Sc.*, St Pétersbourg, série VIII, tom. IV, no. 2.

2 Wakhoucht, *Description géographique de la Géorgie*, tr. Brosset, p. 427.

3 *De Ceremoniis*, II, 48.

4 τὰ ἐννέα κλίματα, *D.A.I.* cc. 10, 11. C. 10 says explicitly that Khazaria and Alania were neighbours (τὰ ἐννέα κλίματα τῆς Χαζαρίας τῇ Ἀλανίᾳ παράκεινται).

5 *Ibid.* c. 42.　　　　6 Migne, *P.G.* CXI, cols. 149 ff.

Mas'ūdī himself describes the king of the Alans as the ruler of an extensive and powerful kingdom;[1] and he names the Alans as neighbours of the Petchenegs, and therefore by inference extending to the mouth of the Don. On the Don itself, the Petchenegs faced the Khazars in Sarkel.[2]

The Russian Chronicle gives the races subdued by Sviatoslav, when he took Beleveša (Sarkel), as "Alans and Circassians".[3] The only nations mentioned by name in the Chronicle as inhabiting these parts are Alans, Circassians and Khazars.

In the thirteenth century the Alan settlements extended to the gates of Cherson.[4]

There is thus no room anywhere in the tenth century for a "great and powerful nation" known as the "Seven Lands". The only place which might be suggested as neither Alan nor Circassian would be Taman (Tmutorakan, Tamatarcha); yet this once great and flourishing Greek community[5] was certainly in the hands of the Khazars in 704,[6] and seems to have remained Khazar until taken by Russia some time in the late tenth

---

1 *Meadows of Gold*, p. 436: "The king of the Alans musters 30,000 brave and strong horsemen; this force gives him the supremacy over other kings. The cultivation of his territory is uninterrupted, so that when the cock crows, he is answered in the whole of his dominions, the country being all covered with inhabitants and cultivation".

2 *D.A.I.* c. 42.

3 "Nestor", I, 90.

4 Cf. the letter of Theodosius, Bishop of Alania (Migne, *P.G.* CXL, cols. 192, 193): ἐπειδήπερ τῆς Χερσῶνος ἐγγὺς ἐν Ἀλανικῷ χωρίῳ φυγάδες ἦμεν (πολυσχιδὲς γὰρ τὸ ἔθνος τοῦτο, καὶ διῆκον μὲν ἀπὸ τῶν Καυκασίων ὀρῶν ἐς Ἴβηρας, τὸ ἀρχαῖον καὶ πάτριον ὅριον· ἀγαπᾷ δὲ καὶ μετοικεσίας πολλοστῶν τινων πέμπειν· ὡς μικρὸν Σκυθικήν τε πᾶσαν καὶ τῶν Σαυρομάτων [here Cumans] ἐκπληροῦν)...Παροικοῦσι τῇ Χερσῶνι καὶ Ἀλανοι, οὐχ ἧττον θελnθέντες ἢ θελήσαντες, ὡς οἷόν τι παρατείχισμα ταύτῃ καὶ περιφρούρημα.

5 Phanagoria was, of course, an ancient Greek settlement. As capital of the kingdom of Bosporus its jurisdiction extended over the whole delta, as far as the mouths of the Cuban, which, according to old writers and maps, flowed both into the Black Sea and the Maiotis. The Anonymous Geographer (*Geog. Graeci Minores*, ed. Gail, II, 207) describes the peninsula definitely as an island, and gives several cities on it: "Phanagoras, Hermanassa, Phanagoria and the Sindian Port, with a Greek population drawn from the neighbouring localities (ἀπὸ τῶν ἐγγὺς ἥκοντας τοπῶν). These cities, which lie apart from one another, are contained in the island (νῆσος) comprising the country along the Maiotis as far as the Bosporus: a large flat district, part of which is protected by the lagoons and rivers, and the swamp opposite part by the sea and lake" (of Maiotis).

6 Nicephorus, *Hist.* p. 40, 28; Theophanes, I, 373.

century.[1] Moreover, Taman could not possibly be identified with the great and independent nation of the "Seven Lands", and it is not easy to identify it with the "Irem"; for Mas'ūdī or his source would surely have known the Khazars, or the name of Taman, under one of its forms. There is therefore no reasonable explanation to be advanced for this people except that suggested above, that the descriptions of "Irem" and the "Seven Lands" are parallel, and that we have mention of one strong and independent nation of pagans, who in part at least were fishermen.[2]

If, on the other hand, Mas'ūdī is quoting here from an old source, and his information dates from the ninth century, all these difficulties disappear. The description fits the Magyars accurately in every respect—a great and powerful nation, pagans, and living, as Constantine tells us, in "seven hordes" without a supreme ruler.[3] In this case, Mas'ūdī and the old report which we are investigating would be mutually confirmatory.

I believe, moreover, that we are justified in assuming that Mas'ūdī is, in fact, drawing in this passage on an old source. The use of the term "Sea of Rūm" for the Black Sea is, as remarked, characteristic of the earlier writers, and Mas'ūdī's own hesitation seems to indicate that he had here an old report which had been in part corrected by later information.

The Ítíl. Gardēzī tells us that "they" (i.e. the Magyars) call their two rivers "the one Ítíl and the other Dūbā". He also

---

1 I go into this question in my "Petchenegs". I am convinced that the Russian appanage of Taman was founded following on Sviatoslav's capture of Sarkel.

2 The name of Írem is very difficult to explain. It might possibly be a real Circassian term, or it may simply be a hopeless corruption of the original. (Can a syllable have dropped out from Ankīradah?) Professor Toynbee, however, refers me to a mythical tribe of the name in the Quran, the word meaning "avenues of pillars" (or "tents"). It might therefore possibly mean "a nomad, tent-dwelling people", in which case it would be applicable to the Magyars.

3 *D.A.I.* c. 38. Possibly the phrase "Seven Lands" may be connected with the word translated by Constantine and the *Toparcha Gothicus* as κλήματα or κλίματα, which appears constantly as describing localities along the Black Sea and in the old (or existing) Khazaria. It appears to have been a popular term (τὰ λεγόμενα κλίματα), certainly in use by the Khazars (τὰ ἐννέα κλίματα τῆς Χαζαρίας) and not improbably of Oriental origin.

tells us that "the river which is to the right of the Magyars goes to Saqlāb and from there dwindles away in the district of Khazar, and that river is the greater of these two rivers". The words "beside Saqlāb" occur also in connection with the other river, the Dūbā, and the "Nandarin", where they do not make sense. It is necessary to take them here as either a corruption, or as a gloss, put in after the Magyar move (which will be gone into below) when the Don actually became the left-hand boundary of the Magyars (looking south).

The *description* of the river fits no other river than the Don—the only river within a vast distance of the Cuban, larger than that great stream, the only river which goes to the country of the Slavs, and afterwards to Khazaria. In old days the Don was, indeed, known as the "river of the Slavs", and appears under that name in a passage of Tabarī,[1] and another of Ibn Khordādbeh.[2] The name probably fell into disuse after the Magyars had crossed the Don and slaughtered or enslaved such of the Slavonic population as still lingered there.

But what of the name? We are told here, quite specifically, that the Magyars call the larger of the two rivers Ītīl. Here we come to a crucial point, which must be dealt with in detail.

The earliest known name of the Volga, as it appears in Ptolemy, etc., is ʻPâ. With the arrival of the Hunnish and Bulgar hordes, however, it appears under the name of Itil, in one form or another,[3] and this name, borrowed by the Turks and Tatars, has remained among them to the present day. All mediaeval Oriental writers describe the Volga under this name, except where they use paraphrases such as "the river of the Khazars". It was asserted by Frähn[4] that the word in its original meaning meant simply "large river", and could therefore be applied indiscriminately to any large river. Frähn

1 Tabarī, tr. Zotenberg, IV, 289: "Merwān se rendit maître de toute la montagne; puis il laissa le pays des Khazars derrière lui, et fit halte près de la rivière des Slaves". It is not easy to conceive that any river other than the Don is meant here.

2 "The Rūs descend the Tanais, the river of the Slavs, and pass by Khamlydj, the capital of the Khazars, where the sovereign takes tithes from them."

3 For a list of references, see Markwart (Marquart), "Kultur- und sprachliche Analekten", *U.J.* April 1929, p. 96.

4 Cit. Dorn, *Mélanges Asiatiques*, VI, 372.

appears to have made this assertion on the strength of the fact that the modern Tatars have such phrases as Čolman itili = the Ural, Kama itili = the Kama, Wätka itili = the Viatka, Aq itili = the Belaja, while the Volga itself is sometimes distinguished as "the Black Itil", or "the Great Itil". Frähn, however, expressly points out that this usage is comparatively modern.[1]

All modern Hungarian writers have adopted Frähn's statement without further question, and have informed their innocent readers that the Magyars made a habit of calling all large rivers Itil. Kuun, in support of this theory, has a touching story of a modern Magyar peasant from Transylvania, who, when first taken to see the Danube at Budapest, exclaimed "what a large Körös!"[2]—an anecdote which, incidentally, rather proves the reverse of his point. It is true that the Magyars ought to know if their own countrymen are addicted to this harmless but confusing mania; but even the foreigner may be permitted to retort that they have never indulged it in Hungary. They might have applied the name of Itil to the Danube, the Theiss, the Save, the Drave, the Raab, the Körös, or any other of the numerous rivers with which their country is watered. But they did not do so. I have searched the atlas of Hungary in vain for the name of Itil, Atel, or Etul.

Failing proof to the contrary, one must agree with Marquart that the name Itil was a specific name for an individual river, very likely transferred, as he suggests, from the τίλ or Togla of the old Oguz.[3] The important point is, that as far as Greek and mediaeval Oriental sources go, the name was applied solely to the Volga. Frähn's later instances, it must be remarked, also refer almost exclusively to tributaries of the Volga or to rivers lying within its system. Here we have to do with a common enough phenomenon, which recurs in modern Hungary; we have the Nagy Szamos and the Kis Szamos, the Nagy and the Kis Küküllo, the Fekete Tisza, etc. But in mediaeval times, only one river, besides the Volga, is *recorded* as bearing the

1 Cit. Markwart, "Ein Arabischer Bericht", etc. *U.J.* Dec. 1924, p. 285.
2 Kuun, *Relatio*, I, 41.
3 Markwart, *Analekten, loc. cit.*

name of Itil. That river is the Don, and the people who so
termed it were precisely the Magyars, as their own chronicles
attest in most specific fashion.

Kezai, in his description of Scythia, tells us that "oriuntur
eciam in eodem duo magna flumina, uni nomen Etul, et
alterius Togora...fluius siquidem Don in Scicia oritur, qui ab
Hungaris Etul nominatur, sed ut montes Rifeos transit difflu-
endo, Don est appellatus".[1] The *Wiener Bilderchronik* has for
these passages, "Don grandis fluvius est, in Scythia oritur, ab
Hungaris Etul nominatur", and later, "fluvius Ethul, id est
Don". Thuroczy begins his description as follows: "Hanc
Scythiam, Hungaricarum primaevi auctores historiarum, in
Europa posuere; illamque versus orientem extendi, et ab uno
latere Ponto aquilonari, ab alio Riphaeis montibus, ab oriente
vero Asia, et ab occidente fluvio Ethewl, quem et Don vocari
dixerunt, includi scripsere". Later we have: "Praeterea in
Scythia grandem flumen Don vocatum oriri, et illum ab
Hungaris Don nuncupari," etc. Afterwards, he refers to
"Fluvius Ethewl, sive Don".[2]

The Anonymus, after locating the Magyars in the east of
Scythia, says that: "fluium Etyl super tulbou sedentes ritu
paganismo transnatauerunt", after which they reached Susdal,
and later came "per ciuitatem Kyeu, fluium Deneper trans-
nauigando".[3]

I do not see how it could be stated in more categorical fashion
that the Hungarians called the Don "Etul", nor with what
right that statement is to be rejected. But there is actually
further evidence that the name Itil was also applied to the Don
by another nation. The Polish chronicler Długocz writes:
"Flumen Tanais, quem Poloni sua lingua Don vocant, Tartari
Edil".[4] Of the Dnieper, it may be remarked, he says that "in
Tartarico vocatur Krsze".[5]

So far as I know, no specifically Turkish name for the Don
is recorded, except this one of Itil. The ordinary name in the

1 Kezai, *Gesta Hunnorum*, I, 1 (p. 87, ed. Endlicher).
2 Thuroczy, *Chronica Ungarorum*, I, 5.
3 *Anonymi Gesta Hungarorum*, cc. 7, 8.
4 *Historia Polonica*, Lipsiae, MDCCXI, I, col. 3.   5 *Ibid.* col. 19.

Oriental writers is Tanais, or some variant of it, such as Tin.
For the Dnieper, on the other hand, Constantine himself, in
a chapter which appears to be derived from a Magyar source,[1]
describes the Dnieper under the name of Βαρούχ—a word of
undoubted Turkish origin, to be paralleled by the Hunnish
name of War for the same river. I will not deny the possibility
that the list which includes this name might be derived from a
source other than that which supplied the remainder of Constantine's chapter; but this is highly improbable, since the list
contains one other name of undoubted Turkish origin—the
name of Τροῦλλος for the Dniester.[2] There is therefore no
reason to suppose that the list does not emanate from the same
source as the remainder of the chapter, and thus gives the name
by which the Magyars actually called the Dnieper.

The only argument advanced against this otherwise obvious
identification is that Constantine, in another passage, says that
"the place where the Hungarians formerly lived is called
Atelkuzu, after the river which traverses it, Atel, and kuzu"
(köz = district). It would seem from what has been said above
that the name Atelkuzu must therefore be interpreted as "the
Don district". In fact, however, this interpretation has been
uniformly rejected by modern Hungarian scholars on the ground
that Constantine represents the Magyars as moving *into* Atelkuzu from another district which they have identified as that of
the Don. They are therefore forced to the conclusion that Atel
must have been the Hungarian name for the Dnieper. But it is
important to realise that they have no evidence whatever for
this assumption, beyond the argument stated here, and any
deductions (and such have frequently been made) that *because*
Constantine is imagined to say that the Magyars called the
Dnieper Atel, therefore Atel-köz is the Dnieper district, is
mere argument in a circle. I propose to show below that there
are manifold and quite insuperable difficulties in the way of
taking Constantine's Atelkuzu as anything except the Don basin;

---

1 *D.A.I.* c. 38.

2 Turla is the regular name for the Dniester which appears in Idrīsī, Abulfēdā,
and other mediaeval geographers, and was in regular use among the mediaeval
Tatars.

in which case, his statement will cease to be an objection to, and become instead a support of, our present identification for Gardēzī's Ītīl as the Don.

This must be added: the transference of the name Itil from the Volga to the Dnieper, which is a long distance from the former river, would be naturally difficult; whereas the transference of the name to the Don is very easy. The Don is, in fact, so closely connected with the Volga that the mediaeval geographers, almost to a man, believed the two rivers to be identical. The conception appears in the writings of Theophanes, Masʿūdī, and a great many other writers; and how tenacious it was may be seen by anyone who troubles to look at the latest edition of *The Times Atlas*, Plate I (Mapping of the World). There he will find the Don and the Volga represented as one river in the maps of Ortelius (A.D. 1570) and De Wit (c. A.D. 1700).[1]

The mistake is obviously due to the fact that the Don and the Volga approach extremely close to each other at one point, where an ancient and very important trade route seems to have led over the *volokh*, uniting the Black Sea and the Caspian via the two rivers. The light ships locally in use were probably transported across the narrow strip of intervening land by human labour—a task which is easier than it sounds today when we remember that the cargoes consisted very largely of slaves. The ships and cargoes were carried in just the same way past the rapids of the Dnieper, as Constantine tells us.[2]

---

1 For example, the whole of Masʿūdī's story (*Meadows of Gold*, I, 297 ff.) of the Russian raid into the Caspian is brought in solely to refute the opinion, which he alleges to have been current among all authors, ancient or recent, to whom he had referred, that the Caspian and the Black Sea were connected by "a canal or strait, or in any other way, except through the river of the Khazars" (the Volga). He accepts, that is, the Don-Volga waterway without question, but denies the existence of any other direct water communication. He tells us that he enquired of sailors, merchants, etc., "and every one of them informed me that one could not come by water into the Black Sea [*sc.* from the Caspian] except the way which had been taken by the Russians". The Russians themselves, in his story, "entered the estuary of the Don, sailed up it as far as the river of the Khazars, went down that river, passed the city of Ītīl and entered through its mouth into the sea of Khazar". Elsewhere he says: "From the upper course of the river of the Khazars an arm branches off, which falls into a narrow gulf of the sea, the Pontus, which is the sea of the Rūs".

2 *D.A.I.* c. 9.

Whether, therefore, the Magyars actually believed in the identity of the two rivers, or not, we need not be surprised that they applied the same name to both, when even geographers with great pretensions at culture did the same thing.

On the other hand, it is not possible to argue, as M. Fehér appears to do, that the Hungarian *chroniclers* took the identification of the Don with the Etul from this old idea. For precisely the geographers on which Kezai draws for his description of Scythia are unacquainted with the confusion. Kezai in his preamble quotes Orosius. Now, Orosius describes the races of Scythia (I, c. 2) as extending "a mari Caspio quod est ad orientem, per oram Oceani septentrionalis usque ad Tanaim fluvium et Maeotides paludes". There is no word here of the Etul, nor of the identification of the Don with the Volga. Kezai appears to have drawn, in one place, not on Orosius, but on Jornandes; but Jornandes, who has a description of Scythia in his fifth chapter, is equally unacquainted with the Etul. He writes of the Don: "In cujus Scythiae medio est locus qui Asiam Europamque ab alterutro dividit, Riphaei scilicet montes, qui Tanain vastissimum fundunt intrantem Maeotida etc."

Precisely the one thing of his own which Kezai inserts into his description of Scythia—the one thing which he does *not* take from his written sources—is the fact that the Magyars called the Don Etul.

So far, then, we may say that we have an *a priori* probability for the Cuban, as being the river which Gardēzī describes as the Dūbā, and another *a priori* probability for the Don as his Ītīl; the two, of course, supporting one another. We will now turn to his mountain.

Gardēzī's mountain. Gardēzī is very brief about his mountain. All that he tells us is: "Above the bank of the river is a great mountain and water flows out on to the side of that mountain, and behind that mountain are a people of Christians whom they call Mirdāt; between them and the Nandar is a ten days' journey".

It may be remarked first that mountains which rise above rivers, and behind which Christians are living, are not found everywhere on the map of South-Eastern Europe in the ninth century. In fact, the Caucasus is the only range to which the description can be made to apply; for there were no Christians in the Urals, and the Carpathians do not fit for many reasons. If we take the Caucasus, which does, in fact rise above the Cuban, we find two very reasonable explanations for the remark about the water flowing out. It might either refer to the Terek flowing through the gorge of Dariel, or else to the famous spring in the fortress of the king of the Alans. One may compare Mas'ūdī's account of the latter: "This fortress (sc. of the king of the Alans) lies on a massive rock.... The fortress built on this rock has a spring with sweet water which gushes out into the midst of it from the highest point of the rock".[1]

The Mirdāt. If the mountain be the Caucasus, as it would indeed appear to be, then the Abasgians, who actually occupied the territory behind it and behind the country of the Alans, must be the "Mirdāt". Professor Marquart, who also makes this identification, has provided a textual emendation showing how the change to this apparently very different name may have arisen.[2] Emendation may not even be necessary, since the different tribes of the Alans bore very various names, often the names of noble families.[3] The description agrees with reasonable accuracy with what later travellers tell us of the Abasgians. It also bears considerable similarity to Mas'ūdī's description of the Nandarin, and given the methods of the Oriental writers, it would be quite possible to make Gardēzī's "they" [are a numerous people, etc.] apply grammatically to the Nandarin. The point is immaterial for my purpose; but it is important to note, in order that absurd identifications for these two nations may be eschewed, that the dress, the religion and the trade relations are alike applicable only to Caucasian nations.

Al-Bekrī's version. If we turn now to al-Bekrī's version, we shall, I hope, be able to confirm all these identifications; explicitly except in the case of the rivers, which follow as a matter of geography.

Al-Bekrī has, strictly speaking, no description of the Magyars

---

1 *Meadows of Gold*, p. 436.   2 *Streifzüge*, pp. 174 ff.
3 Cf. Klaproth, *Reise in den Kaukasus*, ii, 581; Wakhoucht, *Description géographique de la Géorgie*, tr. Brosset, pp. 427, 428.

at all in this section of his work, but only one of their neighbours; and this seems at first to differ very widely from Gardēzī's. The difference can, however, be explained.

When discussing al-Bekrī's methods in an earlier section of
this essay, I showed that he habitually epitomised Džaihānī,
replacing that writer's work, in sundry places, with extracts
from other writers. The three writers whom he used for this
purpose were, respectively, Ibn Jāq'ūb, Ibn Fozlān and
Mas'ūdī. Now, of these three, and indeed, of any Oriental
writers of their day, Mas'ūdī is the only one to give a full
description of the countries of the Caucasus.[1] The full description is contained, as Mas'ūdī himself tells us, in his lost work,
the *Book of Different Sorts of Knowledge*; but there is a shorter
account in the *Meadows of Gold*. Mas'ūdī, where he treated the
same subject more than once, was not averse from repeating
himself; and the passage of al-Bekrī which we are now considering has every appearance of being a terse summary, either
of the account in the *Meadows of Gold*, or of the lost account in
the *Book of Different Sorts of Knowledge*.

It may be said at the beginning that al-Bekrī's mountain,
which extends to Tiflis and Bāb-el-Abwāb, cannot, of course,
be any other than the Caucasus. Thus we have our first point of
correspondence with Gardēzī's report, and our first confirmation
of the identifications made with respect to that report. A
similar correspondence and confirmation will be found to exist
with respect to the nations.

The Ayīn. Al-Bekrī's "boundaries" are, as his first sentence
shows, the eastern and western respectively. At the eastern
end, then, he has a mountain, "and the people who dwell there
are called Ayīn. They have horses and flocks and cultivated
land".

Mas'ūdī's description of the Alans runs: "The king of the
Alans musters thirty thousand brave and strong horsemen; this
force gives him the supremacy over other kings. The cultivation
of his territory is uninterrupted, so that when the cock crows, he

---

1 Istachrī (if al-Bekrī really used him, and not Ibn Fozlān) has some infor-
mation, but not about the countries on the northern slopes of the Caucasus.
Moreover, we possess his works, which contain no passage from which al-
Bekrī could have drawn the present description.

is answered in the whole of his dominions, the country being all covered with inhabitants and cultivation".

The two descriptions thus correspond with sufficient exactitude.

The Awghūna. The emendation of Awghūna to Avgaz—Abkhazians, Abasgians, is easy, requiring only the addition of a few diacritical points.[1] The description, too, shows unmistakable signs of having been imported from Mas'ūdī, subjected, however, to intelligent editing by al-Bekrī.

Al-Bekrī	*Mas'ūdī (Meadows of Gold, p. 452)*
Below this mountain, on the shore of the sea, are a people called Awghūna, and they are Christians, and adjoin the country of those Moslems connected with the country of Tiflis, and it is the beginning of the country of Armenia. This mountain extends as far as the land of Bāb-el-Abwāb and adjoins the country of the Khazars.	We return to the account of the Caucasus, the wall, and Bāb-el-Abwāb.... One of these nations lives on the frontiers of the Alans and has the name el-Ab-chaz. The Abkhaz and Gurz (Georgians) used to pay tribute to the governor of the frontier of Tiflis, since the time when this city was subjected by the Moslems....

Thus we see that al-Bekrī's report, far from being incompatible with that of Gardēzī, is actually another description of the same landscape and peoples, drawn from another source. It confirms the identity of the Mirdāt with the Abasgians, and the rest will follow as a matter of geography. Of the two rivers, the Dūbā is seen to be, in fact, the Cuban, and the Ītīl, the Don.

SUMMARY OF "B"

The Magyars described here are living, then, with their front to the Black Sea, the back of their territory adjoining the land of the Alans. On the south side, the frontier between their land and that of the Circassians is formed by the Cuban; on the north, the frontier is the Don. The locality is an entirely

---

1 Marquart, *Streifzüge*, p. 176.

different one from that described in "A"; nevertheless, the
report (at least in Ibn Rusta's version of it) appears to be
homogeneous, and therefore all of one date. What that date is,
cannot, however, be ascertained. Marquart, in the course of a
long excursus into Georgian and Abasgian history, puts it at
"at least before 240 H. (854/5 A.D.)".[1] As a matter of fact, it is,
as we shall see shortly, probably at least fifteen years earlier than
that.

The territory of these two hordes of Magyars was not
contiguous. It is necessary to insist somewhat strongly on this
point, as otherwise confusion will result. Both M. Fehér[2] and
M. Darkó,[3] each of whom has conceived the whole report as
homogeneous, have come to the conclusion that the territory of
the Magyars reached from the frontier of the Volga Bulgars,
clean down to the Cuban. To a large extent they have been
misled by taking Gardēzī's wording, with its slip of "Bulgars"
for "Petchenegs", instead of the true version preserved by Ibn
Rusta and al-Bekrī, and have thus been misled into imagining
in the first "Bulgars" some nation of Bulgars on the Cuban.
M. Fehér at least is led into further confusion by his erroneous
identification of the two rivers as respectively the Dnieper and
the Don, which thus enables him to assert that "the Magyar
territory reached far to the north, and ran north-east—south-
west along the Don and the Donez".

A little reflection would, however, have shown the impossibility of this theory. The two Magyar nations cannot have been
contiguous, because there are other nations who occupied the
territory thus claimed for the Magyars. Chief among them is
the nation of the Burtās, which, as I have already shown, was
contiguous with the Khazars on the south, the Volga Bulgars
on the north. Further, the merchant's itinerary which I have
quoted shows equally clearly that the "Inner Baškirs", or Ural

1 Marquart, *Streifzüge*, p. 188; but Marquart's reasoning is in any case false,
as it is based on deductions from al-Bekrī's wording, which he assumes to be
that of Džaihānī, whereas al-Bekrī is paraphrasing Mas'ūdī, and thus referring
to conditions a whole century later than those which Marquart details in his
long excursus on Abasgian history.

2 *Beziehungen*, pp. 176–88.

3 "Zur Frage der urmagyarischen und urbulgarischen Beziehungen",
K.C.A. Feb. 1924, p. 299.

Magyars, had Burtās bordering them on the west, Petchenegs on the south. Besides the Burtās, we must reckon with the claims of the Mordvinians, if these were indeed a separate nation, and of various Slavonic tribes.

In the south, it has been proved that the "Ītīl" to which Gardēzī refers is the Don. The Don, then, was the northern boundary of this second nation of Magyars. There was thus a very large stretch of territory intervening between them and their blood brothers in the Urals.[1]

How did this situation come about? It is impossible to say with any certainty; but we can form a general idea, and it is encouraging to note that this idea is exactly confirmed by the results of M. Gombocz' linguistic research. We know, thanks to M. Gombocz, that the Magyars were in close contact with the Bulgars in the region of the Caucasus from about the fifth to the seventh centuries. After the latter date, the linguistic influence of the Bulgarians on the Magyars (those Magyars, that is, from whom the Hungarians of today are descended) ceases to be exerted.

There are two hypotheses which hold the field today. One, maintained with great ability by M. Fehér, is that the Magyars are identical with the Savirs of the Byzantines, the Bulgars with the Onoguri. If that is true, we have a record of how the Savirs arrived and took up their homes above the north-eastern corner of the Caucasus in 561-65, while the Bulgars, inhabiting the "old, great Bulgaria" of Theophanes, lived between the Don and the Cuban, and were thus the Magyars' next-door neighbours on the west.

The second hypothesis, which is fortified by a passage in Mas'ūdī,[2] and is upheld by M. Darkó, identifies the Savirs with

1 M. Darkó supports his argument by quoting the Hungarian Chronicle, according to which the Magyars migrated from their original homes in Scythia via Susdal. But the mention of Susdal is one of the worst anachronisms which the Chronicle contains. Susdal did not even exist at the time of the Magyar migration, and its name in the Chronicle can only mean "Russian territory", according to thirteenth-century usage. One might perhaps add that had the Magyars really occupied all the territory which their descendants claim for them, they would have been one of the most powerful nations in Europe—far too strong for the Petchenegs to defeat or for the Khazars to claim suzerainty over them.

2 *Livre d'Avertissement*, p. 120: "The Khazars are called in Turkish Savir and in Persian Khazarān; they are a sedentary Turkish people". It is, how-

the later Khazars; in which case the Magyars must have lived further west, and in still closer contact with the Bulgars. The result is the same in either case. The pseudo-Avars inflict a devastating defeat on the Savirs, and cause deep perturbation to the Bulgars. They pass on, and are succeeded by the West Turks. After these, the Khazars appear.

From a short time after the arrival of the Khazars, the Cuban Bulgars disappear from history. The Bulgarian legend represents them as being subjugated by the Khazars; a single reference in Tabarī shows them, apparently still as a semi-independent nation, making war against Chosroes II.[1] Then they disappear. There is no later reference to the Cuban Bulgars in history.[2]

---

ever, hard to believe that the name of Khazar is Persian, not only on etymological grounds, but because this name was used by the Russians, Greeks and other nations.

1 Cit. Marquart, *Eranšahr*, p. 65. I have failed to find the reference in the O.T.F. edition of Tabarī.

2 The "Black Bulgars" of Constantine and the Russian Chronicle were certainly *not* on the Cuban. I hope to go into this question more fully elsewhere, and will state my conclusions here in the briefest form.

Constantine refers to Black Bulgaria twice: in the *D.A.I.* c. 12, he notes that "the so-called Black Bulgaria can attack Khazaria", and in c. 42 he mentions the Dnieper as the route used by the Russians "when they go through to Black Bulgaria and Khazaria". In my opinion, the latter passage proves the identity of his Black Bulgaria with Bolgar on the Kama (cf. the parallel references in Ibn Rusta and Gardēzī), while the former statement is based on the latter (cf. the remarks in part III of this essay on the composition of the *D.A.I.*). The treaty preserved in the Russian Chronicle ("Nestor", I, 58 ff.) is more difficult. Article IX runs: "The Black Bulgars come and make war in the land of Cherson; and I command the Russian Tsar not to let them do damage in the said land". It is certainly difficult to imagine the state of Bolgar able, or inclined, to send a force down to make war on Cherson; a land army is out of the question. Westberg (*Die Fragmente des Toparcha Gothicus*) therefore thinks that these Bulgars must be sought elsewhere, and places them in the steppe north of Cherson. In the course of his argument, he shows very convincingly, by elimination, that these Black Bulgars could not have been on the Cuban. I disagree, however, with his conclusion that they were a nomad race north of Cherson; for the steppe at this time contained one race which must certainly have been much more powerful than any other federation of the steppes, to wit, the Petchenegs; and these lived in close proximity to Cherson, as Constantine tells us (*D.A.I.* c. 37: καὶ εἰς Χερσῶνα μέν ἐστιν (ἡ Πατζινακία) ἔγγιστα, εἰς δὲ τὴν Βόσπορον πλησιέστερον). A treaty directed against such a danger from the steppes could not have mentioned the Black Bulgars while preserving silence on the Petchenegs. On the other hand, it must be remarked that the treaty, for all its high-flown preamble, is essentially an *ad hoc* instrument for regulating conditions round Cherson and at thè mouth of the Dnieper. In certain of the districts mentioned, the Russian Tsar is conceived as exercising *de facto*, if not *de jure* sovereignty. It is in his power to stop

On the other hand, we find, 150 or 200 years later, the state of Bulgar on the Kama. This can only be explained by a migration of the Cuban Bulgars north-eastward—whether voluntary, or transplanted to serve as frontier guards, we cannot say.

Nothing is more likely than M. Gombocz' suggestion that the "first frontier of the Magyars" were a horde who became detached from the rest, and accompanied the Bulgars in their journey north. These are not, however, as we shall show presently, the ancestors of the Magyars who entered Hungary. This other group of Magyars either remained on the Cuban, if they were not identical with the Savirs; or if they were so identical, they moved westward to the Cuban to make room for the Khazars, who, on this theory, were a fresh invading race, and whose centre, during the first period of their empire, lay precisely in the territory formerly occupied by the Savirs. The result, from the point of view of this essay, is the same in either case; we get the Magyars who were destined afterwards to enter Hungary, occupying the Don-Cuban steppes vacated by the Bulgars; and we find them there in "B", in the early ninth century. Later, as we shall soon see, they moved across the Don to its right bank.

Relation between Ibn Rusta's report and γ. There can be no doubt that the portion (γ) of "B" found in Gardēzī (and paraphrased by al-Bekrī) and not reproduced by Ibn Rusta, is an addition to the original report. The clumsiness of the editing is so apparent as to make it practically certain that Ibn Rusta's report represents the original text, while the additions constitute an attempt to explain and define that original.

---

these Black Bulgars from committing their ravages. This would not be the case if they were steppe-dwellers; but would be the case if the Bulgars (a) made their raids down the river by boat, in the same way as the Russians themselves raided Ītil; or (b) had a trading depot near the mouth of the Dnieper, similar to the Russian colony in Ītil, or the later Genoese or other colonies in the Black Sea. Either solution leads us back to Bolgar on the Kama. The Black Bolgars are also mentioned in one version of the Russian Chronicle as slaying a son of Dir in battle. No deductions as to their home can be drawn from this. The fact that on one later occasion the Volga Bulgars are described by the Russians as "Silver Bulgars" is, I think, no objection to their earlier identification with the Black Bulgars. The common statement that the παλαιὰ Βουλγαρία ἡ μεγάλη of Theophanes was ever known as "Black" rests on no authority whatever.

But when was this explanatory addition made?

It seems to me excessively difficult to suppose that it was made at a time when it had ceased to correspond to the facts. To suppose that the two rivers of Ibn Rusta are not in reality the Don and the Cuban, as Gardēzī explains them, but two other rivers, to which the Magyars moved later, involves supposing that the author of the addition had known the Magyars on the Don and the Cuban, but was unaware of their move to another locality, although having before him a report describing the new state of things. It also involves supposing that, in their new homes, the Magyars again lived "between two rivers"—a supposition not supported by any other source.[1]

This chain of suppositions seems to me much too difficult to accept, and I think that it cannot reasonably be doubted that α and γ, if not exactly contemporary, at any rate describe the same geographical situation. Thus Ibn Rusta, no less than Gardēzī, is writing of the Don and the Cuban;[2] and the fact that Ibn Rusta's report does not include γ must be explained as a deliberate omission, similar to his omission of the section on the Petchenegs and one sentence in Magyars "C". Thus the original α in Ibn Rusta's report has passed through two stages; the addition of γ by an earlier hand, and its omission again by Ibn Rusta. Džaihānī's version (Gardēzī and al-Bekrī) represents only the first of these two stages.

Were the whole report similarly applicable to the country at the north-western end of the Caucasus, no difficulty would, of course, arise. This does not, however, appear to be the case. The remainder of Ibn Rusta's and Gardēzī's remarks on the Magyars seem to me to describe a totally different situation. It is this situation which must now be considered.

1 We shall see presently that the Magyars themselves called their new home after a single river, the Atel. The fact that the Hungarian Chronicles mention two rivers in their descriptions of Scythia is irrelevant, as these descriptions are drawn from the writings of mediaeval geographers. Hungarian tradition knows only one river, again the Atel. Regino is equally silent respecting any river other than the Don.

2 Historically, indeed, the point is irrelevant, so long as we accept Gardēzī's and al-Bekrī's statements as having corresponded to the facts at any period.

THE REPORT ON THE MAGYARS "C"

In the first section of this essay, I gave my reasons for supposing our archetype to consist, in reality, of two superimposed reports. In my view, for which I gave certain reasons, the break between the two occurs at the end of report "B" on the Magyars; Magyars "C", the report on the Slavs and that on the Rūs form a single and well-defined whole, which represents the Magyars in a different locality from that which we found them occupying in α.

As elsewhere, Ibn Rusta's report seems to be the purer of the two. The differences between his version and that of Gardēzī appear to be due largely to the fact that the latter writer has misread or mistranslated many details, while in more than one case he seems to have misunderstood a passage altogether, and to have redrafted it freely, giving it quite a different sense. Reference to the parallel columns in the Appendix will show where this seems to have occurred; the criticism applies in particular to Gardēzī's mistaken rationalisation of Ibn Rusta's account of the Russian baths (from which he seems to have gleaned only the single idea of the Slavs shutting themselves up in a confined place in winter), and to the concluding paragraph of Ibn Rusta's account of the Magyars, where Gardēzī has transferred his admiration from the Magyars' clothes to their persons. In the section on the Rūs, Ibn Rusta's two paragraphs about the Russian system of justice are paraphrased rather than translated. In the passage on the Russians' clothes, several sentences of Gardēzī's version have got out of place. The most interesting and important variation, however, is in the beginning of the report on the Slavs, where we find, most unexpectedly, the distance given, not from the Magyars, but from the Petchenegs.

It seems clear that we have here a piece of editing by the author of the archetype—the same hand which, in an earlier passage, substituted the word "Slavs" for "Burtās" in the list of the Petchenegs' neighbours. The original text is that preserved by Gardēzī at the end of his report on the Magyars. As

I remarked above, I am suspicious of the whole sentence on the Petchenegs.

Situation as shown in β. I have unfortunately found no very recent discussion by competent Slavonic scholars of the situation as pictured in this report,[1] and hesitate myself to enter upon details. The general situation, however, is perfectly clear—once it is seen that this portion of the report is to be considered separately from what has preceded it.

The centre of the picture is occupied by a great Slavonic kingdom, under a Grand Župan, whose name would appear to have been Sviatopolk ("Suwayyat Balk"). This is not, as has sometimes been assumed, the well-known Sviatopolk of Moravia (870–94), but another king of the same name, ruling north of the Carpathians. Jarwāb or Jarāwāt is recognisably Horvat-Croatia, the great kingdom of White Croatia referred to on more than one occasion even by Constantine Porphyrogenetos himself,[2] and famous in early Czech and Polish legend. Wayīt or Wayīb would appear to be Kiev, which is shown here, interestingly enough, as a frontier city of the Slavs, not of the Rūs. The Slavs are thus still in possession of a considerable and well-organised power north of the Carpathians, and the report is obviously anterior, or drawn from information anterior to the establishment of the Rūs in Southern Russia.[3]

The Rūs are living in the far north, apparently on an island or a marshy place, three days (three days' sail) from the Slavs. This would appear to be the region of the great northern *volokhs* (Novgorod) where, according to the Russian Chronicle, the first establishment of the Rūs in Russia took place. It is very tempting to identify the "Khagan Rūs" with Rurik.

The Rūs are trading with the Khazars and the Volga Bulgars

1 The article by M. Semen Rapoport, "Mahomedan Writers on the Slavs", in the *Slavonic Review*, June 1929, translates Ibn Rusta's version from Harkavy's Russian rendering, but adds practically nothing that is new to Harkavy's interpretations.

2 *D.A.I.* c. 30 gives Βελοχρωβατία as the original home of the Southern Croats, but still existing in the writer's day; similarly c. 31.

3 Marquart (*Streifzüge*, p. 200) quotes a valuable reference, which may be almost contemporary with the present report, to a "ruler of the Slavs", who is coupled with the rulers of the Khazars and of Rūm in connection with events which happened about the year A.D. 855.

—a trade which was certainly in progress at a very early date[1]—
but are not yet settled in Kiev. This gives us a date for the
report earlier than 862, in which year Askold and Dir settled in
Kiev. The report might, however, have been compiled from old
information, and thus be in itself later.

There is, however, one most interesting passage in the report
which makes it probable that we can date it almost exactly. In
the year 839 certain ambassadors arrived in Constantinople
from a dignitary whom they described as the "Khakhan Rūs";
and on their journey homeward asked leave to be allowed to
proceed through Germany, because the steppes were haunted
by a race of savage barbarians, into whose hands they feared to
fall.[2] Thanks to this accident, record of this embassy has been
preserved in the pages of a Western chronicler.

These strange and ferocious peoples were almost certainly
those same Magyars whom we find in the pages of Džaihānī
(which are innocent of reference to any other nomad race in the
same neighbourhood) harrying the Slavs and the Rūs alike; and
the mention of them so fortunately preserved by the chronicler
may do us a double service in enabling us to date the report. The
Russian Chronicle nowhere gives us any foundation to suppose
that the Russian rulers ever in reality took the title of Khagan.
If, indeed, they adopted it in the first flush of Oriental adven-
ture, it soon fell into desuetude. When, therefore, we find the
same title appearing in two such widely different places as
the *Annales Bertiniani* and the present report, we are led to
wonder whether the two statements may not rest upon a
common foundation. Even if this does not prove to be the case,
they will probably be nearly contemporary.

There remains the all-important question of the position of
the Magyars themselves. It is very difficult indeed to imagine
that this report describes the same locality as "B"—the Don
and the Cuban, with the emphasis on the Cuban. Nothing

1 It is mentioned as a regular thing in the ninth century by Ibn Khordādbeh,
and may have been much older still.

2 *Annales Bertiniani*, Part II (*Prudentii Trecensis Annales*, Pertz, *Mon. Germ.
Script.* I, 434): "Quoniam itinera per quae ad Constantinopolim venerant,
inter barbaras et nimiae ferocitatis gentes immanissimas habuerant, quibus
eos, ne forte in periculum inciderent, redire nolunt".

authorises us to suppose that the habitations of the Slavs extended so far eastward in the ninth century as to bring them within the range of a predatory nation living so far to the south. This the more when we remember that the report lays its chief stress on a Slav kingdom situated far to the north-west, and that the Khazars are not mentioned at all in connection with the Slavs.[1] If, then, the Magyars are put at only ten days' distance from the Slavs (the figure need not be taken literally, but it certainly implies comparative proximity), then we must needs seek a fresh home for them. They are living in a marshy district; not very far from the Slavs; and within reach of a Greek port named Karch. The place which best answers this description is the right bank of the Don, near its mouth, the most famous marsh of antiquity. We shall see presently that the Slavonic source of c. 38 of the *D.A.I.* describes the homes of the Magyars by a word which is almost a literal translation of Ibn Rusta's and Gardēzī's description, and that this word signifies the country of the Don. To this may be added Regino's description of the homes from which the Magyars were evicted in 889—"paludes quas Tanais in sua refusione immensas porrigit".

Admittedly there were Greek ports in the ninth century outside the Crimea; but the traditional ports for commerce between the Greeks and the barbarians of the hinterland were in the

---

1 I am not inclined to believe, with Marquart (*Streifzüge*, p. 28) and others, that Ibn Rusta's remark about the ditch, with which the Khazars are said to have surrounded their territory, has anything to do with the construction of Sarkel on the Don. It is true that, as will be shown below, Sarkel was constructed as a defence against the Magyars, and not, as hastily assumed by some, against the Petchenegs; but a ditch is a very different thing from a fortress, and, moreover, Sarkel was probably built just about the time when this report was written, so that its construction could not possibly be set back into the remote past. There was, on the other hand, a famous ditch, dating from very old days, and cutting off the Crimea (in later parlance, Gazaria) from the steppe. This was the great ditch at Perekop (a name which itself means "ditch"), which according to Herodotus was built by the blind slaves of the Scythians. It was famous in antiquity; was noted by the thirteenth-century traveller Rubruquis (pp. 51, 91 in Beazeley's edition, cf. Beazeley's note to p. 91); and was certainly still in existence in the middle of the nineteenth century, and may be still today. If, as I think almost certain, the information in this report was derived via the Greek merchants in these Crimean harbours with whom the Magyars traded—they themselves most likely had it from a Slav slave—it is most natural that this ditch should be mentioned. The sentence occurs in Ibn Rusta alone, and is probably an addition made by him.

Crimea, and this seems especially to have been the case with the slave trade. Further, it may much be doubted whether the ports further to the east, such as Taman, could really deserve the description which Ibn Rusta gives Karakh. Especially if Ibn Rusta's phrase "the ascent of the country of the Greeks" signifies anything, it must refer to the mountains of the Crimea. Finally, as I mentioned above, Ibn Rusta's remark about the Khazars' ditch seems to me to point once again to the Crimea.

Precisely which port is meant it is hard to say. It would be natural, on historical grounds, to expect Cherson, and I cannot myself see that, given the extraordinary mutilations to which foreign names are subjected by the Oriental writers, the philological objections are insuperable. The other obvious alternative is Kerč, as was suggested by Kuun.[1] The objections which Marquart originally raised to this identification seem to have been withdrawn by him on second thoughts.[2]

This later report on the Magyars, then, shows them living in the basin of the Don, and extending both their raids and their trading westward of that district. The situation pictured in Džaihānī β, in other words, is different from that described in Džaihānī α. Before drawing the conclusions which result from this fact, however, I shall adduce the independent evidence covering the same approximate period, and, I hope, show that it supports my findings up to date.

INDEPENDENT EVIDENCE ON THE MAGYARS AND PETCHENEGS

We may now glance at the independent evidence—that is to say, the evidence apart from the old Report and Constantine—for the situations of the Magyars and Petchenegs in the ninth century.

Regino. The only historical account is that of Regino, who shows the Magyars as living at the mouth of the Don until 889, when they were expelled thence by the Petchenegs, and arrived

1 *Relatio*, I, 185.   2 *Streifzüge*, pp. 162, 506.

on the Danube. Regino's story, which is drawn from a lost Byzantine source,[1] runs:

889. In this year of Our Lord the race of Hungarians (gens Hungarorum), a race un-named in earlier centuries, and consequently unknown (retro ante seculos inaudita quia nec nominata), emerged from the Scythian realms and the vast marshes round the mouth of the Don...driven from their own homes by their neighbours, the Pecinacs, because the latter were superior in numbers and valour (eo quod numero et virtute praestarent) and their native land, as said above (ut praemisimus), was insufficient to hold the overflowing multitude. So fleeing from their violence, they bade farewell to their fatherland, and set out to see what country they could dwell in and make their home.

According to Regino, then, the homes of the Magyars were on the mouth of the Don until the year 889, when they were driven westward by the Petchenegs.

The Hungarian Chronicle. The Hungarian national Chronicle, although it does not (for reasons of national pride) mention the Petcheneg defeat, agrees in other respects with this account. In all the descriptions of Scythia contained in the various versions of the Chronicle, the only name which can be ascribed quite certainly to Hungarian national memories is the name Itīl of the river on which they lived; and under this name, as every version of the Chronicle repeats, they understood the Don. All versions of the Chronicle show the Magyars beginning their migration to their present homes from the Palus Maiotis.

Leo Grammaticus. We have actual evidence of the presence of Magyars in the west of this district on various occasions during the ninth century.

---

1 The statement that the Petchenegs were superior to the Magyars in number and valour, although it so scandalised the patriot Count Geza Kuun that he could reproduce it only with a parenthetical (*sic*) (*Relatio*, II, 45), is in point of fact only a translation of a Byzantine formula. So Skylitzes (II, 654, ed. Bonn) says of the Uz that they were τῶν Πατζινάκων ἔθνος εὐγενέστερόν τε καὶ πολυπληθέστερον. The phrase "horum violentia effugati ad exquirendas quas incolere terras, sedesque statuere, valedicentes patriae iter arripuerunt" is strongly reminiscent of Constantine's account of the Magyars (*D.A.I.* c. 38), τράπεντες καὶ πρὸς κατοίκησιν γῆν ἐπιζητοῦντες, and Regino's curious "inaudita quia nec nominata" of Constantine's remark that the Magyars in their earlier homes bore a different name. Regino's form Pecinaci is also Greek (Πατζινάκαι Πατζινακῖται).

The earliest of these is a story preserved by Leo Grammaticus[1] and Georgius Monachus[2] and drawn apparently from
a tenth-century popular source, showing a nation variously
described as Οὔγγροι, Οὔννοι and Τοῦρκοι which appeared
somewhere on the north bank of the Danube, near its mouth,
in alliance with the Bulgars against the Byzantine fleet and the
prisoners settled by Crum north of the Danube. This event, if
genuine (and there is no reason to doubt this), must have
occurred in A.D. 836–38.[3]

St Cyril. About 860[4] the Magyars were encountered again
by no less a person than the holy St Cyril, who had been sent
on a mission from the Emperor to the Khazars to dispute with
them on the Christian faith. He was on his way from Cherson
to Khazaria, immersed in prayer, when he was rudely inter-
rupted by a party of Magyars who rushed upon him, howling
like wolves, "luporum more ululantes"—a very vivid and
convincing touch. Abashed by his sanctity, however, they
withdrew.[5]

Hinkmar. Thirdly, in the year 862 the Magyars raided the
east Frankish Empire—presumably in Pannonia.[6]

We thus have a chain of independent evidence showing the
Magyars in the South Russian steppes from at least the year

1 p. 231, ed. Bonn.

2 p. 818, ed. Bonn; p. 724, ed. Muralt.

3 The later Emperor, Basil the Macedonian, was among the prisoners, and was
at that time twenty-five years old. Basil was born under Michael (811–13). The
date is therefore 836–38. The details of this story are unimportant for the
purposes of this present essay. It is interesting, however, to note that the first
reference to the barbarians is under the name of Οὔγγροι; the second Οὔννοι;
and thereafter, Τοῦρκοι. The story belongs to the later continuation of
Georgius Monachus, and appears to have been committed to paper about the
middle of the tenth century. It looks as though Οὔγγροι was then already the
popular name, as against the literary Τοῦρκοι.

4 See Dvornik, *Slaves, Byzance et Rome au IXième Siècle*, pp. 138 ff.

5 Dümmler, *Vita Constantini*, c. VIII.

6 Hinkmar of Rheims, *ad ann.* 852: "Sed et hostes illis populis inexperti, qui
Ugri vocantur, regnum ejus (*sc.* of Louis the German) populantur". The
Magyar legendeers are fond of attributing the return of the Magyars to Hungary
to traditions of their glorious deeds of valour there as Huns under Attila. It
is much more likely that they were incited in 862 by the princes of Moravia to
help against the Franks, and that what actually led their footsteps was no
Attilian bird or memory, but a guide from the despised Czechoslovak race.
Hinkmar is confirmed by the *Ann. Sang. Maj. ad ann.* 863.

A.D. 835 onward. To these mentions of the Magyars by name must, of course, be added the further passage (the Embassy of the Khagan Rūs) which we now see reason to suppose to be, in reality, a reference to the Magyars. If, then, we look for further confirmation of Regino's story that the Petchenegs drove the Magyars westward towards the Danube in A.D. 889, we shall have to consider two questions: the movements of the Petchenegs, and the movements of the Magyars. We shall find, on the one hand, that the evidence is entirely negative for the Petchenegs having been west of the Don more than a few years before 889; and positive, for the Magyars being subjected to pressure on their eastern flank about that date.

Movements of the Petchenegs: Oriental Sources. Khordādbeh, like Džaihānī, places the Petchenegs east of the Volga. Istachrī and Mas'ūdī know them west of the Don, but both speak of them as having arrived there within so recent a date that the memory of the move has not died. Thus Istachrī writes, in his section on the Turks:

> On the other hand, a body of Turks have left their native country and established themselves between the Khazars and the Rūm. These Turks bear the name of Petchenegs. The country which the Petchenegs occupy is not their original abode; they invaded this country several times and ended by making themselves the masters of it.

Mas'ūdī in his remarks on the "Valandar hordes" in the *Livre d'Avertissement* says that these "hordes" established themselves "between Rome and Constantinople" "after the year 320 H." This remark is, it is true, due to a mere confusion,[1] but Mas'ūdī is himself aware that there had been a move, since he goes on:

> In *The Book of Different Sorts of Knowledge and of What has Happened in Past Centuries* we have spoken of the causes which brought about the displacement from the east of these four Turkish races, of the wars which took place between them, the Guz, the Kharlūkh and the Kimäk, on the borders of the lake of Džordžan (the Aral Sea), of the depredations which they have committed and of the reasons of their establishment in these countries.

1 Mas'ūdī takes the date from the date of the Magyar raid on Constantinople in A.D. 934, which is one of the ingredients in his story.

The Russian Chronicle. The old Russian Chronicle remarks vaguely in its opening pages that "after the Avars appeared the Petchenegs, then the Magyars, who were seen again near Kiev" (*sc.* in 898, according to the Chronicle's chronology).[1] But this is a mere vague generality, on a par with the whole tone of these opening pages. Had the Chronicle been accurate, it must have mentioned the Bulgars, who were the nation which actually appeared after the Avars.

When the Chronicle becomes definite, we get the specific statement that the Petchenegs "appeared" for the first time in "Russia" in 915.[2] Even here, as I hope to show elsewhere, the Petchenegs appear not to have been attacking Kiev, but only seeking for permission to move along the sea-shore.[3] In 916–20, then, we hear of Igor "making war on the Petchenegs".[4] The first Petcheneg attack on Kiev is not until 968, during Sviato-slav's expedition to Bulgaria.[5]

The late Nikon compilation, however, has an entry, omitted in all early versions of the Chronicle, that "Askold and Dir slew many Petchenegs". This late entry might contain a sub-stratum of truth, and may actually refer to the first impact of the Petchenegs on entering Europe, and before settling in the steppes; but it need not refer to any date earlier than A.D. 880.[6]

For the sake of completeness, another entry should perhaps be adduced from the late Stepennaia Kniga, which writes *ad ann.* 866: "Askold and Dir marched on Constantinople, and in their army were Cumans, who were living on the Black Sea". Those writers who insist in identifying Petchenegs and Cumans may possibly take this as evidence of the presence of Petchenegs.

---

1 "Nestor", I, 10. For the real dating of this note, see below, p. 76 (note 3)

2 *Ibid.* p. 54.   3 See my "Petchenegs".

4 "Nestor", I, 55.   5 *Ibid.* I, 91.

6 The traditional chronology puts the murder of Askold and Dir in A.D. 882; so Sir Bernard Pares, *A History of Russia*, p. 18. Hruschewski, on the other hand (*Geschichte des Ukrainischen Volkes*, I, 42), thinks it possible, on inde-pendent grounds, that Dir was still reigning at the end of the eighties. In this case it is not only possible, but extremely probable that Dir, at least, "slew many Petchenegs" while they were wandering about seeking a home. Thus finding their path blocked to the west, they turned to the Don and drove the Magyars away westward.

But this identification is now exploded, and one can only interpret the entry as a false analogy from the writer's day.

The Greek Sources. The Greek sources have no single reference to the Petchenegs before their victory over the Magyars at the end of the ninth century. An apparent—but only an apparent—exception is formed by the story of the fortress of Sarkel on the Don, which was constructed by the Greeks for the benefit of the Khazars in 833–35. The fortress is said by Cedrenus, the later universal chronicler, to have been built as a defence against the Petchenegs; but this is a very obvious slip, as comparison of the three passages which contain references to the event will show at once:

(1) *D.A.I.* c. 42: "Patzinakia extends [*sc.* in A.D. 949] to Sarkel, where there is a city of the Khazars, which was built by Petronas Camaretus, at the request of the Khazars made to the Emperor Theophilus".

(2) Theophanis Continuator, p. 122, ed. Bonn: "About the same time [*sc.* 833–35] the Khagan and the Beg of Khazaria sent an embassy to the Emperor and asked him to build the city of Sarkel. This is a place on the Don, which divides the land of the Petchenegs on the one hand, and of the Khazars on the other'.

(3) Cedrenus, II, 528, ed. Bonn: "Theophilus received an embassy from the Khagan of Khazaria asking him to build a fortress of Markel [*sic*]. For it was seen that this would be a strong fortress against the Patzinaks to stop their incursions across the Don".

These three stories show perfectly clearly how Cedrenus' mistake arose, and it is amazing how scholars, with the original story staring them in the face, should have continued solemnly to deduce the presence of the Petchenegs west of the Don before A.D. 833. Some of these have boggled at the anachronism, and have attempted to make sense of Cedrenus by locating Sarkel far up the Don, on the narrow point where that river approached the Volga. All the evidence, however, shows that Sarkel was situated not far from the mouth of the Don, and as a protection from marauders from the regions west of that river. Those critics who suggest that the fortress was built to check raids from the north-east fail to explain under what conceivable circumstances it could possibly fulfil this purpose. Waterloo is not the best place from which to defend Wandsworth, with bows and arrows, against cavalry attack from Dover.

All evidence goes to show that Sarkel was built near the mouth of the Don, and as a defence against the nation occupying the country immediately opposite it—the Magyars; being the nation which is reported as active in South Russia, for the first time, at precisely this date.

The Georgian Chronicle. Nothing is to be made of the references in the Georgian Chronicle, which mentions the Petchenegs as allied with the Circassians and the Alans in the year A.D. 90 (!) and describing Wakhtang's expedition of A.D. 454, goes on:

After defeating the Ossetes (Alans) and the Qipčak and building the Gate of Darien as a shield against those nations.... Wakhtang then proceeded into the land of the Padchanigs, who were only separated from the Ossetes by the river which marked the frontier. The Djiketh (Zichians) were also in the neighbourhood. Long afterwards the Padchanigs and the Djiketh having been expelled by the Turks, the former emigrated westward, the latter established themselves at the extremity of the Aphkhazeth (Abasgians).[1]

This entry is nothing more than another collection of false analogies from the writer's day; cf. the Qipčak, who did not arrive north of the Caucasus till some 600 years after the date given. The same writer gives the Khazars invading the Caucasus in the year 4000 B.C.

The Armenian and the Western Chronicles, like the Greek, are completely silent on the subject of the Petchenegs during the ninth century. The earliest reference is that in Regino.

Date of Petcheneg arrival. Thus all the external evidence goes to support what is also the Petchenegs' own story, as preserved by Constantine, to the effect that the Petchenegs did not cross the Don until late in the ninth century. It does appear, however, as though they have arrived a year or two before coming to blows with the Magyars. This is indicated by Istachrī's statement that the Petchenegs had "invaded the country which they now

1 *Chronique Géorgienne*, ed. Brosset, p. 159.

occupy several times" before finally becoming masters of it; by
Regino's, that the Petchenegs were "finitimi" of the Magyars
when they expelled them, and by Constantine's own words that
"the Petchenegs were forced to dwell in the land of the Magyars.
War broke out between the Magyars and the Petchenegs".[1]

Magyar movement West. The period can, however, have been
no long one (we are still disregarding Constantine's evidence),
because the outburst of Magyar activity in the West occurred
(with the single exception of the raid of 862), only towards the
end of the ninth century. The recently discovered *Annals of
Admont*[2] report most interestingly two conflicts in 881; the one
with "Hungarians" proper at "Wenia", the other at "Cul-
mite" "cum Cowaris"—a note of most exceptional importance,
as constituting the sole mention of Kavars yet known, outside
Constantine's work. It is quite possible, as we said, that the
Petchenegs first arrived in Southern Russia as early as 880, and
that this notice is an indication of the first pressure on the
feeding-grounds. It might, however, also be an isolated raid;
for when we reach 889, Regino undoubtedly intimates that this
was the *first* appearance of the Magyars. In the same way, the
Annales Sangallenses Majores write *ad ann.* 888 (889): "Et
Arnulphus in regnum elevatur; in cujus tempore Agareni in
istas regiones *primitus* venerunt".

In the next year (890),[3] the Russian Chronicle reports the
Magyars passing by Kiev, evidently on a national migration:
"The Ugri crossed the chain of mountains still today called the
mountains of the Ugri; they approached the banks of the
Dnieper and camped with their chariots not far from Kiev; for
they were nomads, even as the Polovtsi today".

In 892 (893) and 894 the *Annales Fuldenses* and the *Annales
Sangallenses Majores* report the Magyars in the Hungarian
plain, taking part in the fighting between Moravia and the

1 *D.A.I.* c. 38.
2 See E. Klebel, "Eine neu aufgefundene Salzburger Geschichtsquelle",
Mitteilungen der Gesellschaft für Salzburger Landeskunde, 1921.
3 The Chronicle puts the date at 6406 of the world, which should be 894; but
the Chronicle also puts the Greco-Bulgarian war at 6410 (898) whereas it
really took place in 893–95 (see Excursus IV). Therefore there is an error of four
or five years, and the Magyars probably passed by Kiev in 890. See Fehér,
Beziehungen, pp. 111–12.

Empire, and generally ravaging the country. As the Emperor Arnolph was freely accused by his contemporaries of having broken down the Great Wall of Gog and Magog and let the imprisoned nations (including the Magyars) loose upon civilisation, it is clear that they were regarded by their victims as a new pest; this confirms Regino's story of a battle on the Don in 888–89, and is further indirect evidence that the Petchenegs did not cross the Volga much before that date.

In 893–95 comes the Bulgaro-Greek war; and in the winter of 895–96 (probably) the entry of the Magyars into Hungary.[1]

Thus there is evidence to show (even without calling on Constantine) that the Magyars were to be found west of the Don from at least 835 until 889, when they were driven westward by the newly-arrived Petchenegs; but we have still to ascertain two points. Firstly, when did they reach the Don? Secondly, where did they come from?

Date of the Magyar settlement on the Don. As regards the former question, we have only indirect evidence. The fact that the building of Sarkel took place in 833–35, and that a Magyar raid to the Danube occurred about the same time, makes it strongly probable that the Magyars reached the Don shortly before these dates, say about 830. For it is unlikely, if they really menaced the Khazars, that the latter power would have waited very long before taking measures of self-defence.

Where did they come from? This is a more interesting question. If we compare our report "*α*" with "*β*", there seems no doubt that the latter is the later in date. Now "*α*" (Magyars "A" and "B") knows nothing of Magyars on the Don; the Magyars of "A" are east of the Burtās, those of "B" are between the Don and the Cuban. Conversely, "*β*" (Magyars "C") knows no other Magyars than those on the Don.

Therefore, between the time of writing of "α" and "β", the Magyar nation had moved to the Don from one or both of the localities in which they were found in "α".

From which locality did they move—"A" or "B"?

Undoubtedly, from "B".

This can be proved either by linguistic, or by historical

[1] See Excursus IV.

arguments. It has been shown by M. Gombocz that the Magyars of "A" were probably a horde which became detached from the main body of their nation when the Bulgars travelled north-east, and perhaps accompanied the latter on the journey. In any case they are found living next to them in the ninth century. But had these been the ancestors of the Magyars who afterwards entered Hungary, the language of the latter would have borne traces of a later contact than is actually the case, and shown that contact as extending to a northerly region. Further it is difficult to think that the Magyar national tradition would not have retained some trace of this journey, whereas it definitely shows the nation as migrating from the Don.

Moreover, this "first frontier" was still existing when the Petchenegs crossed the Volga, as is shown by their own story; and it continued to exist until at least the thirteenth century—in fact, under another form, until the present day. But if they remained in the Urals, they cannot have migrated to the Don.

It may be added that the explanation advanced in M. Eckhardt's recent history,[1] which makes the Magyars divided by the Petchenegs into "A" and "C", is unacceptable, not only because it ignores "B" altogether, but because a glance at the map will show that a Petcheneg move would not affect the Magyars of "A" at all, except perhaps to push them a little northward; and finally, because the Magyars of "A" were in their places long before the Petchenegs ever attacked them, as the Oriental sources show.

Therefore the Magyars of "C" are those of "B", and crossed the Don between the writing of "α" and "β". This is confirmed incidentally by the Hungarian national legend, which preserves a vague memory of an association with the Alans,[2] as by the linguistic history of the nation, which also shows Caucasian and Alanic influences.

Further, our section "B", together with Mas'ūdī's "Seven Lands", is absolutely the last mention in history of Magyars on the Cuban; for when we come to the tenth century, we find in that region (as shown above) only Circassians on the sea-board,

1 *Introduction à l'histoire Hongroise.*
2 Thurocz, II, 4. It is possible, however, that this reference, like nearly everything in the Hungarian Chronicles relating to the period before they entered Hungary, ought to be disregarded as a borrowing from written sources.

Alans in the hinterland; with occasional mention of Khazars, and the colony at Taman, which was for a time under Russian control.

Therefore it was the Magyars of "B" who, moving across the Don, became the Magyars of "A".

But what led them to make the move?

It was not an attack by the Petchenegs. That is certain for two reasons. Firstly, the move took place a long time before the Petchenegs ever crossed the Volga; for we have seen reason to suppose that the Petcheneg move took place not earlier than about A.D. 880 (and we shall find the Petchenegs' own story in the *D.A.I.* more than confirming this); and secondly, because it would have been a geographical impossibility. For we know from Constantine that the Petchenegs left the Volga because the neighbourhood of the Khazars had become too hot for them. To attack the Magyars on the Cuban, it would therefore have been necessary for them to cross the Volga near Ītīl, the Khazar capital, encumbered as they were with bag and baggage, wife and child, to drive down clean across the vast steppe, and having attacked the Magyars, to follow them across the Don—an obvious absurdity. But if they followed the natural and easy route along the Don, there would be no need for them to attack the Magyars at all, if the latter were south of the Don; nor, if they had done so, could the result have been a Magyar migration westward; since this would involve the Magyars cutting their way clean through the heart of the country occupied by their enemies.

Finally, Constantine tells us that the Petchenegs "found the Magyars in the country over which they now rule"; he also tells us that the eastern frontier of the Petchenegs was the Don. Therefore the Petcheneg attack on the Magyars took place on the Don and not on the Cuban.

Therefore that move of the Magyars from "B" to "C" was due to some other cause.

The Oriental sources will not help us to discover what this cause was; we must turn to Constantine's story. At first sight, this does not seem to help us either; but we shall discover, on looking into it more closely, that *Constantine has actually preserved for us the memory of a defeat inflicted on the Magyars on the Cuban by another nation, not the Petchenegs, in consequence of which the Magyar nation migrated to the right bank of the Don.*

PART II

The De Administrando Imperio

I SHALL now turn to the history of the Magyars and the Petchenegs, as related in Constantine's *De Administrando Imperio*.[1] This work, so much quoted, so little understood, was some years ago subjected to a brilliant critical analysis by Professor J. B. Bury.[2] Bury's analysis again was criticised, more recently, in some cases with effect, by the Hungarian Professor Fehér.[3] I shall have frequent occasion to refer to both of these works.

Bury has pointed out that the bulk of the *D.A.I.* consists of a number of notes, prepared at different times and from different sources, and subsequently thrown together without final arrangement or revision. The chapter headings are mere marginal notes, which often correspond very imperfectly with the text, and it is thus more accurate to speak of sections than of chapters. The sections, then, giving the historical and ethnographical accounts of the various nations, form more or less independent units. Here and there slight attempts have been made to reconcile them; but in many cases, not only is one story duplicated, but the duplications contain glaring discrepancies. An example, taken not from the chapters which we shall chiefly consider, is given by c. 30, which has an account of the Avar capture of Salona duplicating a similar account in c. 29 and differing widely from it; and an account of the coming of the Croats duplicating that in c. 31, and again contradicting it in many points.

But it is not even possible to say that we have clear-cut divisions, each complete in itself and left uncompromisingly for him who will to reconcile. On the contrary, while the broader divisions are kept separate from one another, attempts at

---

1 A translation of the historical portions of these chapters will be found in the Appendix.
2 "The Treatise 'The De Administrando Imperio'", *B.Z.* XIV, pp. 511–77.
3 "Ungarns Gebietsgrenzen in der Mitte des Xen Jahrhundertes", *U.J.* Band II, Heft 1, April 1922. Quoted as *Gebietsgrenzen*.

editing are quite clearly visible *within* several of the divisions. An excellent example of this is c. 40, which is a complex interweaving of a foreign source and of a geographical description. When I come to that chapter, I shall attempt to disentangle the threads; here I will merely ask the reader to look at the chapter in question and see if this be not so. A better example still is the story of the Russian merchants given in c. 9 (and reduplicated, in more detail, in c. 13).[1] The general sense of this passage is clear, and for that reason scholars have not, as a rule, troubled to disentangle the details. Yet the fact that the general sense is clear ought not to blind us to the fact that the story in itself is not coherent, and, taken quite literally, makes doubtful sense. It goes backwards and forwards, picking up threads and dropping them, and duplicating, in a way almost impossible to disentangle.

It is in the light of these observations that we must consider the various accounts of the coming of the Magyars and the Petchenegs. The chapters in question (cc. 37–42) form a rough unit, and there are many signs to indicate that they were received by Constantine in the order in which they now stand. As Constantine received each story, he had in his mind the preceding accounts, and thus modified each slightly to adapt it to its predecessors.[2] He did not, however, attempt to work his three or four stories—the Petcheneg story, the Magyar story, the Kavar story, the Moravian story—into one, but left them standing as parallel accounts. It is in this light that they must be considered, and it will presently be found that we have not four stories, as commonly assumed, but five; c. 38, the Magyar

1 After passing the rapids, the merchants call at the Island of St Gregory. "And after this island the Russians do not fear the Patzinaks until they come to the river Selina. So setting off from it, they sail four days until they reach the lagoon which forms the mouth of the river, in which (lagoon) is also the island of St Eleutherion. Well, landing at this island they rest and refit. But this lagoon is at the mouth of the river, as we said, and reaches to the sea, and opposite the sea lies the island of St Eleutherion. From there they go to the river Dnieper [*sic*] and reaching there, they rest again. But when a suitable season comes, they set out and come to the river called White, and after resting there also, they set out and come to Selina."

2 The most important adaptation is one which remains to be proved—the Κάγγαρ confusion. But the placing of "Great Moravia" is also due to such an adaptation; and there are also minor instances.

story proper, consisting, not of one consecutive account, but of two parallel ones.

I shall now proceed to take each section separately, and in doing so shall compare it with what we have learned from our analysis of the remaining sources to be the rough outline of the Magyar-Petcheneg story, to wit:

That the Magyars at some date in the early ninth century were living in two main bodies, the one east of the Volga, between the Petchenegs (then on the Volga and the Ural) and the Volga Bulgars, the other between the Don and the Cuban.

That at some date, perhaps about A.D. 825–30, the latter body moved north-west for some unascertained reason, and settled on the right bank of the Don, near its mouth.

That in 888 or 889 the Magyars were driven westward by the Petchenegs to the country near the mouth of the Danube, and shortly afterwards entered and settled in their present homes.

I shall now proceed to consider each section of the *D.A.I.* independently, in the light of the above observations.

THE PETCHENEG STORY: c. 37

C. 37 contains far the most simple and straightforward account of the events in question. It is obviously derived ultimately from a Petcheneg source. This is proved, not only by the whole tenor of the account, but by its intimate knowledge of Petcheneg history and organisation, and directly by the various pieces of concealed *oratio obliqua* contained in it—what the Petchenegs say about their Khans, what the Petchenegs call the ruined cities in their country.

We may take it, therefore, that this chapter represents the expulsion of the Magyars and the settlement of the Petchenegs in their new home as it appeared to Petcheneg eyes; and it is noteworthy that the whole story appeared as a single event. The whole course of the fighting, which appears from Regino's account to have extended to several years, is summed up in the laconic and soldierly phrase that the Petchenegs "coming to the country ruled by them today and finding the Magyars in it, conquering them in the course of battle and driving them out, chased them away ". In that light, then, these six or seven years of bickering appeared to the warlike Petchenegs half a century later. The phrase cannot, on the other hand, possibly be taken as describing two great series of operations, separated by a long interval of peace, as it would be necessary to do did we assume that the Petchenegs arrived in Europe much before the end of the ninth century, or even, as some have suggested, in A.D. 830. The picture here is of a single struggle, conceived as a unit from the first defeat by the Uz to the final victory over the Magyars. The account makes no distinction between two parts of the country, occupied successively. "Coming to the country ruled by them today and finding the Magyars in it, they chased them away and settled in it, and are ruling over the said country, as said, etc." The unity of the whole operation could not be more plainly expressed.

Two dates are given. The defeat of the Petchenegs by the Uz and the Khazars is given as "fifty years ago" ($\pi\rho\grave{o}$ $\grave{\epsilon}\tau\hat{\omega}\nu$ $\pi\epsilon\nu\tau\acute{\eta}$-$\kappa o\nu\tau a$), while after the Petchenegs had driven the Magyars into Hungary, they are said to have been "ruling over the said country, as said, fifty-five years" ($\dot{\omega}s$ $\epsilon\ddot{\iota}\rho\eta\tau a\iota$, $\mu\acute{\epsilon}\chi\rho\iota$ $\tau\hat{\eta}s$ $\sigma\acute{\eta}\mu\epsilon\rho o\nu$ $\ddot{\epsilon}\tau\eta$ $\pi\epsilon\nu\tau\acute{\eta}\kappa o\nu\tau a$ $\pi\acute{\epsilon}\nu\tau\epsilon$).

It looks, especially in view of the phrase $\dot{\omega}s$ $\epsilon\ddot{\iota}\rho\eta\tau a\iota$, as though these two dates ought to agree, and Bury makes them do so by emending the former passage through the insertion of the word $\pi\acute{\epsilon}\nu\tau\epsilon$. This, however, has not the effect desired by him. Both dates can now be made to correspond with the date of the Magyar *Landnahme*, by subtracting fifty-five from the year in which Constantine wrote; but the earlier date is now wrong. For we know from Regino that the Petchenegs were across the Don by 889, whereas the *Landnahme* did not take place till several years later.

M. Fehér, on the other hand,[1] ignores the former date altogether; treats with considerable derision the idea that the date of the *Landnahme* can be found from the latter; and calculates his fifty-five back from the year in which the Petchenegs drove the Magyars across the Don. This, however, involves dating the composition of the chapter in 945-46, or considerably earlier than

[1] *Beziehungen*, pp. 107 ff., also in *K.C.A.* I Köt. 2 Szám, p. 123.

any other chapter of the *D.A.I.* (so far as can be judged); and even to reach this result, M. Fehér has to correct Regino's date by one or two years. He also omits to explain why Constantine should have been at pains to give the exact date when the Petchenegs drove the Magyars across the Don, instead of the far more important and obvious date when they became neighbours of Bulgaria; and finally, his explanation involves distinguishing the two stages in the Petcheneg advance, of which distinction their own story bears no trace.

Neither of these explanations, then, is satisfactory, nor will any other explanation which seeks to connect the two dates prove more happy. Moreover, there are at least two considerable objections to supposing Constantine's ὡς εἴρηται to refer to the dates at all. In the first place, the words "as said" would be inapplicable in such a case, since Constantine did not say fifty-five in the first instance, but fifty; and in such respects he is a very careful and even tiresomely pedantic writer, constantly repeating his own earlier remarks word for word. Secondly, the two dates do not refer to the same event. The former relates to the expulsion of the Petchenegs from the Volga, the latter to their settlement on the Don and the Danube. These two events took place in different localities, and different years.

It seems, therefore, clear that we must renounce any attempt to make the two agree, and refer the ὡς εἴρηται, not to the "fifty years" of the Petchenegs at all, but either to the specific verb δεσπόζουσι or to the general sense of the whole sentence (the Petcheneg conquest of the old Magyar territory). We then get the two different dates referring to different events, and the explanation of the discrepancy between them is, as usual in Constantine's work, that they come from two different sources.

The latter date gives the year when the Magyars retired from the frontiers of Bulgaria, and the Petchenegs replaced them. It was an event well known to the Greeks and recorded by their historians, and Constantine's own father, Leo the Philosopher, was prominent in the intrigues which brought it about. Constantine himself mentions some of the incidents connected with it in a later chapter of the *D.A.I.* (c. 51); he was therefore well acquainted with its history. If, therefore, we can discover in what year Constantine wrote these words, thus discovering what he means by his phrase ἡ σήμερον, we can by subtraction arrive at the date of the Magyar *Landnahme*, which will fall in the same year as the final establishment of the Petchenegs in the Magyars' old homes.

It may be noted that Constantine uses the phrase ἡ σήμερον on several occasions in his work, and on three of them he defines it. Two of these (in c. 27[1] and c. 29[2] respectively) occur before this chapter. In each case the formula μέχρι τῆς σήμερον is used, and in each the year of writing is given as A.D. 948–49. It would therefore seem natural to refer the present words back to these earlier definitions, were the distance not too great. I show elsewhere, however,[3] that the distance is not nearly so great as appears on reading the text in its present form. There is strong reason to suppose that both c. 30 and cc. 31–36 are all of them later additions, comprising a συγγραφή on the Yugoslavs which the Emperor promises, in c. 29, to supply at a later date. It is very likely, then, that c. 37 was actually composed immediately after c. 29.

The date of c. 37 would, on this showing, be the same as that of cc. 27, 29, i.e. A.D. 948–49. Subtracting, and using inclusive reckoning (which seems most likely to have been used), we should get a date of 895 for the *Landnahme*. This is also the date at which I arrive, by independent reasoning, from consideration of the Bulgaro-Magyar war, which I discuss elsewhere.[4]

Freed from the bondage of Constantine's "fifty-five", the first date now becomes explicable. It is an integral part of the Petcheneg story, and comes from a Petcheneg source. It is therefore most valuable for our enquiry into the date when the Petchenegs first crossed the Volga. It obviously cannot be taken quite literally, since fifty years back from 949 would give us 899, whereas we know from Regino that the Petchenegs were across the Volga at least as early as 889. It must therefore be taken as an approximation—half a century ago; when the

---

1 p. 120, 25: εἰσὶ δὲ μέχρι τῆς σήμερον, ἥτις ἐστὶν ἰδικτιῶνος ἑβδόμη, ἔτη ἀπὸ κτίσεως κόσμου ,Ϛυνζ´.
2 p. 137, 12: μέχρι τῆς σήμερον, ἥτις ἰνδικτιῶνος ἑβδόμης ἔτους ,Ϛυνζ´.
3 See below, pp. 136 ff.   4 See Excursus IV.

narrator was a little child, or when his father was a young man, or his grandfather in his prime. We must not expect exact chronological reckoning from the Petchenegs. On the other hand, they were not without all historical sense, since they preserved the names of the Khans who commanded them at the time of their great defeat. We cannot therefore strain the meaning of this approximation into signifying more than, say, sixty-five or seventy years at the most. It is inadmissible, on this evidence, to suppose that the Petchenegs crossed the Volga earlier than about A.D. 880.

Constantine's story in c. 37 is based on first-hand evidence. It is clear and straightforward, and agrees with all the evidence which we have yet examined. We must, therefore, be cautious, in examining the next stories, in rejecting this one; if there are found to be discrepancies, the weight of probability is certainly on the side of the Petchenegs.

It may be recalled here that c. 37 gives the Μάζαροι as neighbours of the Petchenegs on the Volga before their move. These Μάζαροι are, as we showed above, the Magyar-Baškirs of Džaihānī's "first frontier of the Magyars".

THE MAGYAR STORY: c. 38

C. 38 is far from being equally clear. According to this story, the Magyars were living in a place called Levedia, next to the Khazars, when they were attacked by the Petchenegs (then known as Kangar), who divided them into two parts. They were then known, not as "Τοῦρκοι", but "for some reason" as "Σάβαρτοι ἄσφαλοι".[1] The one part went south, and took refuge in the Caucasus, where they still bore the name, in Constantine's day, of Savartoi asphaloi; the others were driven west to a place called Atelkouzou. Here they allied themselves with the Khazars; but were attacked by the Petchenegs and driven into their present territory.

Here, then, we have an account of two defeats inflicted on the Magyars, and of a double westward move. The orthodox (I

---

1 Professor Moravcsik, of Budapest, informs me that the MS reading leaves no doubt that these are two words, not one as read in the Bonn text.

believe, indeed, the invariable) explanation has been to take the first of these as being identical with the defeat described by Regino, which occurred in 888 or 889, and resulted in the Magyars being driven westward from the Don to the Danube; the second being that in consequence of which they were forced to enter Hungary. This explanation seems specious at first sight; nevertheless, it teems, on closer investigation, with difficulties of all sorts, military, geographical and chronological. The more closely these pitfalls are examined, the more formidable do they become. We shall proceed now to consider them, and shall, I believe, find them so insuperable that we shall be forced rather to take the second defeat mentioned in this chapter as that which corresponds to the Petchenegs' story in c. 37. In other words, the second defeat in c. 38 covers the whole period of the Petcheneg-Magyar fighting, from the battle on the Don to the flight into Hungary inclusive. This will, of course, involve finding an entirely new explanation for the first defeat mentioned in c. 38. I hope to be able to do this; meanwhile, I shall consider the difficulties which arise on the orthodox interpretation, beginning with the chronological.

The Σάβαρτοι ἄσφαλοι. These words have been interpreted in every conceivable sense, and as part of every known or unknown language, including Swedish.[1] It can, however, no longer be doubted that the interpretation of the word Σάβαρτοι first offered by Thury[2] is the correct one, and that the "Savartoi" are identical with the Sevordik (= "Black Sons") of the Armenians, the al-Sijāwardija of the Arabs—a race which we hear of on several occasions as inhabiting the district of Dous in the province of Oudil, in the Caucasian mountains, north of Armenia proper.

The point is put beyond doubt by Constantine himself, who

---

1 So Zeuss, *Die Deutschen und ihre Nachbarstämme*, p. 249, and following him, Rösler, *Romanische Studien*, p. 150: "ist das Swartiasphali, d.h. die Schwarzen Falen und es wäre dies die Bezeichnung welche ihnen die scandinavisch redenden Waräger in Russland und Constantinopel gaben? Diese Vermutung von K. Zeuss klingt mir sehr beifallswert". But Falen, Falven etc. = (?) Sallow Men, was a Germanic name given to the Cumans; and Rösler himself was well aware that the Cumans did not appear in (later) Russia till 1060.

2 See W. Pecz, *B.Z.* VII, 1898, pp. 201–2. For the controversy which followed, see the same periodical, 1895–97, *passim*.

D

has a second reference to this race in the *De Ceremoniis*. He describes them (in this case under the name of $\Sigma\epsilon\beta\acute{o}\rho\tau\iota o\iota$) as living under three chiefs ($\check{a}\rho\chi o\nu\tau\epsilon\varsigma$), and is even obliging enough to translate the word for us, literally as $\mu a\nu\rho\grave{a}\ \pi a\iota\delta\acute{\iota}a$.[1]

Constantine is therefore quite correct when he tells us that a race of "Black Sons" inhabited "Persia" "till his own day"; by "Persia" of course, understanding, not "Persia" proper, but the Persian Empire, which both under the Sassanides and under the first days of the Chalifate was taken as including the central Caucasian mountains.[2] There is, moreover, no reason to reject his most interesting statement that these Savartoi asphaloi had formed part of the Magyar nation, separated from the rest of the nation and driven into the mountains by an attack from some other nation. Nevertheless a little further examination is necessary.

Our earliest reference to this nation occurs in a passage from al-Balāḍuri, in these words:

Šamkūr. I was informed by some people from Bardha'ah that Šamkūr was an ancient city to which Salmān-ibn-Rabī'ah sent someone who reduced it. It was well populated and flourishing until it was destroyed by as-Sāwardīyah, who after the departure of Yazid ibn-Usaid from Armenia came together and became a source of trouble and misfortune. In the year 240 (H.) the city was rebuilt by the freedman of al-Mutasun and the governor of Armenia, Acharbaijānand Šimšāk.[3]

The date of this raid must have been about A.D. 755–60.[4]

The Sevordik then disappear from history for almost exactly a century; then, for about 50–100 years, references to them are frequent.

According to John Catholicos, Boga captured "Stephen, also named Konsen", who was "of the race called Sievkasievowerkikh in Dous, in the province of Oudil" and dragged him in chains to the court where, despite torture, Stephen confessed

---

1 *De Ceremoniis Aulae Byzantinae*, ii, 48, pp. 687, ed. Bonn.

2 Cf. Vambéry, *Ursprung der Magyaren*, p. 133.

3 *The origins of the Islamic State*, being a translation of the *Kitāb Futāh al-Buldān* of al-Balādhuri, by Philip Khūri Hilli, New York, 1916 (Columbia University Studies), vol. i, p. 319.

4 Marquart, *Streifzüge*, p. 37.

the name of Jesus Christ, and was martyred, dying "in the year 808 of the Roman era (?)", about A.D. 856.[1]

The inhabitants of the province of Oudil recognised the sovereignty of Aschod (who reigned 885–89), "renounced theft and brigandage", and were by him "given chiefs and ischkhans".[2]

In the times of King Sempod (*c.* A.D. 899–900) the Chief Eunuch "marched like a barbarian destroyer against George, Nahabied of the Sevortiens; this family called itself thus on account of its ancestor Sev" [*or* "its bird which was black"].[3] The Chief Eunuch took George and his brother Aronses prisoner and tortured them to convert them to Islam. They refused, and were consequently slain, and "their names are written in the book of life".[4]

In the year 910 we find "the inhabitants of the province of Oudil, called Sevortiens", furnishing troops to Sempat's forces under his sons Aschod and Monschegh, but deserting to the enemy at the critical moment.[5]

Parallel references to the above are made by Moses Katankatvaci, with slight variations, unimportant for our present purpose.

Istachrī, writing *c.* A.D. 950, tells us that "Behind Bardhaʻa and Šamkūr is a tribe (or species) of Armenians called Siyāwardiyya, good-for-nothing, worthless and bandits".[6]

Masʻūdī, writing at almost the same date, describes the "Siyāwardiyya" as living on the Kur, east of Tiflis and west of Bardhaʻa. He describes them as "a kind of Armenians, brave and powerful, according to what has been told us of their deeds. The so-called Siyāwardiyya battle-axes are called after them."

Dimašqi classifies them, with the Čanark and the Kenz (?), as Armenians.[7] It is very doubtful, however, whether Dimašqi is not merely quoting from an old source.

---

1 *Hist. d'Arménie*, cc. XIII, XIV.   2 *Ibid.* c. XVII.

3 The word used is *Sev*, which might mean "ancestor" or "bird". Some have seen in this a reference to the Hungarian falcon legend. Cf. Vambéry, *Ursprung*, p. 274; Kuun, *Relatio*, I, 180 ff.

4 *Hist. d'Arménie*, c. XXXIII.

5 *Ibid.* c. XLVII.   6 See Appendix.

7 *Cosmographie*, tr. Mehren, p. 378: "The Alans and the Borğan are neighbours (of the Rūs) and they say that they are their brethren, similarly the

Thomas Acruni writes:

When the great mourning [for Gurgan, brother of King Gagik, after A.D. 923] was ended, the King put an end to the warlike disturbances in these countries caused by the Persians and the black children of Hagar (Sevordik of Hagar) living in the mountains.[1]

In view of the gap of a century after the first mention, and in view of the fact that this mention apparently refers to a raid; and that long-distance raids by the nomad races were no uncommon things—the Magyars in particular, like the later Cumans, at times covered prodigious distances—it is not necessary from the above references to assume establishment of the Sevordik south of the Caucasus in the eighth century. But it is obviously necessary to assume establishment from a certain time prior to A.D. 853, in order to give the converts time to assimilate the new faith.

Thus it seems reasonable to suppose, from this evidence, that Constantine's statement is so far correct, that the Magyars were actually divided into two by an attack from some people, and that part of them went south to the Caucasus and part westward elsewhere; but if the Petcheneg attack occurred about 889, or shortly before, as we have been led to suppose, then it cannot have been that attack which divided the Magyars, seeing that the Sevordik had already arrived in the Caucasus after the division at least forty years earlier.

The geographical difficulty: Λεβεδία *and* Ἀτελκούζου. But there are other difficulties, no less formidable, which revolve round the names Λεβεδία and Ἀτελκούζου. Many attempts have been made to identify these two localities; but I will pass over the earlier efforts with the remark that each attempt has identified one or the other name, with comparative ease, as the Don valley; but each has found itself in much embarrassment in seeking the second name in some other place.

Levedia. The two things that we are told definitely about Levedia (beyond the fact that it was named after Levedias, to

Azkes (Circassians). All these people are Christians. They are neighbours of the Armenians. They are divided into Saverdiat, Čanariat, Kourdj (Georgians) and Kenz (?) all of whom profess Christianity ".

1 Thomas Acruni, II, 33.

which remark I return later) are, that it contains a river named Chidmas or Činhul, and that it is "next to Khazaria". The latter point really settles the question if we admit (from our report "B" and Regino) that the Magyars were living on the right bank of the Don in the ninth century. But the Petcheneg attack could not in any case have taken place in any other district, since the Petchenegs, according to their own account, "found the Magyars in the country over which they now rule", expelled them thence, and settled in it. But the eastern frontier of the Petchenegs was Sarkel on the Don, as Constantine tells us; and Mas'ūdī also indicates that the Petcheneg frontier was on the Don. This finally rules out any attempt to place Levedia east or south of the Don, not to mention the fact that any such attempt involves us in geographical absurdities.[1]

Furthermore, as Jerney pointed out long ago, the river Moločnaya, which waters precisely this district, is formed by the confluence of the Takmak and the Činhul, and the district is known to this day as Lepedika.[2]

For reasons which I fail to understand, this identification has found little favour with either Fehér or Marquart, although neither has anything material to adduce against it, except, indeed, the comparative insignificance of the river. The same river occurs, however, again, in the form Συγγούλ in Constantine's list of the rivers of South Russia, where it is given as the easternmost of the rivers between the Don and the Danube.[3]

---

[1] See above, pp. 67–8.

[2] *Keleti Utazasa*, II, pp. 47–54; cit. Kuun, *Relatio*, I, 118.

[3] *D.A.I.* c. 42. In the country between the Don and the Danube, Constantine tells us, "are many rivers; two of them, the Dnieper and the Dniester, extremely large; but there are also other rivers, the Συγγούλ and the Ὑβυλ, Ἄλμαται, Κοῦφις, Βογοῦ and many others".

Constantine appears, as Fehér says (*Beziehungen*, pp. 95–6), to be proceeding from east to west, and the Συγγούλ, which is clearly the same as the Χιγγυλούς, must therefore be the easternmost of the series.

There are, however, strong objections against Fehér's identification of the Činhul with the Donez, or with the Upper Don—an identification which he makes on the strength of the fact that Pliny mentions "Sin" as the Scythian name for the Don. For firstly, the rivers in the list are those *between* the Don and the Danube, exclusive (the Danube is not mentioned). Secondly, the Don could not possibly be excluded from the list of larger rivers which included the Dnieper and the Dniester. And although the above objections do not apply to the Donez, yet the description appears to be a merchant's itinerary

It was therefore not unworthy of mention; and being absolutely the only river of any size which flows into the Black Sea between the Don and the Dnieper, was, perhaps, not so unimportant to a nomad cattle-rearing people as it appears to us.

And what of the word Λεβεδία itself? Of the few attempts which have been made to interpret it, Kuun's is easily the most heroic: "Vocabulum lebeda 'chenopodium vulvaria' slavicum esse videtur (lobode in Russia Minore. Rum. lobod, Gr. λουβοδία)", and he links it up with every name remotely resembling the original which he can find. Liddell and Scott translate χηνοποῦς as "goose-weed"; Lewis and Short render "lapathum" as "sorrel", and my Rumanian dictionary explains "lobod", or rather "loboda", as "orach, all-seed, notch-weed". I find it difficult to suppose that many places have really owed their names to local abundance of notch-weed, or even of goose-foot. It is simpler to suppose that Λεβεδία is merely a Slavicised version of a perfectly good Greek word λιβάδιον—a word of decent, if not of great antiquity, used by Plutarch and Strabo in the sense of "water", and then, much later, "in the common dialect", connoting a wet place (Eustathius, Thomas Magister). The word is a somewhat debased, but quite legitimate offspring of the root λιψ, cf. λείβω. Pollux uses γῆ λιβάζουσα for "marshy land". Λιβάδιον was a later vulgarisation which passed, through low Greek, into the common vocabulary of the Slavs. There was a Livada outside Adrianople, where the Cumans defeated the Crusaders; a Tsara Livada today on the junction for Gabrovo on the trans-Balkan line; the famous place near Thebes;[1] and the no less famous Russian resort in the Crimea (this a modern example). Λεβεδία is thus merely a Slavicised form of λιβάδιον, a marshy place—"a country containing many

---

of the coast, which would hardly take account of rivers not debouching into the sea. But finally, it is quite irrelevant whether the Donez or the Moločnaya is meant, since either will suit our purpose equally well.

Constantine has worked in bits of his itinerary into both c. 40 and c. 42. I think it quite likely that the Χιγγυλούς here is merely a note by Constantine himself from this itinerary, the name supplied by the author of the story in c. 38 having been simply Χιδμάς. As any page of the *D.A.I.* will show, Constantine has no scruples whatever about varying his spelling of foreign names.

1 Referred to by Acropolites, p. 183, ed. Bonn, as Λεβαδία.

trees and much water, and the ground is moist", as Ibn Rusta puts it, adequately describing the region of the Maiotis.

A word must be added on the supposed relationship between the name Λεβεδία and the hero Λεβεδίας. The latter appears to have been a historical figure. The Hungarian national tradition has preserved the memory of a certain Eleud, who appears in the Anonymus as one of the "septem capitanei", immediately after Almus;[1] but in the remaining chronicles as Almus' father.[2] Fehér shows in interesting fashion how the Anonymus had his hands tied by family tradition, while the popular saga, tending to group itself round any popular figure (here that of Arpád) naturally assigned Eleud a place in Arpád's family tree. The combination of the two shows that Eleud played an important part in the national life of the Magyars in the generation preceding that of Almus.[3] This is very true; but it is quite another thing to maintain that the district Levedia was actually called after Eleud, as Constantine would have us believe. It has sometimes occurred in the history of nomad tribes that a place has been called after a well-known chieftain; but the practice is extremely rare, and in this particular case, it cannot possibly have happened. For firstly, the name of the chieftain in question was (as we have seen) not Levedias at all, but Eleud. And secondly, by no conceivable method could a country called after either Eleud or Λεβεδίας give the form Λεβεδία. It is, however, easy to suppose that the similarity of the two names confused Constantine's (Slavonic) informant and made him *imagine* this connection; as a result of which the names got pulled out of the straight; the good Greco-Slavonic word "Livadia" only by a vowel or so, but the unfamiliar Magyar name suffering extremely rough handling.

Thus Levedia (Livadia) is the name given by the Slavonic author of this part of c. 38 to the country near the mouth of the Don, and on its right bank. So far, so good; and our identification of Levedia would seem for the moment to support the

---

1 *Anonymi Gesta Hungarorum*, c. 6: "Quorum VII virorum nomina hec fuerunt; Almus pater Arpad, Eleud pater Zobolsu, etc."
2 So Kezai: "Arpad filius Almi filii Elad, etc."
3 *Beziehungen*, p. 93.

orthodox view—although it must not be forgotten that we have a sore discrepancy of about forty years in time to get over. But let us turn now to the name *Atelkuzu.* The name occurs in three passages of the *D.A.I.*:

(*a*) C. 38, p. 169, ll. 11–24, ed. Bonn. The Magyars were attacked by the Kangar and driven west "into the place called Atelkuzu, where the Petchenegs now live".

(*b*) C. 38, p. 170, l. 18—p. 171, l. 13. The story of the Magyars under Arpád being attacked by the Petchenegs and driven into "Great Moravia". Then—a fresh note—introduced by ὅτι: "But the district (τόπος) of the Petchenegs in which the Magyars *were living at that time* (τῷ τότε καιρῷ κατοίκησαν) is called after the name of the rivers in it; the first is called Βαρούχ, the second Κουβοῦ, the third Τροῦλλος, the fourth Βροῦτος, the fifth Σέρετος".

(*c*) C. 40. Another description of the final defeat as a consequence of which the Magyars were driven into Pannonia. "And the Magyars returning and finding their camps desolate, moved into the country which they inhabit today, the land which, as has been said (ὡς εἴρηται) is called after the rivers. But the district in which the Magyars formerly (πρότερον) lived is called after the name of the river which drains it, Etel, and Kuzu (τόπος... ὀνομάζεται κατὰ τὴν ἐπωνυμίαν τοῦ ἐκεῖσε διερχομένου ποταμοῦ Ἐτελ, καὶ Κούζου), in which the Petchenegs are living today."

Now the stumbling-block to all commentators, hitherto, has been the fatal facility of those five rivers mentioned in (*b*). About them there can be no substantial doubt. The Βαρούχ, or Waruch, is the Dnieper (Hun War); the Κουβοῦ the Bug, or Boh; the Τροῦλλος the Dniester (Turkish Turla), the Βροῦτος, as today, the Pruth, and the Σέρετος, again as today, the Sereth. Of these names, Βαρούχ and Τροῦλλος at least are Turkish forms. It therefore seems probable that in Βαρούχ we have what the Magyars really called the Dnieper.

But as it happens, Constantine does not say that this district was called Atelkuzu. He says that it was the district of Petcheneg-land in which the Magyars were living *at that time* when driven into Pannonia. According to Regino, the Magyars were first driven westward *from the Don* in 889, and then spent some years around the mouth of the Danube, i.e. in the very district here described. It may have been called after the rivers in it; but Constantine never tells us that it was called Atelkuzu. Moreover, as the Petchenegs were more numerous than the Magyars, and afterwards occupied the whole territory from Silistra to Sarkel,[1] whereas the Magyars, as we know, moved westward in 889, there is no reason not to distinguish (as Constantine does) the country they were living in in the last period, from that which they inhabited earlier.

It should, of course, be noticed that the remark in question forms no part of the original story of c. 38, but is added as an afterthought, as its position in the narrative, and the introduction of the information by a fresh ὅτι, show.

It takes a mind of extraordinary courage to assert that passages (*a*)—(*c*) above[2] can under any conceivable circumstances be twisted into saying the same thing as passage (*b*). Marquart finds his valour not quite equal to the task, and essays a completely arbitrary emendation of the text, changing τοῦ διερχομένου ποταμοῦ into a plural, and then either changing Κούζου into Κουβοῦ, or else inventing an entirely new river of his own, the Kuz.[3] Hungarians are more tender with the text, but even more unscrupulous with the interpretation; for they calmly put forward a theory, unsupported by any jot or tittle of evidence, that their nation called the Dnieper Ἐτελ, by this means fitting facts to their theories. This in the very face of the fact that passage (*b*) provides them with a different name for the Dnieper in the shape of the Βαρούχ.

It is simpler and easier to recognise the fact that passages (*a*)—(*c*) and (*b*) are not parallel, and that in each case Constantine meant what he said. (*b*) describes the country occupied by the Magyars immediately before they entered their present homes; (*a*)—(*c*), Atelkuzu, the national home from which the Petcheneg attack expelled them.

1 *D.A.I.* c. 42.

2 Strictly, these two passages should only be reckoned as one; for the second was clearly inserted by Constantine in c. 40 from the first. This does not, however, affect the point.

3 *Streifzüge*, p. 33, note 3.

There is no obscurity about the latter. Κούζου is simply the Magyar word köz = district, and it is well attested that the Magyars often called the country surrounding a certain river by the name of that river plus köz.[1] Therefore Atelkuzu is neither more nor less than Etel-köz, the Etel district. But we have shown above that the only river ever testified to have borne the name of Etel, besides the Volga, was the Don; that the Magyars actually, as their own chronicles state, so called it, and even so translate it, since the Dentumoger of the Anonymus, the Dencia of Kezai, etc., seems to be nothing else but a Latin or semi-Latin translation of the native word Etel-köz.

Atelkuzu is therefore where we found Levedia to be—the country on the right bank of the Don, near its mouth.

It is, perhaps, unnecessary to dwell on the extreme difficulty of imagining that the Magyar national tradition should have brought with it simply and solely a memory of a district in which the nation admittedly spent no more than five or six years, and that in continual war with the Petchenegs, rather than of a district in which it spent some two generations at least —perhaps several centuries, if the sojourn on the left bank be counted.

The difficulty of logic. We have therefore shown that Atelkuzu is identical with Levedia, and both describe the country at the mouth of the Don, and on its right bank. But before proceeding to draw the inevitable conclusion, we will imagine ourselves once more attempting to accept the orthodox identification of Atelkuzu with the Dnieper district, and scrutinise the result with the cold eye of common sense.

The Magyars are supposed to have lived as the Khazars' allies for three years, after which the Khagan gave Levedias a noble Khazar woman to wife—not out of friendship, but in order to found a dynasty, which was obviously meant to be under Khazar influence. But Levedias failed to fulfil the purpose, for he had no children by that woman.

Now, the natural thing for the Khagan to do under the circumstances would have been, either to give the whole thing up as a bad job, or else to find someone else in the place of

1 Letter from Professor Németh to the present writer.

Levedias. Did he do so? Not he. First he waited until the
Magyars were separated from his own people by the much
more powerful nation of the Petchenegs, and then he proceeded to make propositions which he was in no conceivable
position to enforce. For neither the Khazars nor the Magyars
were a maritime power, and in that situation, while the Magyars
could very usefully be used as allies of the Khazars, or be hired
by them as mercenaries, they could not conceivably be con-
strained to become vassals. The time for that proposal was when
the two nations were contiguous.

However, the Khagan waited for some time to allow Levedias
to fail to become a father, and then sent word to the Magyars
to send him their first voivode. What made him do that? Why
did he not say, "send me Levedias"—since he must have known
all about him by this time. More extraordinary still: how did
Levedias come still to be no more than a "first voivode"? Had
his marriage made no difference to his status? If so, it must
have been made conditional on his having sons—payment by
results, a very strange arrangement.

However, having got his Levedias, why did the Khagan start
paying him compliments about his birth and virtues? He knew
all about this, and Levedias knew that he knew. The time for all
these flourishes was when the original marriage was concluded,
and the wording of the whole passage loses its point if the
two were already acquaintances. Incidentally, one would have
thought that Levedias, whatever his personal merits, had lost a
good deal of credit by his unfortunate failure to become a father.

But if the Khagan was a fool, Levedias was no better. Why
this unparalleled modesty? Why did he accept the wife and the
added lustre of his position as first voivode, and then suddenly
turn coy when it was proposed that he should become king?
Why, after enjoying all the substance of his position, did he
suddenly refuse when he was offered the glory of it?

It may be added, that on this showing, all parties got a
singularly bad bargain for their pains. The Khagan got nothing
whatever out of either Levedias or Arpád, nor does he appear
to have lifted a finger to help them when they were attacked by
the Petchenegs.

Thus, if we try to read the story in c. 38 as it stands, we get: (1) a chronological untruth, because the Savartoi were separated from the western Magyars some forty years before the arrival of the Petchenegs; (2) a geographical difficulty, because Levedia would seem to be the same place as Atelkuzu; (3) a string of logical absurdities; and we shall therefore be well advised to look about us for a remedy.

C. 38. Two accounts, not one. In doing this, we shall do well to remember the composition of the *D.A.I.*—a series of notes from the most various sources, often duplicating one another, often contradicting one another, and tacked together with the roughest of editing, the chapter headings forming no certain guide to distinguish the different stories. Some small amount of editing does, however, take place, and in particular, in the Petcheneg-Magyar-Moravian chapters, something has been done to gloss a word or phrase by means of an explanation gathered from another passage. Thus the fact that one story contains a word or phrase obviously belonging to the parallel account does not necessarily invalidate a division found acceptable on other grounds, particularly if the word in question is also found in that passage to which it seems more properly to belong. This is said with particular reference to the word βοέβοδος and the name Levedias where it occurs in story *A*.

Division of c. 38. We have found that the place Levedia is identical with the place Atelkuzu. Taking these two names as our pivot, and dividing accordingly, we get the following two stories:

A	B
	There was a war between the Magyars and the [Petchenegs formerly called] Kaggar. The Magyars were defeated and divided into two parts; the one fled eastward and are still called Savartoi asphaloi; the others moved westward with their [voivode and] commander Levedias into Atelkuzu, where the Petchenegs are living today.
The Magyars originally lived next to Khazaria in a place called Levedia [after their first voivode Levedias]. In this place there is a river Chidmas, or Činhul. [At that time they were called, for some reason, Savartoi asphaloi.] They consisted of seven hordes, under voivodes, the chief being [this] Levedias. They lived for three years as allies of the Khazars.	

The Khagan of Khazaria, on account of their valuable military alliance, gave the first Magyar voivode, Levedias, a noble Khazar wife that he might beget children of her; but it chanced that he had no children by the Khazar woman. But the Petchenegs [formerly called Kaggar] were defeated in a war against the Khazars, migrated into the land of the Magyars and drove them out.

After a little while the Khagan of Khazaria sent for Levedias, complimented him on his high birth and valour, and announced his intention of creating him a vassal king, but Levedias declared himself unworthy of the honour, and a young man was chosen instead. But after some time the Petchenegs fell upon the Magyars and chased them away.

I have placed in brackets the phrases which may be regarded as transferred glosses.

It will be seen at once that we have here two closely parallel stories, each quite sensible, coherent and straightforward in itself, and each corresponding closely with the account in c. 37, except that story *B* begins at an earlier moment than either c. 37 or story *A*. It will be noted, moreover, that the two tales, although they relate substantially the same events, are entirely different in tone. *A* is dispassionate. The Magyars were allied with the Khazars; the Khagan formed an alliance with the senior voivode, but he had no children. With that failure, Levedias drops out of story *A*.

B, on the other hand, obviously represents national tradition. It brings in the Magyars of the East, of whom *A* knows nothing. A vast mutual interchange of compliments goes on, ending with the picturesque story of Arpád's elevation to power. All the national heroes come in, including Almutzes (Almus), who really does nothing whatever. There is vivid *oratio directa*, and Levedias does nothing so prosaic as getting deposed for impotency; he abdicates gracefully, just as Almus does in the pages of the Anonymus.[1] When one remembers that among all the Magyars of history (as, indeed, among all other races), the sole difficulty has always been, not to keep existing kings from abdicating, but to prevent half the nobility from trying to be kings at the same time, one cannot but wonder at this extraordinary fact that, if the legendeers are to be believed, two out of the first three kings of Hungary abdicated of their free will.

It must further be noticed that to this difference of tone between *A* and *B*, there corresponds a difference in vocabulary.

---

[1] *Anonymi Gesta Hungarorum*, c. 13.

Levedia is a Slavonic word, Atelkuzu a Magyar. The Slavonic term βοέβοδος undoubtedly belongs really to story *A*, and has only been transported into *B*. Further, the mysterious Savartoi asphaloi, who no less undoubtedly belong originally to *B* (the first mention of them having been transferred to *A* because Constantine imagined himself to be beginning at the beginning of his story with *A*), seem to owe their origin to a Magyar national source. The efforts of Marquart and Darkó to interpret these words as an Arabic or Persian form[1] must be set down as failures. The form Savartoi represents, not an Arabic form, but the Magyar national form of the word—whatever its origin; while ἄσφαλοι can only be regarded, in fact, as the low Greek form of ἀσφαλεῖς—an *epitheton ornans*, derived from popular tradition and Magyar national vanity. Had Constantine not regarded it as a Greek word, it would not have puzzled him, and he would not have qualified it with his ἔκ τινος αἰτίας.

The rather excessive emphasis laid upon the Savartoi is, I would suggest, best accounted for by supposing the source of story *B* to be not a Magyar of the West at all, but one of the Savartoi. We know from the *De Ceremoniis* that the Greek court was in correspondence with this nation. It would seem strange that a Western Magyar source should omit all mention of the Magyar-Bulgar war, but trouble to put in the fact that the Magyars still corresponded with the Savartoi. The mention of the correspondence would, however, derive great point if it was just through one of these letters that the story was derived. Be this as it may, story *B* was certainly derived from a Magyar source, Eastern or Western.[2]

We may now consider these two stories separately.

Story A. Story *A* presents no difficulties. It begins with the Magyars in the Don valley—the earliest home known to the non-Magyar informant. In this place, they are living "next to

1 For a fuller discussion of these attempts, see Excursus III.

2 The use of the word ζάκανα (Old Slavonic законъ) in "B" is no proof against this argument. The word occurs once again in the *D.A.I.* in c. 8, where the Imperial envoy to the Petchenegs is advised to extract an oath from the Petchenegs κατὰ τὰ ζάκανα αὐτῶν. Here it is certain that Constantine is speaking in his own person and his own words. The term was thus one current to himself, and it is necessary to suppose that he put it in himself as part of the popular Greek which he affects.

the Khazars". They are allied with the Khazars for three years.

It may be noted here that it is most unnecessary waste of labour to emend this "three years".[1] Almost every critic—even Bury!—has assumed that Constantine says that the Magyars lived in Levedia for three years. The text does not support this view. Constantine says that the Magyar nation "settled next to Khazaria" (τὴν κατοίκησιν ἐποιεῖτο πλησίον τῆς Χαζαρίας)— a purely geographical statement—at an unspecified date, and formed an association with the Khazars as their allies in war for three years; the word used here—συνῴκησαν—being one which frequently, and indeed usually, bears a certain moral connotation, as of the cohabitation of man and woman. But neither for nations nor for individuals is living next door to them invariably equivalent to living with them. The period of alliance did not necessarily begin with the arrival of the Magyars—indeed, we have seen that the Khazars began by building fortresses to defend themselves against their new neighbours. But neither did these three years cover the whole Magyar-Khazar association. For one thing, if it were necessary to crowd into that short space Levedias' rise to fame, his marriage, his failure to become a father and abdication, Arpád's election and the Petcheneg campaign—then we must credit the Khazar Khagan with requiring poor Levedias to be a lightning lover before whom Hollywood must grow pale. Furthermore, it is not what Constantine says. He tells us that an alliance lasted for three years; then came Levedias' marriage; its failure; and then, after that, Arpád's election; and after that again, the Petcheneg invasion.

The alliance was followed by an attempt on the part of the Khazars to establish a hereditary dynasty; but the attempt failed, and after a time the Petchenegs migrated into the land of the Magyars and drove them out.

Here we have an account parallel in every way with the Petcheneg account in c. 37, and with the general, composite account which we have gathered from the other sources.

---

1 Ranging from 300 (Dankovski), 203 (Schlözer), 200 (Thunmann) to 20 (Marquart), while other writers, such as Kuun, transfer the three years to the time spent by the Magyars in the Dnieper-Danube district, regardless of the fact that the time in question was not three years, but six or seven.

Story B. Story *B* is not quite so easy. The latter part of it, from the arrival of the Magyars in Atelkuzu (= Levedia) onward, is as straightforward as Story *A*, with which it is exactly parallel, except that it represents the Magyar national account. Thus the negotiations between the Khagan and Levedias are told in a far more flowery tone than in the other story. Incidentally, the account of the negotiations provides a further proof that they took place on the Don, and not on the Dnieper. The Khagan tells the Magyars to send him their "first voivode" χελάνδια. Now χελάνδιον is a common Byzantine word for a ship; but those who force themselves to imagine that the Magyars were now away beyond the Dnieper, rather than admit this, tamper with text and sense alike, and evolve the name of a town somewhere near the mouth of the Dnieper.[1] Even to reach this bizarre result, they are obliged to emend the text by inserting an εἰς before the word χελάνδια. But the logical absurdity is worse than the arbitrary textual emendation. The Khagan of the Khazars—not the Beg, who conducted the business of the State, but the mighty and sacrosanct Khagan himself, whose province it was to sit at home in state in his palace[2]—treks across Khazaria, over the Crimea (a journey not only fatiguing, but dangerous to a degree, on the assumption of these authors, who believe the Petchenegs to have been already established on the right bank of the Don), right away to the Dnieper, there to confer with a petty Magyar chief whom he proposes to make a vassal king under himself! The thing is an absurdity. Moreover, take the next sentence: "So Levedias, coming to the Khagan of Khazaria, asked him why he had sent for him". According to these versions of the episode, the question ought to have been why the Khagan had

1 So Kuun, *Relatio*, 1, 208.

2 Cf. Ibn Fozlān on the Khazars (reprinted in Appendix): "The name of the king of the Khazars is Khakhan and he appears only every fourth month walking abroad and his deputy is called Khakhan [our old reports call this man Absad; Ibn Fozlān or his copyist seems to have made a slip here] acting for him, and it is this latter who leads the troops and trains them and manages the affairs of the kingdom and deals with them, and he is visible—day by day he enters the presence of the greater Khakhan meekly displaying humility and remaining silent," etc. Constantine, as we should expect from the author of the *De Ceremoniis*, was well acquainted with this Oriental arrangement. He knows the deputy as the "Beg"; cf. *D.A.I.* c. 42, ὁ χαγάνος ἐκεῖνος, καὶ ὁ πέχ.

come to him, since Levedias would hardly have to move to get to Kalanča.

Finally, the Khagan gives Levedias men of his own and sends him to the Magyars, who, on this showing, were already on the spot.

If χελάνδιον is taken as a boat, the Dnieper theory being retained, some of the above objections vanish; on the other hand, we have to assume here the sole mention in history of a Khazar sea-going navy, whereas Mas'ūdī tells us quite specifically that there was no such thing, even on the Caspian, and that "no nation except the Rūs" navigated the Pontus.[1]

When, on the other hand, we realise that the negotiations took place on the Don, the whole difficulty vanishes. Χελάνδια is an adverbial form, meaning "by boat". The reference is to the Don-Volga waterway. Levedias went to Ītīl like a good vassal, and had his interview with the Khagan there. It was easy for him to do so, since all he had to do was to step on board and be rowed up to the famous *volokh*; and there were no hostile Petchenegs about to make his journey unsafe.

Thus the latter part of story B presents no difficulties, and is parallel to story A, to c. 37 and to the composite account. The early part, however, demands consideration.

We see here the Magyars driven into Etel-köz—into the Don valley—from an earlier home by the Κάγγαρ. Now, we have already shown from our analysis of Džaihānī that some such move took place from the Don-Cuban steppe across the Don, that it took place early in the ninth century and that it was not effected by the Petchenegs. Here, in our story B, we find precisely the same thing; for the separation of the Savartoi—the nation dividing into one part in the Caucasus, one on the Don— can hardly, for geographical considerations, have taken place in any other area except that of the Cuban. But it cannot, for reasons of chronology and geography, have been effected by the Petchenegs.

It would therefore appear as if some confusion lay in the name of the attacking nation; for a single such confusion would explain away all difficulties at one blow.

1 *Meadows of Gold*, p. 416.

The name Κάγγαρ. Constantine's remarks about the name Κάγγαρ call, indeed, for closer examination than has hitherto been accorded to them. It will then be found that the statements in c. 37 and c. 38 are not parallel, although they appear to be so. C. 37 concludes with a note (added after the rest of the chapter has been written, as its abrupt introduction, combined with the formula ὅτι, shows) to the effect that in 949, when Constantine wrote, three out of the eight hordes of the Petchenegs bore the name of Κάγγαρ, this name signifying that they were "braver and nobler than the rest". C. 38, on the other hand, tells us that the whole nation which fell upon the Magyars and sent them flying, part to the west, part to the Caucasus, *at that time* bore the name of Κάγγαρ—quite a different thing.

Secondly, the suggestion that the name Κάγγαρ means nobility and courage at all is one which bears investigation. Vambéry[1] compares the Kirgiz Kangir = agile, and kangirmak = to go out riding; he also suggests kani-kara = black-blooded; but admits that no word with the interpretation suggested by Constantine can be found. Professor Toynbee has been kind enough to suggest to me Turkish qān = blood, plus -ar, the Persian termination of the agent or possessor, so that the word "might mean a red-blooded he-man";[2] but this, too, is extremely strained. Similarly, Professor Németh informs me that he has found a word with the desired meaning in the modern Čagatai speech. I must remark of that that it is not found in al-Kašgarī's Old Turkish dictionary.

On the other hand, the lower rivers of the Jaxartes were known in old times as Kankar, under which name Ibn Khordādbeh describes them as "a river near the kingdom of Schârsch". (The Orkhon inscriptions have a passage describing how (in A.D. 712) the common Türgiz people grew rebellious and marched out against Kängäräs.)[3] Marquart believes that a Turkish people followed the frequent practice of their kind, and took the name of Kängäräs from their feeding-grounds on

1 Vambéry, *Ursprung der Magyaren*, p. 109.
2 Personal communication to the writer.
3 See I. Thomsen, "Alttürkische Inschriften aus der Mongolei", *Zeitschrift der deutschen morgenländischen Gesellschaft*, Neue Folge, Bd. III (Bd. LXXVIII) (1924), p. 153.

the Jaxartes. Afterwards, being pressed westward, they formed a federation with other hordes (Bxux?), the whole taking the name of Bedjnāk.[1]

Even more probable than this river-derivation is, I think, the old association, adopted by several earlier scholars, of the word with the Turkish qān (Čagatai gāng) = chariot. For the Petchenegs were not merely hamaxobiotic; they were, to their neighbours, *the* hamaxobiotic people *par excellence*. Out of many possible examples I will quote only a few, which could easily be multiplied. Leo Diaconus' terse description of the Petchenegs runs:[2] Πατζινάκαι—ἔθνος νομαδικὸν τοῦτο καὶ πολυάνθρωπον, φθειροφάγον τε καὶ φερέοικον ἐφ᾽ ἀμαξῶν ὡς τὰ πολλὰ βιώτευον.

Anna Comnena tells us how at the beginning of her father's reign:[3] καὶ ὁ Κέλτος ἐκεκίνητο καὶ ἐδείκνυ τοῦ δόρατος τὴν ἀκμὴν καὶ ὁ Ἰσμαὴλ τόξον ἐνέτεινε καὶ τὸ νομαδικὸν ἅπαν ἔθνος καὶ Σκυθικὸν ὅλον ἀμάξαις παμμυρίαις ἐπέβρισεν.

Nicetas Choniates ends his account of John Comnenus' great victory:[4] κατὰ χιλιοστύας τοίνυν πίπτει τὸ ἀμαξόβιον.

Prodromos even uses the term as a proper name:[5]

Ἀλλ᾽ ἐπειδὴ καὶ τῶν Σκυθῶν ὁ λόγος ὑπεμνήσθη,

Μικρὸν ἐνδιατρίψωμεν κἂν τοῖς Ἀμαξοβίοις.

Nicephorus Gregoras seems to do the same.[6]

The Russian Chronicle uses the corresponding term in the same way.

In 1151 we read of "the Brodniki with their heavy *kibitkas* (chariots) and the Torks with their black caps".[7] The "Brodniki" are one of the new names under which the nomads of the steppes, but especially the Petchenegs, came to be known to the Russian Chronicles.[8] *Ad ann.* 1162 occurs the phrase:[9] "The

---

1 Marquart, *Komanen*, p. 35.   2 IX, 12, p. 157, ed. Bonn.

3 II, 289.   4 p. 22, ed. Bonn.

5 In a poem printed in the *Recueil des historiens des Croisades: Historiens Grecs*, vol. II, p. 130.

6 His description of the nations of the steppe panic-struck by the Mongol invasion includes ἀμαξόβιοι which may describe remnants of the Petchenegs.

7 "Nestor", I, 70.

8 This point will be treated in full in my "Petchenegs".

9 "Nestor", II, 98.

Polovtsi advanced to Kiev, destroyed a great number of *kibitkas* on the way, and slew Voibolu". Here the word *kitbitkas* is being used simply = ἁμαξόβιοι, and is a term for the Petchenegs.

Constantine's statement is evidence that the three Kangar hordes still retained a certain distinction from the rest in the tenth century. The attempts which have been made[1] to show that this distinction had any great practical effect must, however, be regarded as unsuccessful, although the fact that these hordes are named first in his list seems to show that they claimed a certain superiority. This is not the same thing as saying that the name actually signified courage, but it might make easier the confusion with a name which had that meaning.

But, against all these possible derivations for a name or nickname to be applied to the three leading Petcheneg hordes, must be set the quite undeniable fact that all evidence goes to show that the nation as a whole *never* bore any name except "Petcheneg" in its many variations.[2] The nation certainly bore that name as early as the day of our old report and of Ibn Khordādbeh, well before it swam into Constantine's ken; and of all the barbarous nations, known in the case of the Magyars, Cumans and others by so many names, the Petchenegs, of them all, are never known, by Arab, Persian, Armenian, Georgian, Greek, German, Magyar, Pole, Frank or Englishman, by any other name except Petcheneg (such pseudo-learned generalities as "Scythians" alone excepted), or "chariot-dwellers".

The statement that the whole nation ever bore the name of Κάγγαρ is, therefore, exceedingly unlikely; and we should do well to look round, if only for that reason, for another name which did bear the meaning required, being, if possible, not so wholly unlike Κάγκαρ in sound as to make a confusion unlikely;[3] the fact being that if Constantine's words in c. 38 be read with care, it will appear sufficiently plainly that the nation which

---

1 So the articles by Czebe and Németh in the *K.C.A.* 1 Köt. 3 Szám, June 1922.

2 I give a list of these in my "Petchenegs".

3 It may be worth noticing that the form in c. 37 is Κάγκαρ (which transliterates gäng-äris very closely), while in c. 38 the invariable form is Κάγγαρ. I do not, however, want to insist on this point.

made the attack recorded in the opening lines of story *B* was not the Petchenegs at all, but some nation with a name meaning "courage and nobility"; the identification with the Petchenegs being supplied by Constantine or his informant, perhaps as an unlucky afterthought.

Let memory now recall Mas'ūdī's description of the Circassians—the nation which were the Magyars' southern neighbours on the Cuban, and known to them as the Nandarin. "The meaning of their name", says Mas'ūdī, "which is Persian, is 'pride and arrogance'." It is entirely irrelevant to the present argument whether Constantine's mistake arose through a confusion between the *meanings* "pride and arrogance" and "nobility and valour", or between the somewhat similar words Κάγγαρ and Nandar. In any case, the people in question which divided the Magyars can hardly have been other than the Circassians; because none other was situated geographically in a position to bring about the cleavage which occurred, except perhaps the Alans; and it is by no means out of the question that the Circassians, when the war took place, were acting under Alan, or even under Khazar suzerainty.

It has been suggested that the Circassians were too weak to defeat the Magyars. Against this objection, one may quote Mas'ūdī's estimate of their potential strength, in the above passage; and there is yet another passage, from a later writer, that I should also like to quote:

This nation [*sc.* the Circassians] from the extent of its territory which runs for nearly six degrees of longitude, and for its courage and military genius, might become most formidable, if all the peoples composing it were united under one chief. But a nation of mountaineers, which subsist on the produce of their herds and are forced to settle on river banks, soon forget their origin, and are soon divided into hostile tribes. This principle of disunion is the reason why the Circassians of the Cuban are so impotent, and are hardly known even by the Russians, who confound them under the general name of Cuban Tartars, which they share with the Abkhaz and the Nogais, their neighbours.[1]

Origin of the confusion. It is not difficult to see how Constantine fell into the single and fatal confusion out of which all

[1] Gegewin, *Mémoires historiques et géographiques sur les pays situés entre la mer noire et la mer Caspienne*, Paris, 1797, p. 25.

later difficulties have arisen. The *De Administrando Imperio* has not really been so misnomered as recent critics have maintained. It is only incidentally a historical and ethnographical encyclopaedia; in essence and purpose it is a manual of statecraft compiled by Constantine for his son's benefit. The earlier chapters are really a treatise on the balance of power, the supremely important factor of which was, in the Emperor's eyes, the position of the Petchenegs. The cardinal point in the North European situation—the point to which, in his preoccupation, he returns again and again—was the overwhelming power of the Petchenegs, as evinced by the defeats which they had inflicted, or could again inflict, on other nations. It is fair to say that the relative strengths of the Petchenegs and the Magyars interest Constantine much more than the individual character of either; and thus preoccupied, it is not truly surprising that he should have tripped up over the word Κάγγαρ.

Story *B* has thus been reconciled, in its later part with *A*, c. 37, etc., in its earlier part with the data afforded by linguistic research and by our analysis of the old Oriental report—an analysis which, thus confirmed, we may now hope to be correct. The history of the Magyars in the ninth and tenth centuries may be summed up shortly as follows:

Living on the Don and Cuban, they were attacked in the early part of the ninth century by the Circassians, and divided into two parts; the one went to live in the Caucasus (the Sevordik); the other moved west to the mouth of the Don. About 888/9 the latter was attacked by the Petchenegs and driven west to the Dnieper-Danube district; and in 895 again attacked by Petchenegs and Magyars, and migrated into Hungary.

Date of the Magyar move, and of the Magyar-Khazar alliance. We now see that the story in c. 38 gives us no date either for the Magyar move across the Don, or for the Magyar-Khazar alliance. For the former, we have seen that it is probable that it took place shortly before the building of Sarkel and the first Magyar raid on the Danube, i.e. about A.D. 825–30. For the latter, we get a certain clue from the genealogy at the end of c. 40 of the *D.A.I.*

Here we learn that at the time of writing (*c.* 949) Arpád and all his sons were dead. Arpád's grandson, son of his third son, was "ruler" of Hungary; and one great-grandson was of an age to have come recently (ἀρτίως) on an official mission to Hungary.

At the beginning of the same chapter, we learn that Arpád's son Levente (not one of those mentioned in the genealogy) led the Magyar troops in the first campaign against the Bulgars in 895.

If we take—as a very rough guess—twenty-five years for an average generation and sixty for a lifetime, we should get the following:

Arpád's four sons born *circa* 880–90, d. 940–50 (the Hungarian Chronicles give Zoltan as dying 947).

His grandsons born *circa* 905–15.

His eldest great-grandson born *circa* 930 (and thus old enough to accompany an official mission in 948).

To Arpád himself, we should therefore ascribe a date of birth of *circa* 855.

On the other hand, the appearance of Levente as a military leader in 895 disposes me to put the date of Arpád's birth as little further back; for I hardly think it likely that a general should have a father much under fifty. On this reckoning, Arpád would be born *circa* 840.

This makes the gap between Arpád and his sons a rather unusually long one; but I think that this must actually have been the case. For, as I read it, there could have been no possibility of passing over Almus, Arpád's father, except on the single ground that he was no longer capable of marrying afresh and starting a Khazar dynasty.[1] Therefore when Arpád was raised

---

1 The Hungarian Chroniclers know of Almus (Ἀλμύτζης). So in Kezai (*Gesta H.* II, 1): "Arpad filius Almi, filii Elad, filii Uger, de genere Turul"; *Wiener Bilderchronik* and Thuroczy (as below): "Almus genuit Arpad". All the chronicles, however, like Constantine, make Arpád lead his nation into Pannonia. The sole exception is the Anonymus, at the beginning and most mythical part of his tale—that "first act", in fact, which he fraudulently inserts, largely in order to have an excuse to bring in the "Cumans". This he does, as a general rule, by making the fathers of the names in the Chronicle his actors. Thus for Kezai's seven leaders, Arpád, Zobole, Iula, Urs, Cund, Lel, Werbulchu, the Anonymus gives us Almus pater Arpad, Eleudunec pater Zobolsu, Tuhutum avus Geula, Cusad (a Cuman) pater Ursuuru, Ensee pater Urcum, Tosu pater Lelu, Bogat pater Bulsu. Having then to get rid of his Almus, the Anonymus makes him abdicate on entry into Pannonia.

on the shields, Khazar fashion, he was already a man of ripe age, and Almutzes already an old man.

The curious circumstance that Levente is entirely unknown to the genealogy, and also that the Hungarian Chronicles do not mention the children of Arpád at all, with the single exception of Zoltan, leads me to conjecture that Levente may have been actually an older son of Arpád's—possibly illegitimate—and that the genealogy in c. 40 only gives us the princely, or Khazar branch of the family. If the Anonymus is correct in telling us that Arpád died A.D. 907, and that he bequeathed the throne to his son Zoltan, who was then a minor of twelve or thirteen years of age,[1] we should get the explanation why the names of Arpád's eldest sons were not preserved by the Chroniclers. At the time of the famous *Landnahme* they were too young to take any prominent part, or to take their places among the "septem capitanei"; and the probability is that they were all killed off in the subsequent years of fighting, perhaps even before their father.

I will say, then, no more than this; it seems on the whole more likely than not that Arpád was born about A.D. 840, and that his second (Khazar) marriage took place about A.D. 880.

The original Magyar-Khazar alliance must be dated at least several years earlier than this, to give Levedias time to distinguish himself, to marry, and to fail to produce a progeny. I think it just possible that we may find a clue to a more exact date in the pages of the Russian Chronicle.

A strange episode which has never really been wholly cleared up is the subjection of parts of Russia to the Khazars. The first mention made by the Poviesti[2] is obviously derived direct from Byzantine sources, and refers to the growth of the Khazar power

---

1 *Anonymi Gesta H.* c. 52, tells us that Arpád died A.D. 907: "Et successit ei filius suus Zulta...transactis quibusdam temporibus, dux Zulta cum esset tredecim annorum, omnes primates regni sui, communi consilio et pari voluntate, quosdam rectores regni sub duce prefecerunt". In this chapter the Anonymus seems to be following the genuine Hungarian tradition; at least he agrees to a large extent with the other writers, if he adds rather more genealogical detail. The *Wiener Bilderchronik* (c. XI), followed by Thuroczy, tells us that "Almus genuit Arpad, Arpad genuit Zoltan, Zoltan genuit Toxun". In the earlier chapters, on the other hand, where he tells us of the birth of Zoltan (c. 50) Anonymus is clearly romancing.

2 "Nestor", I, 10.

in the seventh century. It is otherwise with the statement that
in 859 "the Polanians, the Severians and the Viatiči" were
tributaries to the Khazars; they paid one squirrel per house.[1]
Then when Askold and Dir reached Kiev shortly after 860:
"they discovered a city built on a hill. They asked 'whose is
this city?' It was answered to them: 'Formerly it belonged to
three brothers, Kii, Šteček and Choriw, who built it; but they
are dead, and at present we pay tribute to the Khazars'. Askold
and Dir, learning this, established themselves in this city, called
to them a great number of Varangians, and began to reign over
the Varangians and their country".[2]

In 885 Oleg further conquered the Radimici from the
Khazars.[3] It has been well pointed out that the wording of the
passage about Kiev mentions no prince, but only the city.
Hrushewski concludes from this that the Khazars had established themselves in Kiev in the eighth or even the seventh
century.[4] I should like, on the other hand, to point out that
the old Oriental report gives no justification for this suggestion.
On the contrary, it shows us a strong Slav state in White
Croatia, to which, to all appearances, Kiev also belonged, as a
frontier city, and it makes no reference whatever to the Khazars
in the west of Russia.

Now there is one phrase in Constantine's report which ought
not to be ignored: it is that the Magyars, in their alliance with
the Khazars, "fought with them in all their wars", in the course
of which Levedias apparently distinguished himself by his
valour. I think that some attempt ought to be made to explain
what these wars were. The Magyars may, of course, have
undertaken distant campaigns on the far frontiers of Khazaria;
but it seems far more likely that these two nations were combining in their common interest. In this case, I cannot but
think it likely that we have in this phrase an echo of the campaign against the Slavs which ended in the break-up of the great
White Croatian Empire, and the establishment of the Khazar
dominion over Kiev as also over the Radimici. For we have no
real grounds for supposing the Khazar power decadent in the

1 *Ibid.* p. 19.   2 *Ibid.* p. 21.
3 *Ibid.* pp. 30–31.   4 Hruschewski, *op. cit.* 1, 405.

ninth century A.D. This assumption is largely made on the strength of the building of Sarkel, but it is unsupported by any other evidence, while the report of Ibn Fozlān still testifies to a strong military organisation of the Khazar state.

This is, of course, all very conjectural; but it is at least an attempt to explain various events and statements between which it would seem very probable that there might be a connection. This would place the beginnings of the Khazar alliance at some time between 840 and 860; and perhaps it was this very offensive, rather than their mutual discord (which is hardly apparent from Ibn Rusta's report), which caused the Slavs to invite Rurik.[1] It is certainly tempting to connect this disunion among the Slavs, plus the fact that so many of them were now paying tribute to the Khazars, with the disappearance of the powerful White Croatian Empire testified as existing at an earlier date, and the alliance between the two powerful and warlike nations of the eastern steppes.

THE KAVAR STORY: CC. 39, 40.

Chapters 39, 40[2] of the *D.A.I.* contain yet another account of the arrival of the Magyars, which does not contradict any of our other stories, but differs from them very widely, selecting quite a different set of events upon which to lay stress, as the following comparison will show:

C. 38 (*as analysed*)	Cc. 39, 40
The Magyars were attacked by the Circassians, and part of them driven west beyond the Don. Here they allied themselves with the Khazars; but after a while were attacked under their prince Arpád and defeated by the Petchenegs, and after seeking a place to settle, ended by migrating to Great Moravia.	The Kavars seceded from the Khazars, fled to the Magyars and formed an alliance with them. After a while they were invited by the Greek Emperor to make war against Symeon of Bulgaria and duly took part in the campaign under Liountinas, son of Arpád. When the campaign was over, Symeon made a treaty with the Petchenegs, fell on the Magyars while they were away on a raid, slew their guards and took their women and children. The Magyars returned, found their homes ravaged, and settled in their new territory.

1 "Nestor", I, 20.

2 The chapter division of the *D.A.I.* is very bad here; cc. 39–40 should be one chapter.

Now, there is no *a priori* reason for rejecting one of these stories in favour of the other, and they are not, in fact, mutually incompatible; but they certainly look at things from very different angles. The defeat mentioned in c. 38 is that of 888–89, as a consequence of which the Magyars were driven westward from the Don to the Danube, and this chapter passes over the whole story related in c. 40 with the simple words that "the Magyars turning and seeking a place to dwell in came and chased away the inhabitants of Great Moravia". The Bulgar-Magyar war is not mentioned at all. On the other hand, c. 40 is at least disingenuous in so far as it never mentions the first defeat by the Petchenegs, preferring the truth (which was not, however, the whole truth) that the Magyars were invited by the Emperor Leo to the war against Bulgaria.[1] Moreover, the course of the war is described in a manner eminently flattering to the Magyar army, as will be seen on comparing the other versions of the same story.[2] The defeat inflicted by the Magyars on the Bulgarians is given; the subsequent crushing victory won by Symeon over the Magyars is passed over in silence, and the only part assigned to the Petchenegs in the whole story is that they combined with the Bulgars, slaughtered the Magyar guards and carried off their "families" while the fighting men were away on a campaign abroad.

More important still, of course, is the fact that while neither half of c. 38 so much as mentions the Kavars, cc. 39–40 assign to that race an absolutely preponderating role in the Magyar state. We are told that "proving themselves stronger in war and more courageous than the (eight) hordes, and leading in war, they were chosen to be the leading hordes. And there is one ruler ($\check{a}\rho\chi o\nu\tau a$) among them, that is, in the three hordes of Kavars, who exists until today". The Kavar horde is given the first place in the list of tribes, the name of Magyar ($M\epsilon\gamma\acute{\epsilon}\rho\eta$) appearing only as that of the third horde. Further, at least if we take strict grammar, the expedition against the Bulgars is

---

1 This may, however, be due partly to the fact that Constantine, as his wording shows (cf. the description of Leo), is here writing in part from the Greek point of view.

2 See below, Excursus IV, for an analysis of the accounts of this war.

described as undertaken by the Kavars; and it is worthy of note that this army, whether Kavar or Magyar, is described as having "Liountinas the son of Arpád as ruler ($\check{\alpha}\rho\chi o\nu\tau a$)"; the same word as is used above to describe the chief of the Kavars. The other chroniclers of the war do not mention this personage; they tell us only that the Emperor Leo, when arranging the campaign, made his contract with the Magyar "heads, Arpád and Cusan".[1] There is no confusion here between Arpád and his son; on the contrary the one represents the executive power, the other and younger man is the leader of the military forces.

When, then, we find one narrative not troubling to mention the Kavars at all, and the other assigning them in every way the preponderating role, the obvious conclusion is that the second narrative comes from *a Kavar source*. But the most interesting point is that, as it happens, we are in possession of information which makes it probable that we can identify this source, and by doing so, throw considerable fresh light on early Magyar history.

In the year 943, as we learn from the Byzantine Chronicles, the Magyars made a great incursion into Byzantine territory. The Greeks, however, concluded a peace with them, which was sealed by an exchange of hostages, and was to last for five years.[2] In the year 948, then—the year in which the truce expired—Constantinople received visitors, apparently with a view to arranging a permanent peace in place of the five years' truce. Under this date (948) Cedrenus tells us:

> The Magyars did not cease to ravage the Byzantine dominions, until Bulosudes, a prince of theirs, pretending to embrace the Catholic faith, came to Constantinople and was there baptised by Constantine, and returned home, having been endowed by him with patrician rank and great gifts.

> Not long afterwards Gylas, another prince of Hungary, came here also for the same purpose; and being baptised and treated in the same way as above, took back with him Hierotheus, a monk celebrated for his piety, whom the patriarch Theophylactus appointed bishop of Hungary. And when he came to Hungary, he converted

---

1 Leo Grammaticus, p. 478, $\tau a\hat{\imath}s$ $\kappa\epsilon\phi a\lambda a\hat{\imath}s$ $\text{'}A\rho\pi a\delta\grave{\eta}$ $\kappa a\grave{\imath}$ $Kov\sigma a\nu\acute{\eta}$.

2 *Ibid.* p. 507; Cedrenus, II, 631; Incertus Continuator, p. 267; Symeon Logotheta, p. 491; Georgius Monachus, p. 590.

many from their barbarous delusions. And Gylas remained firm in the faith, undertook no raids against Byzantine territory, and cared for Christian prisoners. But Bulosudes recanted from his contract with God, and made a raid against the Greeks with all his men. Trying the same thing against the Franks, he was captured and impaled by their King John.[1]

Zonaras has a rather different version of the story.[2]

The Turks (we said above that the Hungarians [Οὔγγροι] were so called), who at other times were wont to ravage Byzantine territory, were quiet at the time. For their commander, Bolosoudes, and another man Gylas, who was also the ruler of a part,[3] came to the Emperor, and being both initiated into the holy baptism of new birth, and imbued with the secrets of our religion, and also enriched with patrician dignity and loaded with gifts, returned home, taking with them a priest through whom many attained to the knowledge of God. And Gylas remained in the faith; but the other, breaking his pledges, fought against the Greeks; and having tried to do the same against the Franks, was captured and crucified.

The story about "Bulosudes" is thoroughly well authenticated. He is the "Bulchu" of Kezai; the Pulszi of the *Annales Sangallenses Majores*,[4] the Bulgio of the *Gesta app. Camerae*,[5] the Bulsu of Giesebrecht,[6] from whom we learn that it was at the battle of Augsburg that he was captured and hanged. Moreover, he is mentioned by Constantine himself, at the close of c. 40, where he tells us that "Βουλτζοὺς ὁ Καρχᾶς", i.e. the third dignitary of the Hungarian state, is "the son of Καλή" the Καρχᾶς and "recently" (ἀρτίως, a short time before Constantine composed the chapter in question) "came to Constantinople on a friendly mission, accompanied by Termatzu, son of Teveles".[7]

Bury, in agreement with Professor Marczali,[8] draws the very natural, and indeed irresistible conclusion, that the information contained in cc. 39, 40 was derived from these Magyar visitors. But he is on far weaker ground when he proceeds to identify the

---

1 Cedrenus, II, 634, ed. Bonn.   2 Zonaras, III, p. 484, ed. Bonn.

3 καὶ ἕτερος δ᾽ αὖθις Γυλᾶς, καὶ αὐτὸς μέρους ἄρχων.

4 *Ad ann.* 955.   5 I, c. 75.

6 *M.G.S.* ed. Pertz, I, 418–25.

7 Bury has pointed out the strange mistranslation in the Bonn edition.

8 *A Magyar honfoglatas kutfoi*, p. 128.

Gylas with Termatzu, who accompanied Bultzu to Constantinople. For Cedrenus makes it perfectly clear that there were two separate visits, the Gylas coming after the Karchas, and Zonaras, although less explicit, will be seen, if read carefully, to say the same thing. Incidentally, it is not very likely that Termatzu, who can hardly have been above twenty years of age at the time when Constantine wrote, should already have been filling the office of Commander-in-Chief of the Magyar forces—for the Gylas was little less.

Furthermore, the visit of the Karchas took place in 948; and Constantine does not appear to have begun compiling his work before the end of that year, at the earliest.

The natural interpretation of Constantine's notes is that they were made a short time after the Karchas, accompanied ·by Termatzu—the latter as representative of the royal house of Arpád—had shortly before (ἀρτίως) visited Constantinople. They were taken down from a second source, which was none other than the Gylas, who had come soon afterwards on a mission of his own. The independent position of the Gylas is quite correctly noted by Zonaras, who describes him as "καὶ αὐτὸς μέρους ἄρχων". In this case, since we have guessed that the information in cc. 39, 40 comes from a Kavar source, it follows logically that the Gylas (as the name itself would encourage one to suppose)[1] was the leader of the three Kavar hordes.

This is not, indeed, the usual view. The earlier generation of Hungarian critics was accustomed to assume that not the Gylas, but Arpád was the Kavar. This view, however, rested on no authority whatever, but only on the assumption that the Khagan would probably choose his leader from among the most powerful tribe. But the view is not even logical; for Arpád was only elected after Levedias had been tried and rejected; therefore we ought to assume—if we think that the Khagan had dealings with the Kavars at all—that Levedias, not Arpád, was the Kavar. The argument that both the names Almus and Turul, which are

---

[1] Gylas was undoubtedly a Turkish title. Γύλα was the name of the third horde of the Petchenegs, that which settled nearest to the Magyars, cf. *D.A.I.* c. 37.

numbered among Arpâd's ancestors,[1] are of Turkish origin,[2] is not a strong one; for there is linguistic evidence to suppose that the Magyars had received Turkish elements at an early date, and even that "a dominant Bulgaro-Turkish caste was the true organiser of the Hungarian nation".[3] But this earlier assimilation of a Bulgaro-Turkish warrior caste apparently took place long before the arrival of the Kavars, whose association with the Magyars, to judge from the relative scarcity of Turkish words of the middle period in the Magyar language, was a comparatively short one.

Still less is it possible to agree with the fashionable modern Hungarian view that the Kavars never occupied at all the position which is claimed for them by Constantine, but were merely an inferior tribe, driven before the Magyars into battle as the Tatars afterwards drove the conquered Cumans and Mordvinians. For this view presents us with a dilemma. There is no getting round Constantine's words. If we take the Gylas as their source, we are able to allow for a certain exaggeration owing to self-praise; but if we take the source to have been a Magyar one, then this allowance cannot be made, and unless we make the ridiculous assumption that some modest Magyar was depreciating his own nation's exploits in favour of the Kavars, the latter must have played *at least* as important a part as Constantine assigns to them.

Certainly by far the easiest solution is to see in the author of cc. 39–40 the Kavar Gylas.

The story of the Gylas. The Gylas is mentioned first in our report α as the *de facto* commander of the whole nation; the reference being, apparently, to the Magyars of the East. As, moreover, it is certain that the name Gylas was a title and not a proper name (as Constantine explicitly assures us), it appears

---

1 Simon de Keza, II, I, "Arpad filius Almi, filii Elad, filii Uger, de genere Turul".

2 Almus = Turkish *Almys* (taken), the name of the prince of the Volga Bulgars who accepted Islam (see Ibn Fozlān's report). Turul = Turkish *toghrul*, turul, a bird of prey. Arpád on the other hand is a Hungarian derivation from a naturalised Turkish word. See Szinnyei, *Die Herkunft der Ungarn*, pp. 34–5.

3 See Gombocz, "Die bulgarische Frage und die ungarische Hunnensage" *U.J.* I, 203.

that the institution must have existed in the original Magyar state, before the arrival of the Kavars.

The Gylas then reappears in the Hungarian national legend; but his story is related in a confused fashion which betrays the chroniclers' own confusion between various holders of the title. Kezai has simply: "Tercii quidem exercitus Jula fuit capitaneus, hic cum aliis in Pannoniam introisset, in partibus Erteulu tandem habitavit". He has no further mention of the name or the place, until we find the laconic notice that St Stephen, after slaying the "dux Cupan" who had led a rebellion against him, brought his uncle Jula, with his wife and two sons, "de septem castris in Pannoniam", and "adjunxit septem castra Pannonie".[1]

The natural implication of this account would be, of course, that the first Gylas conquered Transylvania at the very outset of the occupation of Hungary. This immediate conquest is also testified by the Anonymus, who has not failed to make out of it one of his romantic stories—a story which, by its light-hearted introduction of a certain "Gelou, dux Blacorum", has sorely embarrassed his countrymen in later centuries, who would give much to explain away this inopportune mention of the Roumanians in Hungary at the time of the Magyar occupation. There, however, the story stands. The Hungarian champion, who is not referred to as Jula, but as "Tuhutum, father of Horca", hears of the "goodness" of Transylvania and asks permission of Arpád to conquer it. Having received gracious permission, he defeats Gelu and takes possession of Transylvania for himself and his posterity until the time of St Stephen "and they would have held it longer, if Gyla the younger (minor Gylas) had been willing to become Christian, and had not always thwarted the saintly king, as will be told hereafter".[2] This Tuhutum, we are told, was the leader of the seventh army, and "the father of Horca whose sons were Gyla and Zombor, from whom the race of Moglout is descended".[3]

The fall of the last Gylas is retold at greater length as follows:

Tuhutum begat Horca, Horca begat Geula and Zubor, Geula begat two daughters of whom one was called Caroldu and the other Sarolta, and Sarolta was the mother of the holy king Stephen. Zumbol begat Gyla the younger, the father of Bue and Bucne, in whose day the holy king Stephen subjugated the land of Transylvania (terram ultrasylvanam), and led Geula prisoner into Hungary, and kept him all his days imprisoned, because he was vain in the faith and would not become a Christian, and did much to thwart the holy king Stephen, although a relative of his mother's.[1]

Thuroczy, on the other hand, has yet another genealogy, agreeing in part with the above, in part differing from it. I must quote him in the Latin, as his obscurity lends itself to various translations:

Tercius vero capitaneus Gyula fuit, unde Gyula, filius Ladislai, derivatur. Eratque iste Gyula, dux magnus et potens, qui civitatem magnam in Erdeulu, in venatione sua invenerat, quae jam pridem a Romanis constructa fuerat. Habebatque filiam, nomine Saroltam, pulcherrimam...quam Geysa dux, consilio et auxilio Beliud qui terram Kulam possederat, duxit in uxorem legitimam. Isti Beliud, Kulam dedit filiam suam, ut contra fratrem suum kean bellaret, et post obitum suum, terram suam idem Beliud haeritavit. Tandem cum Gyula, Hungaris in Pannonia habitantibus, infestus esset et multipliciter molestus; per sanctum Stephanum regem in Pannoniam est deductus. Non tamen iste Gyula capitaneus, sed ab illo tertius.[2]

The story of the last Gyula's defeat and capture by St Stephen is told substantially as the Anonymus has it.[3]

The story of the last Gylas is well authenticated. The Annals of Hildesheim, under the year 1003, note: "In this year Stephen King of Hungary marched against his uncle king Julus (avunculum suum regem Julum) with an army": and the chronicler Ditmar is even more explicit. From him we learn[4] that the name of this Gylas was Procui, and that King Stephen did not keep him in perpetual captivity, as alleged by the Anonymus, but even restored to him his wife free, as he was unable to ransom her; and Procui afterwards became warden, under the king of Bohemia, of a city on the frontiers of Bohemia and Hungary. Of St Stephen's mother, Sarolta,[5] we learn that

---

1 *Anonymi Gesta Hungarorum*, c. 27.
2 Thuroczy, *Chronica Ungarorum*, II, 5.　　3 *Ibid*. II, 29.　　4 VIII, 3.
5 "White" or "fair lady" from Turkish *sarai*; similarly "karoldu", black, Turkish *kara*. The derivation of the latter part of the word is disputed.

she was called in Slavonic Beleknigini, or the fair lady, and that she "drank to excess, rode like a man at arms, and once slew a man in an outburst of rage. Better had it been if her hand, thus stained with blood, had wielded the spindle and taught her wild spirit patience". A trying mother for a saint; but, as the patriotic Hungarian historian Mailáth gravely remarks, "these faults did not, in those violent days, seem so reprehensible as they do to us".

Thus the end of the Gylas dynasty is well authenticated, and there is no reason whatever to doubt that the last Gylas possessed, as the Hungarian chroniclers tell us, an extensive kingdom in Transylvania, although not, indeed, extending over the whole of what is now known under that name. It is equally certain that the grandfather of the last Gylas must have been the Γυλᾶς mentioned by Cedrenus as having visited Constantine in Constantinople. But it is not equally clear whether the first Gylas, the "capitaneus", possessed the same domains. For his conquest of them, we have primarily the authority of the Anonymus, whose tale contains, quite indisputably, large elements of romance. Kezai also tells us that this first Gylas ended by living in Transylvania; but the wording of Thuroczy shows that this first "capitaneus" was a somewhat shadowy figure compared to his much better-known grandson, and it is quite possible that the possession of Transylvania has been transferred in Kezai's story from the latter to the former.

According to Kezai, Arpád, the national leader, settled round Székesfehérvár; Zobola round Csakvár; Verbulchu south of Lake Balaton; Lel in eastern Slovakia; Urs and Cund in the extreme north-east, near the passage by which the Magyars appear to have entered Hungary. Thus for Gylas we are left, not only Transylvania, but the whole of the central plain of the Theiss—that part of Hungary, in fact, which has always proved the most irresistible to the true nomadic, Turkish races which have occupied it successively.

Now the description of the Magyars' homes in c. 40 of the *D.A.I.* must be noted. After describing various "old monuments" and cities, such as Trajan's Bridge, Belgrade and Sirmium, "beyond which is the great, heathen Moravia which the Magyars destroyed", Constantine goes on: "The part above this, where all the settlements of the Magyars are,[1] they now call after the names of the rivers in it. These are, first the Temes (Τιμήσης), second the (?) Bega (Τούτης), third the Mures (Μορήσης), fourth the Körös (Κρίσος) and another the Theiss (Τίτζα)".

Now if this list comes, not from Constantine's private knowledge, but from his informant (and in favour of this supposition, we have firstly the statement that the *Hungarians* now call it ἀρτίως ὀνομάζουσι, secondly, perhaps, the name-forms of the rivers),[2] it is inconceivable that its source should be—say—an emissary from Arpád's own horde near Székesfehérvár. It can only have come from a semi-independent chieftain, occupying the plain of the Theiss.[3] I shall return later to a closer consideration of the composition of these chapters; meanwhile, I may perhaps be allowed one or two remarks of a more general character.

Turks and Finns. It is proverbial that the true Magyar national life is to be found on the pusztas of the Great and the Little Alföld. The student of Hungarian history, even the superficial student, may, however, find some cause for astonishment in this, and may wonder whether the West is not inclined to regard the life of the Alföld as typically Magyar, merely because it is most unlike the life of the other nations of Europe. The Magyar language, with its roots of Finnish and Turkish, is typical of the course of Magyar history, which has always shown this dualism between the Finno-Ugrian and the Turkish strains.

1 τὰ ἀνώτερα τούτων, ἐν ᾧ ἐστὶν ἡ πᾶσα τῆς Τουρκίας κατασκήνωσις.

2 Professor Melich claims all these for Bulgaro-Turkish forms ("A honfoglaláskori Magyarország", M. Tud. Akad. 1925, 1926), thence deducing theories of Bulgarian rule in the Hungarian plain. E. Moór, on the other hand, combats this and maintains that practically all old name-forms in the Hungarian plain are of Slavonic origin (U.J. Dec. 1926, pp. 434 ff.). It may be remarked that the form for the Theiss used in the Old Bulgarian inscriptions (in Greek language) is ἡ Τήσα (see the collection reproduced in the *Izvestia* of the Russian Archaeological Society (Sofia, 1909)).

3 Constantine himself is obliged to qualify his statement in c. 42, where he writes: καὶ κατοικοῦσι μὲν οἱ Τοῦρκοι πέραθεν τοῦ Δανούβεως ποταμοῦ εἰς τὴν τῆς Μοραβίας γῆν, ἀλλὰ καὶ ἔνθεν μέσον τοῦ Δανούβεως καὶ τοῦ Σάβα ποταμοῦ. The former statement is copied from c. 40; the latter is a better second thought.

The former seems, like Arpád of old, to have sought for preference the hills and woods; the latter, the boundless plains of the puszta. The former has become in the course of time blended with a medley of strains, Slavonic and Teutonic; and it is proof of the astonishing vitality of the race that it has absorbed them and impressed its language upon them. More than this: the Magyar strain has proved itself capable of absorbing the Turkish strain itself. After the Kavars, the Magyars have experienced two great waves of Turkish immigration: the Cumans, and the Osmanli Turks, of whom the former entered the country in the thirteenth century in such large numbers as to endanger its religion and life, while the latter ruled over most of Hungary for a century and a half. Besides these, there were the minor, but not inconsiderable reinforcements of Petchenegs, some Bulgars, and the remains of the Avars.

Until comparatively recent times, the occupants of the great plains were to be distinguished from the Magyars proper, both in manner of life and in language itself. If the linguistic distinction is now gone, the difference in manners remains, and it is probably true to say that those special characteristics of the inhabitants of the Alföld were as alien to the true Magyars as they were to the Slavs or the Teutons.

It is, I think, very probable that precisely the same process took place in the tenth century as in the fourteenth and fifteenth, only much more swiftly. The bulk of the Magyar nation, the true Finno-Ugrians, comparatively (although not very) pacific and sedentary agriculturalists, made their homes in the undulating country of the true Pannonia, west of the Danube.

The plain of the Alföld was occupied by the nomadic race of Kavars, true Turks, herdsmen, horsemen and fighters, the driving force and the army of the nation. This was the race which in Constantine's day still occupied pride of place as the "first of the hordes of the Magyars". It was, I believe, chiefly this race of Kavars which raided the Slavs and Russians from the steppe; led the campaign against the Bulgars in 895; in large part and for more than half a century afterwards, was the terror of half Europe. I have for myself never wholly believed in the softening of the Magyars' hearts which changed them from those wild raiders of whom the monkish chroniclers have handed down such tales of horror into the comparatively sedate citizens of St Stephen. Much argument has turned round the work known as the "Tactica" of the Emperor Leo. It has been shown long since that the methods of warfare attributed by Leo to the Magyars are simply word for word (with few changes) what earlier historians described of the true Turks. The Magyars in the ninth century, then, must have been using those very peculiar and characteristic tactics employed since time immemorial by every Turkish nation —Huns, Avars, Turks, Petchenegs, Cumans—and by no other. In the early days of the tenth century, when their name was the dread of Europe, they employed the same tactics, as the chroniclers show; but one or two centuries after, what do we find?

A complete change. In the pages of Bonfinius and Thuroczy we find, indeed, light cavalry using the old devices of simulated flight, of shooting while fleeing, of sudden charges with fearful, wolf-like howling. But the authors of these tactics are not the Magyars themselves; they are Petchenegs and Széklers. The Magyars proper are fighting and demeaning themselves very much like their neighbours, the Slavs and Teutons.

I do not believe that this was due to a deliberate adaptation to changed conditions. It was due at least as much to a change in the racial proportions of the Magyar nation itself. The brunt of sixty years of restless and remorseless warfare fell on the Kavars, whose ranks must have been thinned by it to an extraordinary extent. Meanwhile the true Magyars, living in comparative peace, increased their numbers. The turning-point came under St Stephen, who at last was strong enough to crush the Kavars of his cousin, the Gylas. From that day until the next great immigration of a Turkish race, Hungary had nearly 250 years in which to consolidate and assert the predominance of the Finno-Ugrian element; for the remnants of the Kavars and Avars and the immigrant Petchenegs were too weak to challenge that supremacy, and by the time the Alföld was once more occupied by a Turkish race—the Cumans—it was too late, if only just too late, to tip the balance back to the side of the Turks once more.

Nor, while we are on this subject, can I think it without significance that the centre of the pagan reaction and of the opposition to the royal house, throughout the tenth and eleventh centuries, was always the east of Hungary, while not infrequently, as in the case of the luckless Salomon, the opposition seems to have allied itself with the Cumans and Uz in the plains of Bessarabia and Walachia.

The name of Τοῦρκοι. It is impossible to extract from any of our written sources any evidence of the date at which the Kavars joined the Magyars. One can only conjecture, from the absence of mention in any sources outside Constantine and the single reference in the Admont Chronicle, and from the fact that the two nations were not assimilated in Constantine's day, that the junction probably occurred not very long before the close of the ninth century.

I believe, however, that it is possible to say that this Kavar association furnishes the reason why Constantine and the other Byzantine writers of his age referred to the Magyars habitually as Τοῦρκοι.

The simple explanation, adapted by Vambéry and his school, that the Magyars were called Turks because they were Turks, has been disproved by the researches of philologists; nor can I really believe that the nation as a whole had become so mixed with Turkish elements, and had so far adopted Turkish characteristics, as to have earned the name of "Turks". For this name, it must be pointed out, is not a vague, generic one among the Byzantines. It is used, to my knowledge, to describe five nations, and five only. Firstly, to the Turks proper, the founders of the great Turkish Empire of the sixth century, the Tu-kiue of the Chinese annals. This Turkish Empire extended in 568 over the Volga and in A.D. 576 reached as far as the Maiotis. Its tide soon receded: it was succeeded in the west by the Khazars, who had previously formed part of the Turkish Empire, and were themselves—it seems quite clear—true Turks by origin. During the first half-century of its existence, the Khazar Empire remained under Turkish suzerainty, and it is for this reason that Theophanes, when he first has occasion to mention the Khazars, refers to them explicitly as "east Turks, known as Khazars".[1]

In subsequent mentions of the Khazars, the specific name of the horde alternates with the wider name of the race, the former gradually coming to predominate, until in the pages of Constantine it is unchallenged. This being the case, it is, I think, surely impossible that the name "Turk" should have been applied to the Magyars as having previously formed part of the Khazar-Turkish Empire, when the name had been abandoned for the Khazars themselves.

The other nations known to the Byzantines as "Turks" are, besides the Magyars, the Seljuk and the Osmanli Turks—again, Turks in the very truest sense of the word, and in each case coming from the east towards Constantinople through Asia Minor. The word is in no single instance used by the Byzantines to denote invaders from the steppes of South Russia, and that although the Empire had to suffer from three several waves of invaders, all of whom were true Turks, and with all of whom they became—to their cost—exceedingly well acquainted. These were the Petchenegs, the Uz and the Cumans. It is true that these races were not always referred to by their distinctive names; but when an alternative appellation is used, this is regularly " Σκύθαι ", or occasionally " Οὖννοι ";[2] the term Τοῦρκοι is reserved, after it had ceased to be used for the Magyars, for the Seljuk and Osmanli Turks. Thus the suggestion made by Professor Darkó[3] that the name Τοῦρκοι, as used for the Magyars, has merely "a geographical and cultural significance" is to be dismissed. Particularly as regards Constantine, it is

---

1 *Chronographia*, p. 315, οἱ Τοῦρκοι ἐκ τῆς ἑῴας, οὓς Χαζάρεις ὀνομάζουσι.

2 Constantine calls the Petchenegs by that name alone; Attaliotes, Anna Comnena, Nicephorus Bryennius, Nicetas Choniates, Glykas, Cinnamus, Cedrenus, Skylitzes, Zonaras, all use Σκύθαι indiscriminately with Πατζινακῖται or Πατζινάκαι. Attaliotes and Anna use Οὖζοι and explain it as Οὖννοι; Cedrenus, Skylitzes and Glykas Οὖζοι, explained as Σκύθαι. Anna, Choniates, Glykas and Zonaras use both Κόμανοι and Σκύθαι, or else Κόμανοι only. For the Seljuks, the term Τοῦρκοι is used by Attaliotes, Anna, Bryennius, Glykas, Cedrenus, Skylitzes, Zonaras and others. Only Attaliotes has also Οὖννοι and Οὖννοι Νεφθαλῖται; and Cinnamus has Πέρσαι.

3 In his essay "Die auf die Ungarn bezüglichen Volksnamen bei den Byzantinern", *B.Z.* XXI (1912), pp. 422 ff.

inconceivable that so pedantically careful a writer should have been content with a vague generic term in the case of a nation in which he took so deep an interest. Indeed, Constantine himself twice employs such a generic term to denote the nations of the north; and in each case, the term which he uses is "Scythians", or simply "Northern".[1]

On the contrary, it is abundantly clear that Constantine throughout uses the word Τοῦρκοι of the Magyars, and even of their country (Hungary) as a regular, current, official term. There can be no doubt that it was by this name that the Magyars were commonly known to the Byzantines in his day. But when did the name become current, and how long did it remain so?

Professor Darkó, in the essay mentioned above, has compiled a list of the names used by the Byzantines for the Magyars. As, however, the list omits some of the most important writers, including that one writer to whom the name is actually to be traced, and in other cases confuses the issue by showing later sources, such as Zonaras, as using the name, when they are merely quoting verbatim from earlier chronicles, I will do no more here than refer the curious reader to his list.

In the sixth and seventh centuries we find two extremely doubtful, but possible occurrences of the name of Magyar. Theophylactus Simocattes, in a single passage,[2] describes a Byzantine campaign in the year A.D. 587 in which an ancient fortress known as τὸ Ματζάρων is mentioned as existing in the south-western corner of Armenia. This seems a rickety basis indeed for Professor Darkó's assertion that "some of the Magyars had passed the Caucasus and pushed southwards even before the second half of the sixth century"; but as the racial name Magyar is obviously (as proved by its appearance in the ninth century south of Bolgar) of great antiquity, it may, perhaps, stand. The reference is, however, to a local appellation, and implies no direct Byzantine knowledge of the Magyars.

Malalas gives the name of a Hunnish king near Cimmerian

---

1 *D.A.I.* c. 13: Ἴσθι οὖν ὅτι ταῖς βορείαις ἅπασι γένεσι φύσις ὥσπερ καθέσ-τηκεν.... Εἰ ἀξιώσουσί ποτε καὶ αἰτήσονται, εἴτε Χάζαροι, εἴτε Τοῦρκοι, εἴτε καὶ Ῥῶς, ἢ ἕτερόν τι ἔθνος τῶν βορείων καὶ Σκυθικῶν.... c. 43: Ἀλλὰ μὲν περὶ τῶν βορείων Σκυθῶν ἱκανῶς σοι δεδήλωται.

2 p. 818, ed. Bonn, τὸ Ματζάρων (φρούριον δὲ καὶ τοῦτο).

Bosporus in the year A.D. 520 as Μούγελ,[1] and Theophanes (who is here merely copying from Malalas) repeats the name as Μουάγερις.[2]

Theophanes mentions two incursions by Τοῦρκοι through the Caucasus into Armenia in the eighth century. The two passages in question run:

(1) In the 23rd year of Constantine's rule [i.e. A.D. 763], the Τοῦρκοι, sallying out of the Caspian Gates, having slain many in Armenia, collected numbers of captives and returned home.[3]

(2) In the 24th year the Τοῦρκοι made a second irruption into the Caspian Gates and Iberia, and joined battle with the Arabs, in which many of each side were slain.[4]

These two passages have usually been ascribed to the Khazars, but Darkó considers that it is here "absolutely necessary to understand the Magyars". The point is, I think, a very open one, since the invaders might almost equally well have been Khazars, Magyars, or Magyars acting under the initiative of the Khazars.[5] In any case, however, there was no direct contact between the Byzantines and the Magyars on these occasions. One would expect the information to have been gathered, either from Arabs, or from Armenians. If the former, the Arabs would normally refer to the Khazars by that name, the Magyars as either "Magyars" or "Baškirs". One would expect the strange name, had it occurred, to have struck Theophanes' source, whereas he would translate "Khazars" by Τοῦρκοι without further demur. If the source was Armenian, the same argument applies. If the invaders were Magyars, why were they not described as Sevordik?

The alleged ninth-century reference to Georgius Monachus is out of place, as this story is a late one, belonging to the middle of the tenth century; but at the close of the ninth century we

---

1 p. 431, ed. Bonn.   2 p. 165, ed. de Boor.

3 *Ibid.* p. 364.   4 *Ibid.* p. 366.

5 Cf. Tabarī, IV, 269 ff. (O.T.F. edition). In the year 106 H. the Khazars, who had been defeated in the previous year by the Arabs, appealed to "all the infidels their allies" and invaded Azerbaidjan. They were driven out and defeated by the Arabs. In the next year came the great Arab invasion of Khazaria as far as the Don. These events are referred to by Theophanes, pp. 340–1, in which passage both names Χαζάρεις and Τοῦρκοι occur.

get at last, in the Emperor Leo's "Tactica", a quite unmistakable and undeniable description of the Magyars as Τοῦρκοι.
It is important to note in what circumstances this occurs. The
Emperor undoubtedly bases his work, at least so far as the
description of tactics is concerned, on the pseudo-Mauricius
of early days, who described, under the name of Τοῦρκοι, the
true Turks. On the other hand, the Emperor Leo has not taken
over pseudo-Mauricius' descriptions absolutely slavishly, but
has made certain slight adaptations and alterations which prove
that he actually considered the tactics of the Magyars and
reproduced the old description with full consciousness of what
he was doing. Hence it follows that the Magyars in the
Emperor's day really pursued practically the same tactics as
were used by the Turks in the days of pseudo-Mauricius.

These tactics were known to Leo only through the Greco-
Bulgaro-Magyar war of 893–95.

The Emperor Leo the Philosopher is the first Greek writer
of whom it can be said with certainty that he describes the
Magyars as Τοῦρκοι; and he does so because their tactics in war,
as evinced in 895, were exactly similar to those of the true
Turks.

The next writer to use the term is also omitted by Darkó.
He is the Patriarch Nicolaus, the "mysticus" of Leo the
Philosopher, who became Patriarch of Constantinople in A.D.
895, and afterwards played a very important political role, being
closely in touch with the Emperor. In his twenty-third letter
to Symeon of Bulgaria[1] the Patriarch, writing in 917, warns
Symeon that unless he makes peace the Emperor will bring
about a coalition against him of τῶν τε Ῥῶς, καὶ σὺν ἐκείνοις
τῶν Πατζινακιτῶν, ἔτι δὲ καὶ Ἀλανῶν, καὶ τῶν ἐκ τῆς δύσεως
Τούρκων.

In a second reference,[2] we find simply the term Τοῦρκοι.

It has been suggested that the Khazars are to be understood
under this name; but this interpretation is not tenable. In the
first place it must be remarked that Nicolaus knows the Khazars
under their specific name.[3] Secondly, as M. Czebe justly

1 Migne, *P.G.* cxi, cols. 149 ff.   2 *Ibid.* col. 154.
3 *Ibid.* col. 268 (letter LVIII).

remarks,[1] the Magyars, alone of the nations enumerated, could be described by a Byzantine as living "in the west".

If, which is *a priori* unlikely, Nicolaus still had in mind at all Theophanes' old description of the Khazars as οἱ Τοῦρκοι ἐκ τῆς ἑῴας then, by contrast, he must understand the Magyars by οἱ ἐκ τῆς δύσεως Τοῦρκοι. M. Czebe is also justified in comparing Constantine's *D.A.I.* c. 38, where the two divisions of the Magyars, after their separation by the Κάγγαρ, are distinguished as those living πρὸς τὴν ἀνατολήν and οἱ πρὸς τὸ δυτικὸν μέρος οἰκοῦντες Τοῦρκοι.

The fact that Magyars and not Khazars are meant here is supported by a second passage in the *D.A.I.* where we are informed that during the latter part of the war in question, which extended from 915–17, Michael, Prince of Zachlumia, informed Symeon that Peter of Serbia (897–917) had been persuaded by the Greek Emperor to attack Bulgaria, in collaboration with the Hungarians.[2] The attack does not appear to have come off; Symeon was still too formidable a foe. But after concluding peace with the Greeks, he marched at once against the Croats, was defeated, and died soon after. On hearing of his death, at once the "Τοῦρκοι, Serbs, Croats and other neighbouring nations prepared to make war on Bulgaria".[3]

One other writer has been adduced as referring to the Magyars in the early tenth century. The *Life of St Clement*, formerly attributed to Theophylactus of Bulgaria and printed by Migne as an appendix to his works,[4] has been considered by many to be rather a document of the early tenth century. The last chapter contains a reference to Bulgaria's being ravaged by the "Σκυθικὴ μάχαιρα"[5] and this has been interpreted (as by Migne) to the Hungarian raids in 934, etc.

---

1 G. Czebe, "Turko-Byzantische Miszellen, II", *K.C.A.* 1 Köt. 4 Szám, Feb. 1924, pp. 306 ff. I should say that I came to my conclusions independently of M. Czebe, and before reading his article.

2 *D.A.I.* c. 32: ζηλοτυπήσας δὲ πρὸς τοῦτο Μιχαὴλ ὁ ἄρχων τῶν Ζαχλούμων ἐμήνυσε Συμεὼν τῷ Βουλγάριον ἄρχοντι ὅτι ὁ βασιλεὺς Ῥωμαίων δεξιοῦται διὰ δώρων τὸν ἄρχοντα Πέτρον πρὸς τὸ συνεπαρεῖν τοὺς Τούρκους καὶ ἀπελθεῖν κατὰ Βουλγαρίας· ἐγένετο δὲ κατὰ τὸν καιρὸν ἐκεῖνον καὶ πόλεμος εἰς Ἀχελὼν μεταξὺ τῶν Ῥωμαίων καὶ τῶν Βουλγάρων.

3 Cedrenus, II, 308, etc.

4 *P.G.* cxxvi, cols. 1193 ff.   5 *Ibid.* col. 1240.

On the other hand, M. Jugie[1] has shown by theological arguments that the *Life* was in all probability revised by Theophylactus, in which case this last paragraph is most likely an addition from the late eleventh century, and the Σκυθαί in question are the Petchenegs. Even if this were not so, the term Σκυθαί is used in a wide general sense; thus Comeniates uses it constantly of the Slavs of Macedonia.[2]

The next writer who uses the term Τοῦρκοι constantly for the Magyars of his day is, of course, Constantine Porphyrogenetos, to whom they are known by no other name (except Σάβαρτοι ἄσφαλοι, the old and unexplained name).[3] The same use occurs in Symeon the Logothete, pseudo-Symeon, Genesius, Theophanis Continuator—in other words, in the writers who compiled their works in conjunction with or under the direction of Constantine. Where the term is found in Skylitzes, Cedrenus or Zonaras, these later writers are merely copying from the group of writers under Constantine, and their practice cannot be adduced as proof that the name was ever in use after Constantine's day.

It is at this point that we should consider the reference in Georgius Monachus. The passage in question was written probably under the regency of Nicephorus Phocas, but based on a popular legend. The occurrence of no less than three names for the Magyars, and, more particularly, the order in which they occur, is most significant. First we hear of Οὔγγροι. Then a slightly more learned form—the writer picks himself up—Οὔννοι. Finally, as the writer swings away from the popular into the learned tradition, Τοῦρκοι. The impression that we gather from this anecdote is that, while the learned and court tradition still preserved the name Τοῦρκοι, the popular custom, at least among the Slavs, already referred to the Magyars as Οὔγγροι, while the slightly more "learned" form, which was very likely that current among the more sophisticated Greeks, was Οὔννοι.

---

1 "L'auteur de la vie de St Clément de Bulgarie", *Échos d'Orient*, no. 133, Jan.–March 1924.

2 Ed. Bonn, pp. 496, 499, etc.

3 Constantine did, however, hear the national name Magyar and wrote it down without understanding it; it appears (in the form Μεγέρη) as the name of the third horde in c. 40 of the *D.A.I.*

And already, only a few years later, we see the name gone altogether. Leo Grammaticus practically tells us the true state of things in his day. For him, the Magyars are "the 'Scythians', vulgarly called 'Huns'".[1] Leo, it should be noted, loves the antique. For him the Bulgars are "Mysians", the Russians "Tauroscythians" or "Scythians", the Magyars "Scythians" or "Huns". I am personally very dubious whether in his day the Magyars were vulgarly called even "Huns"; I suspect that they were called "Hungarians"; but Leo could not bring himself to set down the unrefined term.

The latest use of the name Τοῦρκοι for the Magyars which I have found in any author purporting to write as a contemporary occurs in the anonymous military essayist edited by R. Vári.[2] But even here, the writer's independence is very doubtful. In one phrase he uses Τουρκία indubitably of Hungary, but in wording strongly reminiscent of Constantine.[3] In two other passages the name Τοῦρκοι occurs in each case in close conjunction with Ἄραβες.[4] In both these cases, then, there can, I think, be no doubt whatever that the reference is to Turkish soldiers fighting as mercenaries of the Arabs.

Kulakovskiy has argued plausibly for assigning to this treatise a date during the Bulgarian wars of the Emperor Basil Bulgaroctonos (994–95). Vári himself places the date in the time of Nicephorus Phocas. In any case, it seems not to be later than the end of the tenth century. This is the last instance which it is at all possible to quote as an independent reference to the Magyars as Τοῦρκοι; but it would, I think, be more accurate to set this aside as a quotation from Constantine.

The report of Hārun b. Yahya (967) on Turkish guards in

---

1 Σκύθαι (Οὔννους δὲ τὸ ἔθνος κατονομάζουσιν). After this introductory mention, the Magyars are referred to indiscriminately as Σκύθαι and Οὔννοι.

2 *Incerti Scriptoris Byzantini Seculi X, Liber de Re Militari*, ed. R. Vári, Teubner, 1901.

3 p. 29, ll. 9–15: οὐ μόνον δὲ εἰς τοὺς Βουλγάρους ἔξεστι τῷ δομεστίκῳ καὶ τοῖς ἀκρίταις στρατηγοῖς κατασκόπους ἔχειν, ἀλλὰ καὶ εἰς τὰ λοιπὰ γειτονοῦντα ἔθνη, εἴτουν εἰς Πατζιvακίαν καὶ εἰς Τουρκίαν καὶ Ῥωσίαν, ἵνα μηδὲν τῶν ἐκείνων βουλευμάτων ἄγνωστον ἡμῖν ᾖ.

4 p. 21, l. 1: προσήκει δὲ διά τε τοὺς Ἄραβας καὶ τοὺς Τούρκους θρασύτερον ἐφορμῶντας ταῖς παρατάξεσι, κ.τ.λ. p. 22, l. 6. Rest on the march to let stragglers catch up, μὴ καὶ ἀφυλάκτοις τούτοις οὖσι παρατυχόντες οἱ Ἄραβες ἢ καὶ οἱ Τοῦρκοι καταβλάπτωσι.

Constantinople[1] refers surely to true Turks. I am less convinced regarding the passage in the *De Ceremoniis* (taken from the *Kletorologion* of Philotheos, compiled A.D. 900) where places at table are assigned, among the ἐθνικοὶ τῆς ἑταιρείας, οἷον Τοῦρκοι, Χαζάρεις καὶ λοιποί, despite Czebe's arguments; but believe that when I give my own explanation, this particular dispute may become irrelevant.

We thus see that, so far from its being the usual Byzantine custom to refer to the Magyars as "Τοῦρκοι", this custom was actually a very restricted one. It was introduced by the Emperor Leo the Philosopher, after the Greco-Bulgarian-Magyar war. It was adopted by his Patriarch, and by his son; and by the writers who compiled their works under the son's directions. Immediately afterwards, it dropped out even of learned contemporary use. Zonaras, for instance, when using the name in copying from earlier writers, finds it necessary to explain that he means the "Οὔγγροι" by this term. It was thus obviously unintelligible to his readers in his day.[2] It is therefore incorrect to say that the Byzantine described the Hungarians as Τοῦρκοι. We should say simply that Leo the Philosopher so described them—for he is the *fons et origo mali*. So far my conclusions have led me in agreement with M. Czebe, and apparently with M. Darkó himself, on second thoughts.[3]

Why did Leo fall into this error?

The answer is, that it was not really an error on his part. The warriors whom Leo saw and described during the war of 895 were in truth Turks. They were Kavars, "a race of Khazars", who were themselves Turks. But more; they were part of the Khazar standing army, which was recruited, like the standing armies of many other powers of the day, from among the

1 Cit. Marquart, *Streifzüge*, pp. 216 ff.

2 III, pp. 443 and 484, ed. Bonn.

3 Darkó says himself (*B.Z.* xxiv, pp. 376–7) that "the similarity in military methods of these two peoples [the Turks and the Magyars] occasioned the identical nomenclature in Leo's *Tactica*; Constantine Porphyrogenetos then carried on the imperial tradition, and the writers who wrote under his influence took it from him. To this is due the fact that the name Τοῦρκοι stuck to the Hungarians in Byzantium for more than 200 years". "200 years" is erroneous; the period during which the term was in use hardly exceeded fifty years.

recognised condottieri of Eastern Europe, the necessitous and pugnacious Turks.

Dimašqi[1] describes under the year 254 H. (A.D. 867/8 corrected by Marquart, *Streifzüge*, p. 4, to 354 H., A.D. 965) a palace revolution in Khazaria. The State was attacked by an (unnamed) tribe of Turks, whereupon the "Khwārismians" refused to fight unless the Khazars accepted Islam. In their extremity, the whole nation consented and was converted, except the Khagan. The "Khwārismians" now attacked and repelled the invaders, whereupon the Khagan likewise accepted Islam.

These "Khwārismians" are undoubtedly mercenary Turks from Khwārism, in permanent service with the Khagan of Khazaria. Their relations with the Khagan, as we know from yet another story, were not always happy. Ibn Fozlān tells us of a considerable difference of opinion, which he dates at A.D. 922. The actual secession of the Kavars to the Magyars seems to have been the result of some such contest between the army and the local authorities. The defeated mercenaries fled across the frontier to a nation which would treat them with greater deference; and as a professional fighting class, they naturally took the lead in all such enterprises as the war of 895.

Leo therefore described the Magyars as Turks because the Kavars (the only class of the mixed nation with which he came into contact) actually were Turks, and more than probably described themselves as such to enquirers. Constantine was led to carry on the tradition of nomenclature, largely out of natural piety; but it must not be forgotten that the same circumstances were still operative up to his own day. Contact between the Hungarians and the Byzantines during the first half of the tenth century was infrequent, and was very largely confined to military matters, which lay for the most part under the direction of the Kavars. There was the embassy of the Cleric Gabriel, described in c. 8 of the *D.A.I.* which must probably be dated at A.D. 943; then there were the Magyar raids into Byzantine territory in 934 and 943; and finally, the embassies of the two Magyar leaders in 948 and 949. It was only on the last-named

1 *Cosmographie*, p. 380.

occasion, as we have seen, that Constantine himself obtained any first-hand, direct information as to the Magyars, and then it was through a Kavar source. It is, indeed, logically absurd that he should distinguish, as he does in c. 39, the "Turks", i.e. the Magyars proper, from the "Kavars", from whom the name "Turk" was originally derived. But given the fact that the name "Turk" was already firmly fixed in his head for the Hungarian nation, as it undoubtedly was, since the composition of his father's work, and given also the fact—which emerges very clearly from his text—that up to the time of the Gylas' arrival he had been unaware of the dual nature of the Hungarian nation, then the logical absurdity becomes a logical necessity.

It was the more easy for the name "Turk" to disappear in later centuries, since the Kavars gradually became killed off, and the Turkish elements in the Hungarian nation diminished and were absorbed by the Finno-Ugrian.

PART III

Further Remarks on the Composition of the De Administrando Imperio

CONSTANTINE himself explains in his preface the plan which he has set himself in the *D.A.I.*

"First I shall show you", he writes, "what race can be useful, and how, to the Greeks and how it can harm them, and how and by what race each of them can be made war against and subdued, then concerning their greedy and insatiable minds, and what things they demand unreasonably to be given, then also about the differences from other races, the genealogy of races and their way of living, and the situation and extent of the land inhabited by them and its measure and extent also, and of what has happened at what time between the Greeks and divers nations, and after that what novelties have been introduced in our policy, and also in all the land of the Greeks, at what time. These things I learned for myself and had noted down for you my dear son...."

The four main divisions of the book fall as follows:

(1) How to manage the ἔθνη, cc. 1–13, paragraphs 1 and 2.

(2) How to treat their demands, remainder of c. 13.

(3) Ethnography, geography, etc.

    A. Of Saracens, Spain, Italy, cc. 14–25.

    B. Italy, Franks, Venetians, cc. 26–28.

    C. The Southern Slavs, cc. 29–36.

    D. The Petchenegs, Magyars and Moravians, cc. 37–42.

    E. The Eastern ἔθνη, cc. 43–46, except last paragraph.

(4) Certain relations between the Empire and the ἔθνη, cc. 46 fin.–48 med.

(5) Internal innovations, cc. 48 med.–52.[1]

(6) C. 53, which is parallel and belongs partly to Section (1), partly to Section (3) D.

In spite of Bury's epoch-making work, and Fehér's criticism of it, there are certain further remarks to be made which, I venture to think, can throw some new light on this treatise, and

---

[1] This analysis is based on that in Bury, *op. cit.*

in doing so, help to clear up the situation, in particular of the Magyars in the tenth century.

Bury has pointed out that the chapter headings are inaccurate and misleading, and I have remarked above that we should consider the work in sections rather than in chapters. If we take Section (3), as above (ethnography, geography, etc.), we shall find this confirmed.

Section (3) A. *Saracens, Spain, Italy*, cc. 14–25. Bury has subjected this section to a particularly close analysis, and has shown that it consists of no less than three independent series of notes, combined "in a purely mechanical fashion and badly at that, without any attempt at working the sets of material into an ordered whole"; nevertheless, these chapters, as they stand, form a unit in themselves. There is nothing to indicate the date of this composition.

Section (3) B. *Italy, Franks, Venetians*, cc. 26–28. Bury ascribes c. 28, with something like certainty, to Liutprand of Cremona, who arrived in Constantinople on September 17th, 949, and stopped there some six months. C. 27 was written in 948/9, by Constantine's own admission.[1] The section on Venice cannot be dated.

Section (3) C. *The Southern Slavs*, cc. 29–36. In c. 29 Constantine tells us that he is writing in "the seventh indiction, in the 6457th year after the creation of the world", i.e. A.D. 948/9. In the same chapter he promises to give a further sketch (συγγραφή) on the Serbs and Croats.[2]

C. 30 differs altogether in style from the remaining Southern Slav chapters. It is introduced by a short preface in the classical style, and the formula ὅτι or ἰστέον ὅτι is absent from it altogether. Further, it contains an account of the capture of Salona which is duplicated with differences in c. 29, and an account of the coming of the Croats and of their conquest of the Avars which is duplicated, with differences, in c. 31. The differences between c. 30 and c. 31 are numerous. C. 30 makes the Croats emigrate from "White Croatia" under five brothers,

---

1 εἰσὶ δὲ μέχρις τῆς σήμερον, ἥτις ἐστὶν ἰνδικτιῶνος ἑβδόμη, ἔτη ἀπὸ κτίσεως κόσμου ͵ϛυνζ΄.

2 μέχρι τῆς σήμερον, ἥτις ἰνδικτιῶνος ἑβδόμης ἔτους ͵ϛυνζ΄.

Κλουκάς, Λόβελος, Κοσέντζης, Μούχλω and Χρώβατος,[1] and two sisters, Τοῦγα and Βοῦγα. C. 31 makes Heraclius invite their prince at the time being "the father of Πόργα". C. 30 makes the White Croats live on the best of terms with the Magyars;[2] c. 31 knows only hostile relations between the two nations. C. 30 makes the White Croats vassals of the Franks;[3] in c. 31 they are "preyed upon" by them; etc., etc.

It is, therefore, obvious that Bury is right when he separates c. 30 from cc. 31–36, and M. Fehér, in ascribing cc. 30–36 to one author, evinces small feeling either for style or for logic. He is also mistaken in arguing that the introduction to c. 30 need be anything more than the preamble to that chapter itself. It consists of precisely four and a half lines in the Bonn edition— no long period for a Byzantine to wind himself up in—while the chapter itself is of the very respectable length of 165 lines. It is, on the other hand, almost equally inexplicable when Bury suggests that the author of c. 30 was the same as the author of cc. 29, 31–36, and that in writing c. 30 he has "forgotten" that he had already told much of his story, and told it differently.[4] On the contrary, the difference in style (not to mention the preface) makes it clear that we have here a separate account by a different author. It seems very probable that this was, as Fehér suggests, a Dalmatian.[5]

Bury couples c. 29 with cc. 31–36; believes them all to have been written practically simultaneously, and interprets cc. 31–36 as the συγγραφή referred to in c. 29. He puts c. 30 as a later addition, owing to the mention in it of a king of the White Croats who is subject to "Otto the great king of Frankia and Saxony". Westberg in his work on Ibrāhīm ibn Jā'qūb's report on the lands of the Slavs[6] identifies Constantine's "Βελοχρώβατοι with the kingdom of "Braga, Biūma and Krkūia" (Bohemia, Moravia and Silesia and Breslau) ruled over by

---

1 καθ' ὃν μέλλει τρόπον ῥηθήσεσθαι ἐν τῇ τῶν Χρωβάτων καὶ Σερβλίων συγγραφῇ.

2 συμπενθερίας μετὰ τοὺς Τούρκους καὶ ἀγάπας ἔχοντες.

3 πραιδευόμενοι παρά τε τῶν Φράγγων τε καὶ Τούρκων καὶ Πατζινακιτῶν.

4 Bury, *op. cit.* p. 525.

5 Fehér, *Gebietsgrenzen*, p. 60.

6 *Zapiski* of the Ac. Imp. de St Pétersbourg, sér. VIII, 1893.

Boleslav I, who was, in fact, reduced by Otto the Great in May or June 950. I think that Bury and Westberg have proved their point here conclusively. The arguments advanced by M. Fehér against the identification seem to me to be devoid of foundation.[1]

We must therefore put c. 30 at after July 950, and, as Bury says, since "the manner in which Constantine speaks of the subjection of the Bohemian kingdom to Otto does not suggest that the words were written in consequence of an immediate announcement of the German king's success, we can say with probability that c. 30 was written after 950".

But it is very doubtful whether cc. 31–36 were contemporary with c. 29 either. C. 31 says that "when Miroslav, after ruling for four years, was slain...and dissensions and many civil wars

[1] M. Fehér argues that, according to Mas'ūdī and the *Legend of St Wenceslaus*, the Croats of the north were independent of Bohemia, and it is not possible to deduce from this or any other of Constantine's references to the White Croats an identification of their country with the kingdom of Bohemia. Although, it is true, Westberg fails to prove that the kingdom of the White Croats in 950 was co-extensive with that of Bohemia in 965, no evidence to the contrary is available. Mas'ūdī's *Meadows of Gold* were compiled in 943–44, and the work is thus no evidence for the situation in 950; particularly as the information contained in his section on the Slavs is by no means of the latest (cf. Marquart, *Streifzüge*, pp. 96 ff.). What he does say is ambiguous. In enumerating the Slavonic nations, he mentions the Serbs, then "the Moravin, the Chorwatin, the Čáchin, the Guššanin, Braničabin". There follows a description of "the kingdom of al-Dīr", which is "the first of the Slav kingdoms" and "possesses extensive cities, numerous cultivated lands, large armies and much munitions of war....Next to this Slav kingdom is the kingdom of al-Firāg (Prague), which possesses a gold mine, cities, many cultivated lands, large military forces and a powerful army. It makes war on the Rūm, Franks, Bažkarda and other peoples, and war is waged between them with varying fortunes. Next to this Slav kingdom lies the land of the Turks".

Thus, if the Moravians and Croats are not explicitly given as subject to Bohemia, they are mentioned in one breath with the Czechs, and neither nation is given the honour of separate description as a kingdom. The old Slovene *Legend of St Wenceslaus*, it is true, considers the Croats as definitely independent of Bohemia, since it says that after the murder of Wenceslaus, "his mother, fearing death, fled to the Croats; for...Boleslav sent after her, but did not catch her". The Croats must, then, have been independent at the date of the murder; but the reference in question is to the year 935 or 936, and the legend itself was composed not long after, as Vondrak has proved ("Zur Würdigung der altslowenischen Wenzelslegende", *S.B. der Wiener Akademie*, CXXVII, 1892, 13). As Wenceslaus had himself been forced in 929 to swear fealty to the German king, it was only after his death that his murderer, Boleslav, was able to shake off the German yoke and defeat the German forces sent against him in 936. It is obvious that the independence of Croatia in the very year of Boleslav's accession is as little a proof that the same independence survived till 950, as Jāq'ūb's testimony that Prague and Cracow were united in 965 is proof that the union was completed by 950.

came over the land, the armed forces over the Croats were weakened ". The death of Miroslav was in 949; this chapter, with its reference to subsequent civil wars, can therefore hardly have been written before 950.

Similarly in c. 32, Bosnia is represented as belonging to Serbia. This again can only have been after the death of Miroslav.

Thus cc. 31–36, equally with c. 30, are written after c. 29; and though, as we saw, c. 30 stands apart, while cc. 31–36 hang together, it is quite admissible to consider with Fehér that the whole of the complex cc. 30–36 comprises the συγγραφή promised by Constantine in c. 29. He merely got two different accounts made, inserted them at a later date, and did not trouble to put them to further editing.

Section (3) D. We now come to the section which chiefly interests us: the chapters on the Petchenegs, Magyars and Moravians.

We have already seen that the date for c. 37—the Petcheneg chapter—can be deduced from that of the Bulgaro-Greek war as A.D. 949. It seems probable that in his composition, Constantine passed straight on from c. 29 to c. 37, thus making possible the reference back of the words μέχρι τῆς σήμερον in c. 37 to the definition of the same phrase in c. 29.

The chapters on the races of the north, more than any others in Constantine's work, form a unit. They are, indeed, derived from numerous different sources, but an attempt is evident to work them up and make of them a coherent whole—an attempt which on at least one occasion led to disastrous results.

It is probable that the chapters were composed in the order in which they stand, for this reason, that while the later chapters show signs that the writer, in compiling them, was acquainted with the information contained in the earlier chapters, the converse is not the case.

Thus c. 37, as remarked before, is plain and straightforward, and presents no difficulties.

C. 38 is a confused story, and it is very probable that the confusion is definitely due to the note at the end of c. 37 regarding the Κάγκαρ. When Constantine learned this piece of information (which was clearly a postscript, as its position in the chapter shows), he probably had c. 38 already in his hands, and made the unlucky editorial alteration which has taken so much unravelling.

C. 38 shows a certain acquaintance with c. 37; the remark that the Petchenegs had "taken up arms against the Khazars" seems to me to have been imported with the name of Petcheneg when "they" was substituted for the original word.

The last sentence of c. 38—the fatal list of rivers—is again a postscript, but appears from the forms of the names to be derived from the Magyar source "B" of c. 38.

Cc. 39–40 were clearly written after c. 38, since c. 38 shows not the smallest knowledge of so much as the existence of a nation called Kavars. Cc. 39–40, on the other hand, certainly imply some knowledge in the writer's and reader's minds of cc. 37 and 38. This is clear from the abrupt introduction (without further explanation) of the Τοῦρκοι and the τῶν Πατζινακιτῶν γῆ. Certainly the second reference to Etel-köz (the parenthetical sentence beginning ὁ δὲ τόπος) is inserted from c. 38 by Constantine himself.

C. 41, the legend of Great Moravia is, as Fehér remarks, a popular legend grouped round the *person* of Sviatopolk (not round the country of Great Moravia);[1] and Fehér is clearly right in deducing the source to be a popular legend, probably South Slavonic, and in comparing the reference to a similar source in c. 31.[2] But this chapter again was composed after cc. 37–40; for the last clause in it—εἰς δὲ τοὺς Βουλγάρους—is simply drawn from the description of the Kavars' neighbours in c. 40.

C. 40 is, however, complicated by the introduction of a second source—a geographical description, which forms a part of a larger whole which reappears also in c. 42, and again in c. 53. It has been added to the earlier information in c. 42, like the second set of notes on the Saracens, "in a purely mechanical fashion, and badly at that". It is very probable that this second source dates from after the composition of the Southern Slav chapters; since at least one remark in c. 42 (the Magyars live in

---

1 *Gebietsgrenzen*, pp. 54, 56.
2 C. 31, p. 150, 4, λέγουσιν οἱ αὐτοὶ Χρώβατοι.

Great Moravia, but also between the Save and the Danube) would seem to be based on later knowledge than Constantine possessed in 949.

When this addition was made, Constantine did a certain amount of editing. We thus find in c. 40 no less than three threads which must be distinguished: the Kavar story, the geographical description, and the parenthetical sentences which represent Constantine's attempts at editing.

Of these, the Kavar narrative, as we saw, is probably derived from the Gylas who came to Constantinople in 949 ("shortly after" the earlier visitors in 948). Another evidence of dating is given by the description of the Kavars' neighbours, as "the Bulgars on the East, the Patzinaks on the North, the Franks on the West, the Croats on the South". Allowing for a geographical error of half a quadrant, due to the source of the information,[1] this description seems to represent the actual situation in A.D. 949, the date which must be assigned to this chapter. As Fehér correctly points out, the absence of the Serbs from among the southern neighbours of the Bulgars proves that this description was written before Serbia became master of Bosnia, and thus before c. 31.

Thus the directly Kavar portions of cc. 39–40 were written in A.D. 949, after c. 38 but before c. 41; the geographical description was inserted later, and Constantine's notes later still.

Naming these three sources respectively α, β, and γ and assigning the symbol γ' to such changes as Constantine made to α, immediately he received it, in order to adapt it to cc. 37, 38, we get the following results:

C. 39 is entirely α, except, as I pointed out, that the phrase εἰς τὴν τῶν Πατζινακιτῶν γῆν might be described as γ', since Constantine's hand is visible in it.

C. 40 up to the phrase εἰς τὴν γῆν εἰς ἥν, κ.τ.λ. is almost pure α, although the influence of γ is visible in the account of the

---

[1] M. Fehér points out that "the description of the points of the compass in Constantine agree with our own elsewhere, as many passages in the *D.A.I.* and the *De Thematibus* show"; but fails to draw the conclusion that the difference, in this instance, is due to the different source (Oriental instead of Greek). For the Turkish orientation of the compass, compare the similar error in the Petchenegs' description of their neighbours in our old report.

invitation to the Kavars by "the Christ-loving and respectable Emperor Leo". The next lines τὴν ἐπονομαζομένην...εἰς ἣν νῦν οἰκοῦσιν are γ. This is proved, firstly by the parenthetical nature of these lines; secondly by the fact that in the opening clause the words ὡς εἴρηται are out of place as they stand. For actually, the fact that this particular country (the plain of the Theiss) was called "after the rivers in it", is mentioned after and not before the clause in question. The words κατὰ τὴν ἀνωτέρω, ὡς εἴρηται are therefore only explicable as a later addition, and a clumsy one at that, which had in mind the statement that τὰ ἀνώτερα...ἀρτίως ὀνομάζουσι, but did not edit with sufficient skill to change the "above" in the writer's mind into "below" to fit the text. The next sentences ἐν αὐτῷ δὲ τόπῳ...ὁδὸν ἔχον ἡμερῶν δύο are β.

Next comes a sentence καὶ ἀπὸ τῶν ἐκεῖσε...Σφενδόπλοκος which must be ascribed to γ. It is based simply and purely on the statements in cc. 38, 41 that the Magyars destroyed Great Moravia and occupied Sviatopolk's territory, and on the description of the Kavars' homes which follows this note, but was actually written before it.

We go back to β for the little one-line summary ταῦτα μὲν... γνωρίσματά τε καὶ ἐπωνυμίαι. Then comes the description of the Kavars' homes in 949, running down to πρὸς τὸ μεσημβρινὸν οἱ Χρώβατοι.

This whole description is undoubtedly due to source α (the Kavar informant). This is proved by the following facts:

(1) Constantine explicitly says, not that the country "is called", but that "they now call it" (ἀρτίως ὀνομάζουσι). This habit of the Magyars of calling a country after the rivers in it is an attested one, and it is obviously more likely that he should have got the information from a Magyar (Kavar) source than from any other.

(2) The phrase below ὁμονοίαν ἔχουσιν, κ.τ.λ., which unquestionably comes from α, seems more natural if the "rivers" had previously been mentioned.

There remains the possibility that the names of the rivers alone are a gloss from β or other information in Constantine's possession; but against this too there are the following arguments:

(1) The name-formations are apparently Bulgarian or Slav (which would have been adopted by the Magyars) and not Greek.[1]

(2) The geographical description is not a general geographical survey, but a route, running the whole way from Belgrade to the Caucasus. Where resumed in c. 42 it sticks almost wholly to the sea-coast, and does not show any intimate knowledge of districts lying off the direct line.

(3) Having got from the Kavars the fact that they called their country "after the names of the rivers flowing through it", Constantine would naturally take down their answer, and would hardly correct it, just as he does not explain the Magyar Etel by its Greek name.

I have shown above that the description of the Magyars' neighbours comes from α.

The remainder of the chapter is obviously α.

C. 42 is an interesting chapter. The greater part of it is composed of that geographical description which we have called above β. Embedded in this is a sort of footnote which tells the story of the building of Sarkel, and constitutes the only information on the Khazars in the whole *D.A.I.* But there are also one or two notes which we may ascribe to Constantine, and thus represent by γ. These are the following:

εἰς δὲ τὰ ὑψηλότερα...τὴν ἄφιξιν and the second remark about the Russians on the Dnieper.

ἐξ οὗ καὶ οἱ Ῥῶς, κ.τ.λ. These seem reminiscences of the Russian chapter—c. 9—a chapter which is quite out of place where it stands, in the first part of Constantine's work, and ought by rights to be in the ethnographical and geographical section among the northern races.

The second description of Patzinakia ἡ δὲ Πατζινακία πᾶσαν τὴν γῆν...καὶ τῶν λ´ μερῶν seems to be based similarly on c. 37.

Section (3) E, *The Eastern* ἔθνη, calls for only one remark here: it forms a compact whole, and was written some three years after the Italian, Dalmatian and Petcheneg chapters, as a remark let fall in c. 45 shows.[2]

---

1 See above, p. 121, note 2.

2 Μέχρι τῆς σήμερον ἥτις ἐστὶν ἰνδικτιῶν ι´, ἔτη ἀπὸ κτίσεως κόσμου ,ϛυξ´.

Of the last pages of the *D.A.I.*, all that interests us is the final chapter, c. 53; but that is exceptionally interesting. It contains a very long history of Cherson; and appended to it, in the final lines of the *D.A.I.*, are, firstly, the conclusion of the geographical description β from cc. 40, 42, and secondly, a few sentences of direct advice from Constantine to his son, absolutely parallel with, and only with, cc. 1–13.

We must now turn to the opening sections of the *D.A.I.* (cc. 1–13).

Sections (1) and (2): cc. 1–13. It is in dealing with these chapters that Professor Bury and M. Fehér seem to me to have gone furthest astray. Both have assumed, apparently, without further thought, that because they stand first, these chapters were the earliest written in the book. Nothing whatever warrants this assumption, which is in any case *a priori* improbable; for since cc. 1–13 contain political precepts which are based on certain geographical and historical facts, it would seem most unnatural to suggest that the precepts had been composed before the facts were ascertained. Obviously, the natural order would be the opposite of this. In fact, a little study of these chapters will prove that they were composed after cc. 37–42 (and, consequently, after cc. 26–29, which we know to have preceded c. 37). On the other hand, it seems quite probable that they were composed before the other Southern Slav chapters, and before the chapters dealing with the Eastern ἔθνη.

It is perfectly clear that cc. 1–13 (with the added fragment at the end of c. 53) do not really represent the last word on "how to administer the Empire". In point of fact, they are composed solely with reference to what Constantine calls "the northern and Scythian races". This we see to have been intentional; for not only are no other nations mentioned in the precepts regarding the balance of power, but in c. 13 inordinate demands of the ἔθνη are presupposed to be coming only from such northern races.[1]

---

1 Εἰ ἀξιώσουσί ποτε καὶ αἰτήσονται, εἴτε Χάζαροι, εἴτε Τοῦρκοι, εἴτε καὶ ῾Ρῶς, ἢ ἕτερόν τι ἔθνος Βορείων καὶ Σκυθικῶν. And again: Εἰ γάρ ποτε ἔθνος τι ἀπὸ τῶν ἀπίστων τούτων καὶ ἀτίμων Βορείων γένεων αἰτήσεται, κ.τ.λ.

Actually, these chapters deal only with the following races: Petchenegs, Khazars, Magyars, Russians, Bulgars; with one or two incidental references to Alans, Uz, Black Bulgars and Franks. One might almost add the Chersonites, who are treated with at least as much mistrust as the foreign ἔθνη.

All this is obvious; but when we turn to the sources on which the precepts in question are based, we get some interesting results; for we find that they are based almost exclusively on the historical and geographical chapters dealing with the ἔθνη in question.

In saying this, we must, of course, reckon the longer chapter on the Russians (c. 9) as the equivalent of the chapters on the Petchenegs, Magyars, etc. The shorter chapters on the Russians (cc. 2 and 4) belong, on the other hand, quite properly to the hortatory chapters—and the fact that c. 2 is quite obviously based on c. 9 should in itself have sufficed to show the true composition of this part of the essay. The omission of an account of the Bulgars seems rather remarkable, since they are certainly included among the "northern and Scythian races". It is probably due, not to the unfinished state of the *D.A.I.*, but to Constantine's pious imitation of his father's practice in avoiding a description of the tactics in war of this Christian and therefore *ex hypothesi* friendly nation.[1] Nevertheless, Leo's whole description of the Bulgaro-Greco-Magyar war is really aimed at the Bulgars; and similarly, Constantine does not mind showing how the Bulgars can be kept in check by the Petchenegs, even if he does not give an account of their methods.

The same may perhaps be the case with regard to the Khazars, and conceivably, also the Alans. The absence of a description of the Uz and the Black Bulgars is due, however, to lack of information.

The main sources of cc. 1–13 are, then, cc. 9, 37–42 inclusive and c. 53 of the *D.A.I.* To these must be added a certain amount

[1] Leo, *Tactica* (ed. Migne, *P.G.* cvii, col. 945, c. 18): "Since the Bulgars have embraced peace in Christ and pledged faith in Christ with the Greeks, since God took vengeance on them for their perjury and breach of faith, we will not arm our hands against them; therefore we do not venture to describe their order of battle against us, nor ours against them, since we are joined together like brothers, and now that they are said to have submitted to our exhortations".

of "palace information" in Constantine's possession about his own father Leo, about Romanus Lecapenus, and about Leo the Khazar (this information is incorrect); and finally, a very considerable amount of further information, chiefly on the Petchenegs, but also on the position at Cherson, and on the Magyars, which would appear to have been gathered in the course of various embassies, chiefly to the Petchenegs.

The last-named source includes one embassy mentioned by name—that of the "Cleric Gabriel" to the Magyars (c. 8); but embassies have clearly also been sent to the Petchenegs, and the ambassadors have brought back many interesting and intriguing details on the subject of that race. When these embassies took place we cannot tell for certain; but I think it more than probable that M. Fehér's excellent conjecture is correct, and that all of them were undertaken in connection with the Russian threat on Constantinople in 943/4.[1]

Both Bury and Fehér have attempted to assign to the Cleric Gabriel's mission more importance, as a source for Constantine's information, than it deserves. The sources for Constantine's cc. 1–13 need not, in the vast majority of cases, be sought further afield than cc. 9, 37–42, 53. What is more, the information in these explanatory chapters, which should more properly be regarded as appendices to cc. 1–8, 10–12, has been utilised in a most mechanical and unintelligent fashion, which alone has given rise to most of the difficulties in the hortatory chapters, and in particular to the difficulty regarding the situation of "Great Moravia".

The best example of this is seen at the end of c. 9 and c. 10—the notes on the Uz. We read:

"The Uz can make war on the Petchenegs."

"The Uz can make war on the Khazars, being their neighbours."

It would be the greatest mistake to imagine these sentences to mean that the Uz were actually across the Don when Constantine wrote. They are drawn in each case solely from c. 37. In that chapter the Uz are represented as having defeated the Petchenegs. Therefore, Constantine argues, they can defeat the

1 *Gebietsgrenzen*, pp. 45 f.

Petchenegs again. Similarly, in c. 37 we learn (and Constantine learned) that the Uz, on expelling the Petchenegs, took their feeding-grounds and thus became neighbours of the Khazars. This is the source of the second statement. The same blind reliance on c. 37 is responsible for the absence of a suggestion that the Petchenegs can make war on the Khazars; not, as Rambaud suggests that Constantine did not want to destroy the Khazars utterly; but because in c. 37 the boot was on the other leg; it was the Khazars who had made war on the Petchenegs. Similarly c. 12 is merely an echo of the mention of Black Bulgaria in c. 42.

More interesting and more illuminating is the question of "Great Moravia".

The following are the references in the *D.A.I.* to that country:

(1) C. 13. "The following races are the neighbours of the Magyars; to the west of them Francia, and to the north the Patzinaks, and to the south side Great Moravia, that is, the land of Sviatopolk, which was utterly destroyed by the Magyars and occupied by them. But the Croats are next to the Magyars on the mountain side."[1]

(2) C. 38. "The Magyars turning and seeking a land to live in came and chased away the inhabitants of Great Moravia and settled in their land, in which the Magyars are living today."

(3) C. 40 describes certain important points on the south side of the Danube: "and after them (ἀπὸ τῶν ἐκεῖσε) is the Great, Unbaptised Moravia, which the Magyars destroyed, which Sviatopolk formerly ruled over. These are the things of mark and names along the Danube; and above them, where are all the settlements of the Magyars, they now call after the names of the rivers in them": Temes, Tut, Mures, Körös, Theiss. "And the neighbours of the Magyars are: on the east the Bulgars, where the Danube separates them, north the Patzinaks, west the Franks and south the Croats."

(4) C. 41 does not describe the locality of Moravia, only saying: "and the Magyars, coming, destroyed them altogether and conquered their country, in which they also live today", and the remains of the people were dispersed and fled to the

---

1 οἱ δὲ Χρώβατοι πρὸς τὰ ὄρη τοῖς Τούρκοις παρακεῖνται.

neighbouring nations, to the Bulgars and the Magyars and the Croats and the other races.

(5) C. 42. "And the Magyars live beyond the Danube in Moravia, but also inside it, between the Danube and the Save" (καὶ κατοικοῦσι μὲν οἱ Τοῦρκοι πέραθεν τοῦ Δανούβεως ποταμοῦ, ἀλλὰ καὶ ἔνθεν μέσον τοῦ Δανούβεως καὶ τοῦ Σάβα ποταμοῦ).

Bury, observing the discrepancy between the two accounts of the Magyars' frontiers, deduced that the account in c. 13 was written before the destruction of Moravia by the Magyars, i.e. within a few years after the *Landnahme*. He brings the account into relation with the embassy of the "Cleric Gabriel" mentioned in c. 7, and does not shrink from placing Great Moravia actually in the south of the present Hungary.

The account in c. 40, he thinks, represents the state of affairs in Constantine's own day.

But if this were the case, as Fehér points out, we should have to assume that "Great Moravia" in the south was actually cut off from Moravia in the north; for otherwise the Franks could not have been described as the western neighbours of the Magyars. It is certainly impossible to transfer Moravia bodily to the south; for there is no doubt whatever that the core of that kingdom was situated in that country still called Moravia today, even if its frontiers were much more extensive then than now. Fehér's own ingenious explanation is that the "Croats" of c. 13 are not the Southern Croats at all, but the "Βελοχρώβατοι" of the north; but having already given the Patzinaks in the north, the Franks in the west, Constantine has no point of the compass left for the White Croats, so placed them "πρὸς τὰ ὄρη". The southern frontier was not mentioned, because the description was given by some envoy who "only wanted, as regards the frontiers of Hungary, to describe what his master could not know, that is, its eastern, western and northern neighbours". This report "then served Constantine as a model for the other description of the frontiers in c. 40". The author was perhaps after all the Cleric Gabriel; but his mission was undertaken in 943-4.

But while correcting Bury's misapprehension, Fehér has fallen into an equal error. It is difficult to believe that Constantine, who knew the Croats so well, should suddenly refer, under that name, to the quite different nation of White Croats, about whom he knows hardly anything. Equally unlikely is it that he should describe the northern Carpathians (with which he shows no acquaintance whatever) under the airy title of τὰ ὄρη; particularly when we compare his phrase πρὸς τὰ ὀρεινά[1] in speaking of the northern frontier of the Dalmatian Croats.

Fehér is, however, fully justified in repudiating Marquart's amazing *a priori* statement that "Great Moravia must beyond any doubt be sought in Southern Pannonia"[2]—an assumption which he then bases on a violent emendation of Constantine's text, to make it read what he wants it to say, which is, roughly, the opposite of what it does say. We have no evidence that Pannonia was ever a part of Moravia. It is true that in 882 and 883 Sviatopolk ravaged Pannonia cruelly, and we read that "Pannonia de Hraba flumine ad orientem tota deleta est".[3] The Annals speak, however, of its destruction and not of its loss. It has been suggested that when Sviatopolk did homage to the Emperor in the following year, he might have been ceded Pannonia; but even were this so (and we have no ground to suppose it, other than the theory based on Constantine), the arrangement must have been of very short duration; for we find Brazlovo, who in 884 did homage to the Emperor for the land between the Save and the Drave,[4] entrusted with the defence of "all Pannonia" with his seat in Moosburg on the Zala in 896.[5]

About the country on the left bank of the Danube—the Danube-Theiss plain—we have no certain information. A considerable portion of it in the south seems at one time to have belonged to the Bulgarian Empire—exactly how much we are not called upon in this essay to consider. It is, however, difficult to believe that Bulgarian rule, north of the present Banat, was either very extensive or very secure.

It must be remembered that until the coming of modern methods of cultivation, the whole of the Theiss-Danube plain with its limitless marshes, its sandy wastes, its frequent droughts

1 C. 30, p. 146, l. 11.   2 *Annales Fuldenses, ad ann.* 882, 883.
3 *Ibid. ad ann.* 884.   4 *Streifzüge*, p. 119.
5 *Annales Fuldenses, ad ann.* 896.

and still more frequent and devastating floods, was wholly unsuitable to any settled peasant life; and all parties probably left it gratefully enough to the only nation which liked that sort of thing, viz. the remnants of the Avars. Regino, indeed, describes the country in question as "Avarum Solitudines", and I see no reason to take this as a mere anachronism.[1] It was not, however, the habit of mediaeval (nor indeed of modern) rulers to leave such large districts on their frontiers entirely independent, and it would seem reasonable to suppose that Bulgaria at one time claimed suzerainty over these Avar fragments. But by 890 this suzerainty, such as it was, had probably passed to the growing power of Moravia. The Frankish embassy to Bulgaria in 892 had to travel by water via the Kulpa and the Save,[2] on account of the danger from Sviatopolk's hordes, which reads as though the Moravian power had extended some distance southward by that date. The fact that in 886 Sviatopolk accuses the Duke of Carinthia of collusion with the Bulgars with whom he had had war in the previous year[3] also seems to show that the "desert" had been bridged over by that date, and Moravia and Bulgaria became neighbours. And when we read in the letter from the Bavarian bishops, quoted elsewhere, that the Moravians had "shaved the heads of their pseudo-Christians, Hungarian fashion (*more eorum*) and sent them against us", I cannot read this as referring to Slavs; it seems far more likely that Avars, who had a natural affinity with Magyars, should have joined them under the auspices of the Moravians.

If the district on the left bank of the Danube, down to the mouth of the Save or thereabouts, was under Moravian suzerainty in the '90's (further south was surely Bulgarian, for otherwise the envoys of 892 would not have been safe in taking that route), we should get a locality which could be described as Great Moravia and which was actually occupied by the Magyars immediately on their entering Hungary. Moreover, this

1 Regino, *ad ann.* 889: "Primo quidem Pannoniorum et Avarum solitudines pererrantes, venatu ac piscatione victum quotidianum quaeritant. Deinde Carantaniorum, Marahensium ac Bulgarorum fines irrumpunt".

2 *Annales Fuldenses, ad ann.* 892. It is as a "desert" that King Alfred knows it. "East of Carinthia beyond the desert is Pulgaraland, east of that Greece. And east of Moravia is the land of the Vistula and east of that Dacia."

3 *Annales Fuldenses, ad ann.* 886.

country was actually—in practice if not in theory—ἀβάπτιστος
—an epithet which could not possibly be applied either to
Pannonia or to Moravia proper. We should then be able, by
bearing in mind the order in which Constantine wrote his
various chapters, to realise how Constantine comes to place
Great Moravia in the south.

First in order comes the statement in c. 38, which gives no
indication of the situation of Great Moravia, but only says that
the Magyars destroyed and occupied it. *On this first statement,
all the others are built up.*

Second comes c. 40 (source α), which gives the localities
inhabited by the Magyars (actually the Kavars). These are on
the Theiss and its tributaries. Ergo, according to Constantine,
that district was Great Moravia.

Third comes c. 41, in which the words "to the Bulgars and
the Magyars and the Croats" are simply taken from c. 40. It
must be noted that Constantine imagines the Magyars to have
come in from the north (cf. his description of Patzinakia as
lying north of Hungary); therefore he represents the Moravians
as fleeing southward.

Fourth comes the geographical description in cc. 40–42
(sources γ, γ'), which is built up on the preceding statements,
supplemented in c. 42 by the remark that the Magyars also lived
in Pannonia.

Last (*not* first) comes c. 13, a thoroughly unintelligent deduction from the above. Constantine has already got the idea that
the Magyars came from the north, so that Moravia should be
south of them; and he fills in the list so mechanically from his
previous writings that he does not even perceive that a state
"utterly destroyed" by another can no longer be a neighbour
of it.

I may end with the suggestion that these lines at the beginning
of c. 13 were actually among the very last written of the whole
D.A.I. I certainly think that πρὸς τὰ ὄρη implies knowledge of
the phrase πρὸς τὰ ὀρεινά in c. 31; and it seems very probable
that this note represents the embryo of a second treatise on the
balance of power, this time centring round the Magyars, as
cc. 1–12 (described by Constantine as τὸ περὶ Πατζινακίτων
κεφάλαιον) centre round the Petchenegs.

EXCURSUS I

The Abrégé des Merveilles; *the Works of al-Garmī*

FOR a summary of the main historical and stylistic difficulties in the way of attributing the entire *Abrégé des Merveilles* to Masʿūdī, see M. Carra de Vaux' introduction. An important point is the fact that Masʿūdī, who is fond of quoting his own works by name, never mentions a book with this title. Masʿūdī is cited by name as a source three times in the *Abrégé*; the formula ("al-Masʿūdī says") is inconclusive as evidence of authorship in either direction, as it might be used, either by a different writer quoting Masʿūdī, or by Masʿūdī himself, to indicate that he was speaking from his own knowledge. On the other hand, it proves that the passages where it occurs are based on Masʿūdī's work, and he was undoubtedly a main source for much of the book. In particular, the chapter on the Sons of Japhet, which contains the section on the Burǧan, has numerous and close parallels with Masʿūdī's *Livre d'Avertissement*, which is itself a compendium of his earlier works, most of which have been lost. Compare the extracts given in the Appendix with certain parts of the *Livre d'Avertissement*, e.g.:

The King of the Rūmīs (*L. d'A.* p. 257).

The conversion of Constantine (*L. d'A.* pp. 195, 196).

Spain (*L. d'A.* p. 429).

The Ihtāradah, or Ankīradah (*L. d'A.* pp. 244, 245, and *Meadows of Gold*, pp. 446 ff.). The last-named passages are particularly interesting, since the *varia lectio* Ankīradah in the *Abrégé* shows that the fourth "Valandar horde" of Masʿūdī's story, on which so much ink has been spilt (cf. Marquart, *Streifzüge*, pp. 60 ff.), are none other than the Hungarians.

The use of the term Burǧan. The chapter in question contains mention of a number of events which occurred about the time that Masʿūdī was writing, but none of later date. This looks as if he had made it up into the form in which it has come down to us. Some of his material, however, was much older. The section on the Burğan describes that nation, not only as heathens, but as semi-nomads. It was therefore undoubtedly composed before the national conversion to Christianity (A.D. 865). The mention of wars with the Khazars, if it means anything, points to a very early date. Further, the emphasis laid on the wars between the Bulgars and the Greeks, and on the ritual observed when they concluded peace, seems to indicate that the report was written not very long after the death of Khan Krum (A.D. 844), after which a peace was concluded with Greece which lasted for many years, being regularly renewed.

It seems likely that we can assign an author, and thus an approximate date, to this report. Mas'ūdī (*Livre d'Avertisse-ment*, p. 257) mentions a certain al-Garmī, who was among the prisoners of war ransomed at Sozopetra in 231 H. (A.D. 845/6), of whom he says:

He dwelt in the frontier fortresses, and knew the Rūm and their lands. He wrote on the history of the Rūm, on their kings and dignitaries, their land, its roads and routes, the dates of the raids into it and campaigns against it, and the neighbouring kingdoms, the Burğan, Avars, Burgar, Slavs, Khazars and others.

Ibn Khordādbeh begins his description of the Greek Empire by quoting al-Garmī; and it looks as though his whole descrip-tion of that empire (in which he regularly uses the form Burğan for the Danube Bulgars) was taken from al-Garmī. Mas'ūdī certainly used him largely, as will be seen by comparing the above list of al-Garmī's writings with a passage [1] in which Mas'ūdī refers the reader to his lost *Book of Different Sorts of Knowledge*, telling us that in this and other books he wrote "the history of the peoples of the east and of the west, of the north and of the south, such as the Indians, the Chinese, the Turks, the Khazars, the Alans, the peoples who dwell in the Caucasus, such as the Lesghians, those who dwell in the neigh-bourhood of Bāb-el-Abwāb and not far from that mountain, such as the Alans, the Serīr, the Khazars, the Georgians, the Abasgians, the Senarieh, the Kašāk, the Kāšah, etc., *then the*

---

[1] *Livre d'Avertissement*, p. 249.

Avars, the Burǧan, the Rūs, the Burgar, the Franks, the Slavs,
etc."

Mas'ūdī is here obviously enumerating various accounts
which he has drawn from various sources, as the repetitions
show; and his last sentence (that which I have italicised; it is
clearly distinguishable, grammatically, from the preceding lists)
is, despite the minor variations, unmistakably identical with
the list which he attributes to al-Garmī. We thus not only learn
the approximate scope of al-Garmī's work, but we see that
Mas'ūdī incorporated it, probably with few alterations, in his
Book of Different Sorts of Knowledge.

Al-Bekrī might, of course, have taken his account of the
Burǧan direct from al-Garmī; but since he uses Mas'ūdī in
other parts of his work, and since Mas'ūdī was much the more
popular author of the two, it seems far more likely that al-Bekrī
knew al-Garmī only at second-hand.

It would be a fascinating task to try to reconstruct al-Garmī's
lost work. In one instance, I believe that this can be done.
Abulfēdā has the following curious passage:

Burǧan. A city of the sixth climate. According to Ibn Said, it is
the name of the capital of the people of Burǧan, a nation formerly
remarkable for their courage, and afterwards vanquished and exter-
minated by the Germans, so that today there exists no more even a
remnant of it, not so much as a trace.[1]

Now, this description is totally inapplicable to the Danube
Bulgars who were never vanquished by the Germans, and never
disappeared so completely as would seem indicated here. On
the other hand, it is exactly true of the Avars, and is strongly
reminiscent of their dreadful fall, which was so spectacular that
the Russian Chronicle wrote: "God smote them, they all died,
not one of them remains. Hence there came a proverb, still
current among Russians in our day: 'They perished like the
Obri, of whom not a trace remained'".[2] It may be true, as
Šafařik argued[3], that the "visitation of God" upon the Avars
really referred to an outbreak of plague among them; but their

---

1 Aboulfeda, ed. Reinaud, II, 313.
2 "Nestor", I, 10.
3 *Slavische Alterthümer*, II, 59.

destruction at the hands of the Franks was no less complete, and undoubtedly became proverbial (cf. the story preserved by Suidas, of how Khan Krum made enquiries of the surviving Avars, how they came to have fallen so low from their former greatness).

It therefore seems as though we had here al-Garmī's description of the Avars, attributed erroneously by Ibn Said to the Bulgars.

For the rest, Marquart persists in attributing almost the whole of Ibn Rusta's and Gardēzī's report to al-Garmī;[1] but this convenient suggestion is not tenable. For we have seen that Mas'ūdī made very extensive use of al-Garmī, whereas the curious but important fact is that Mas'ūdī's extant works contain not so much as a hint that he was acquainted with any portion of our report. The same objection applies to the suggestion that Ibn Khordādbeh might have taken over the report. Further, al-Garmī's lists contain no mention of either the Petchenegs or the Burtās. Finally, al-Garmī is not mentioned in Ibn Rusta's list of sources.

It will not be possible to identify any more of al-Garmī's work with any certainty. Probably there are many echoes of it in the *Livre d'Avertissement*, and in the *Abrégé des Merveilles*. In the latter work, the last part of the section on the Turks describes the Khazars, as the reference to Judaism shows. This may be al-Garmī's description of that nation. Possibly most or all of the section on the Slavs, in the same chapter, also comes from him; and he may well have a hand in Mas'ūdī's description of the Burgar, to which, however, much later material has been added from Ibn Fozlān and elsewhere. A really thorough investigation of the chapter in the *Abrégé* might well repay some scholar's trouble.

1 *Streifzüge*, p. xxxii.

EXCURSUS II

Magna Hungaria

THE story of the travels of Hungarian friars in search of what was imagined to be the original home of their nation is a very romantic one; but exaggerated conclusions must not be drawn from it.

Although the Magyars are interested to a quite extraordinary degree in genealogies, national and personal alike, it does not appear as though they were so much as aware of, much less interested in, any relatives of theirs in the Urals before the twelfth century. Even their correspondence with the Sevordik, noted by Constantine, must have died away soon after he wrote; for nothing more is ever heard of it.

It is only towards the close of the twelfth century that the idea of a "Greater Hungary" in the East begins to appear. So Godfrey of Viterbo (1133–1196/8) has a note *ad ann.* 1185: "Hungarorum regne duo esse legimus, unum antiquum apud Meotidas palus in finibus Asiae et Europae et alterum quasi novum a primo regno in Pannonia derivatur, quam Pannoniam nonnulli novam Ungariam vocant. Ungari etiam Huni sunt appellati".

Vincent de Beauvais, a little later, writes: "Hungaria duplex est secundum Orosium. Maior quidem est in ulteriore Syria (!) ultra maeotides palus, a quo Hunni venationis gratia primitus exeuntes" etc., etc.

These quotations betray quite clearly their origin; it was not Hungarian national tradition, which had preserved practically nothing but the name of Etel-köz; it was the pseudo-learned belief, now become current, and accepted by the Magyars themselves, of their identity with the Huns. That the report happened to be true of the Magyars also was pure coincidence, owing to the fact that both nations came to Europe from the Palus Maiotis.

But although the idea of a "Greater Hunland" in the East was thus now become current, there is nothing in Orosius, or his imitators, to suggest that it was still inhabited by Huns,

Christian or pagan. If, then, this belief arose in Hungary about the '30's of the thirteenth century, we must look for a further explanation.

There is one most obvious source, from which the rumour undoubtedly sprang; the Cumans.

The real nature of the Cuman power has never yet been worked out in detail.[1] I hope in a later essay to deal with it more fully; but I will remark here that the centre of it remained, till the very last, in the area known as the Dešt Qypčaq, viz. the Don-Volga steppe. There were certain periods during which the Cumans pressed further west; notably was this the case during the years 1080–1103, not long after the first arrival of the Cumans within European ken. But after Vladimir Mono-mach's great victories, the flood ebbed back eastward again, and henceforward the Cumans were for a long period no more than occasional visitors to the frontiers of Hungary.

The establishment of the second Bulgar (Bulgaro-Vlach) Empire in 1186 brought them further west again; and it was shortly after this date that Hungary began to take a more active interest in her Eastern frontier. In the year 1211 Andrew II granted the Teutonic Knights the Burzenland, with permission to fortify it and defend it against Cuman incursions.[2]

Immediately after this, attempts were made to convert the Cumans to Christianity. An "Episcopus Cumanorum" appears as early as 1217.[3] The Teutonic knights and other settlers were pushing their conquests down into the plains beyond the mountains;[4] in 1229 the conversion of "no small multitude of Cumans" is reported.[5] In 1233 Bela, later Bela IV of Hungary, but then Crown Prince, reckons among his titles that of Cumania.[6]

Like the Cossacks six hundred years later, the Cumans must

1 Professor Bruce Boswell's article in the *Slavonic Review*, July 1927 ("The Kipchak Turks"), has no fault except brevity; but it does not go into detail.
2 The documents relating to the Cumans are printed in various collections, but I have used here the convenient *Documente Privitóre la Istoria Romanilor*, ed. Densusianu, vol. 1 (Bucharest, 1887). The original grant to the Teutonic Knights is no. XLI in Densusianu's collection.
3 Densusianu, no. XLV.
4 *Ibid.* nos. LX, LXIII, etc.—references to "terra transalpina".
5 *Ibid.* no. LXXXVI.   6 *Ibid.* no. XCIX.

have addressed the Magyars as Baškirs, and brought with them vague tidings of cousins (that is, of the real Baškirs) dwelling far to the east. They cannot, however, have been lucid in their explanations, as we see from the most interesting document which records the first journey undertaken in search of these distant relatives.[1]

This document begins with the statement that "it was found in the Deeds of the Christian Hungarians that there was another Ungaria Maior, whence the Seven Chieftains had issued". Reading this, the Hungarian Preaching Friars, "pitying the pagan situation" of the other Magyars, sent out four Preaching Friars to find and convert them. They knew that the other Hungary was somewhere in the East; but they knew nothing more exact. The four friars searched for over two years, but without success; only one of them, a certain Otto, talked with some "of that tongue" who told him where they were to be found; but he did not enter their land, but returned to Hungary and died a week later.

A second group of four then set out "cum ducatu et expensis domini Bele nunc Regis Ungarie";[2] they travelled through Bulgaria to Constantinople; thence by boat to Matrica (Taman) and thence to Alania. Here two returned home; the other two, after a long wait to find guides, the whole country being afraid of the Mongols, at last made their way across the steppe to the "terram Saracenorum que vocatur Vela in civitatem Bundam". Here they were not taken into any house, but were kindly received by the prince "because both the prince of that district and the people say commonly that they are soon to become Christians and be subjected to the Church of Rome". Here one of the monks died, but the survivor, Julian, attached himself to a Mahomedan merchant who was going to Magna Bulgaria. Arriving there, he found the same rumour about approaching conversion to Rome: "sic enim a suis sacerdotibus audiverunt". In "one great city of this province, whence it is said that 50,000 warriors can issue", he found a Hungarian woman, who directed

---

1 Printed in Theiner, *Mon. Hist. Hung.* I, 151; Fejer, *Codex Diplomaticus*, IV, 1, p. 50; Densusianu, no. CXVIII, etc.
2 Bela IV ascended the throne in 1235.

him. Two (or ten) days (the readings vary) away he found the
"Hungarians" "juxta flumen Ethyl".

The "Hungarians" received him with pleasure, conducted
him "per domos et villas eorum" and listened to all he had to
say, "quia omnino habent Ungaricum ydioma, et intelligebant
eum, et ipse eos". These "Hungarians" are described as savage
pagans; "sicut bestie vivunt; terras non colunt"; they had been
attacked by the Mongols, but not conquered; they had, in fact,
beaten them off in the first encounter, after which the two
nations had joined hands, and "together totally devastated
fifteen kingdoms". Here Julian found a man who told him that
the Mongols were near at hand, and proposed to invade
"Alemaniam", but were waiting for an army to return from
Persia. The friar was invited to stay, but decided to return;
firstly, because if the "regne Paganorum" and Russians heard
that the "Hungarians" were to become Catholics, they would
block the roads for fear the two Hungarian nations should
conquer them all; secondly, because he did not want to die
before passing on his information. He therefore returned
through the country of the Mordvinians. These were pagans,
but had sent to the Prince of Vladimir ("ad ducem Magne
Laudamerie") asking for baptism; but he had answered: "that
is not my job, but the Pope's; for the time is near when we shall
all have to adopt the Roman faith and become obedient to
Rome". Julian arrived home on December 27th.

This ingenuous little narrative was subjected to a most
destructive criticism by Professor Vambéry,[1] who came to the
conclusion that it was simply a romantic forgery. I am bound
to say that I find his arguments, from first to last, inconclusive.
As they are partly based on historical reasoning, it may be well
to summarise, extremely shortly, the history of the Mongol
operations on the Volga.

The Mongol war with the Khwārism Shah broke out in 1218.
Džordžan (Urghendj) fell about the end of 1220. Džuči,
Chinghiz Khan's eldest son, quarrelled with his brothers over
the siege of Džordžan, and established himself to the north of
the Aral Sea. He had been ordered to invade the country of the

1 *Der Ursprung der Magyaren*, pp. 454 ff.

Cumans, but did not do so,[1] and this may partly have been due to the fact that Chinghiz Khan only gave him 4000 Mongol troops with which to rule his vast appanage. It is said, however, the local tribes voluntarily submitted to him;[2] but these certainly did not include the Qypčaq on the Volga, nor the Bulgars.

In 1222 or 1223, however, another force under the famous general Subutai, who had been operating in Georgia, crossed the Caucasus from the south and defeated the Cumans, over-running their territory as far as their port Soudaq, in the Crimea. The Cumans, having appealed to the Russians for help, the latter marched out against the Mongols, but suffered a devastating defeat on the Kalka (probably in June 1223). At the end of 1223 Subutai's troops attacked Bolgar on the Kama, but were severely defeated.[3] They then retired via Saqsīn on the lower Volga,[4] and "went to join Chinghiz Khan". How far Džuči co-operated in these movements is obscure. I can find no evidence that he was concerned in them at all, although he may have sent troops to help Subutai.[5] It is certain, however, that, the raids over, the Mongols disappeared as suddenly as they came.

1 d'Ohsson, *Histoire des Mongoles* (Amsterdam, 1852), I, 353, 447.

2 Abulghazi, a late epitomiser of Rešid-ed-din, *A General History of the Turks, Mongols and Tatars* (London, MDCCXXX, I, 143), says that Džuči "retired into Dešt Qypčaq, where he was received with open arms by the inhabitants, who, becoming acquainted with his merit, voluntarily submitted to his obedience". Dešt Qypčaq, for the historians of the Mongol invasion, was taken as covering the whole area from the Don to the Aral Sea (the later Empire of the Qypčaq horde).

3 See Marquart, *Komanen*, p. 145, who points out that d'Ohsson has mistranslated Ibn el-Athir at this point, making a Mongol victory out of their defeat by the Bulgars.

4 Saqsīn is described by al-Bakouwy as "a great city of the land of the Khazars". It was an important trading centre, afterwards destroyed. It was on the Volga; but its exact site is unknown.

5 I can find no evidence for Wolf's statements regarding Džuči's co-operation (*Geschichte der Mongolen und Tataren*, Breslau, 1872, p. 101). He is perhaps misreading the Tarikh Džihankušai (d'Ohsson, I, 446–7), which says that Subutai's troops, after passing Derbend, "went to join the troops of Džuči in the Qypčaq steppe". But this refers to their movements *after* the defeat at Bolgar, which the Tarikh passes over. In any case, according to the Chinese biography of Subutai, the attack on the Russians was followed by one on the Kangli, north of the Aral Sea, which looks as though Džuči at that time had been further east still. Cf. Bretschneider, *Mediaeval Researches* (London, 1888), I, 298–9.

There was no more serious fighting in the west for some years. It appears that in 1229 Ogotai sent an army against the Qypčaq, Bolgar and Saqsīn, but obviously without great success.[1] The Russian annals report that in that year certain Saqsīn and Cumans, fleeing from the Mongols, took refuge in Bolgar.[2] At the same time, news arrived that the Bolgars had been defeated on the Ural. It appears, however, that they were driven back across the Ural in 1234.[3]

In 1235, however, a great effort was made to conquer the "As (Alans), Bulgar, Qypčaq and Rūs". The army moved forward very slowly, gathering in reinforcements as it went, and must have crossed the Ural River in 1236. The Mahomedan writers say that after marching the whole summer, they arrived in the autumn at the horde of the sons of Džuči, not far from Bolgar.[4] In the winter Subutai was detached to take Bolgar, and he did this, massacring the inhabitants or dragging them away into slavery.

The dates of these events are fixed with some certainty by the Russian annals, which say that Batu, the Commander-in-Chief, wintered near the Volga in 1236/7, while Bolgar was destroyed in the autumn of 1237.[5]

Simultaneously with the attack on Bolgar, another force on the lower Volga defeated a Cuman chief named Pačman, after a stubborn resistance.[6]

In the same year (the summer of 1237) the centre of the army attacked the "Bokšas and the Burtās".[7] The fighting with these tribes cannot have been severe. They had long been at enmity with the Russians, particularly the principalities of Vladimir-Susdal, to which some of them were tributary.[8] They appear to have welcomed the Mongols and assisted them readily. They acted as guides to the Mongol army when it advanced into Russia, and even accompanied the army (though probably unwillingly enough) as far as Germany.[9]

---

1 d'Ohsson, II, 15, quoting the Tarikh Džihankušai.
2 Karamsin, *Histoire de Russie*, tr. St Thomas et Jauffre (Paris, 1819), III, 335.
3 Wolff, *op. cit.* p. 124.   4 d'Ohsson, II, 699.   5 Karamsin, *loc. cit.*
6 d'Ohsson, II, 623; Bretschneider, II, 311–12.   7 d'Ohsson, *loc. cit.*
8 Karamsin, III, 333.   9 Rubruquis in Densusianu, p. 296.

From this short sketch, it will be seen that there is nothing whatever impossible, historically speaking, in "brother Julian's" letter. There is indeed no actual evidence that Batu's army was reinforced by troops from Persia; but there is also no reason to suppose the contrary, as desultory fighting had gone on in that region ever since it revolted on the death of Chinghiz Khan.[1] Nor are the details of the friars' alleged journey impossible, nor even improbable, as Vambéry maintains. They are, however, admittedly, extremely confused.

Further, very strong confirmation of the general authenticity of the document is found in the report of Rubruquis, who made his famous journey to the Mongol court in 1254.

Rubruquis has the following passage:[2]

Postquam iveramus duodecim dies ab Etilia [the Volga], invenimus magnum flumen, quod vocatur Iagas [the Ural] et venit ab Aquilone de terra Pascatir, descendens in praedictum mare [the Caspian]. Idioma Pascatir et Hungarorum idem est; et sunt pastores sine civitate aliqua. Et continguatur majori Bulgariae ab occidente. Ab illa terra versus orientem in latere illo aquilonari, non est amplius aliqua civitas. Unde Bulgaria maior est ultima regio habens civitatem. De illa regione Pascatir exierunt Huni, qui postea sunt dicti Hungari. ...Hoc quod dixi de terra Pascatir, scio per fratres Praedicatores, qui iverunt illuc ante adventum Tartarorum.

It is surely impossible to doubt, without prejudice, that Rubruquis is here echoing the very words of "brother Julian's" report, which is thus proved to be in any case anterior to 1254. There is further internal evidence for the approximate date of its composition, such as the use of the expression "Bulgaria Assani" for Bulgaria—a contemporary appellation[3] which afterwards fell into desuetude.

Brother Julian's journey, then, was actually undertaken; and the date of his return from it was probably the end of 1236. It is only when we come to look into certain details of the report, that we find that this pious friar was no reliable reporter. He was, to put it bluntly, a blatant liar.

Patent lies of the worst type are those which describe the pagans of "Vela" and the Bulgars as expecting conversion to

1 Wolff, pp. 121–2.   2 Densusianu, p. 273.
3 Cf. Densusianu, nos. cxxvii, cxxxii, cxxxiii, etc.

Christianity. As regards the latter, the remark of Rubruquis may be quoted: "I wonder what devil brought the law of Mahomet to Great Bulgaria.... These Bulgarians are the worst Saracens (i.e. Mahomedans), and adhere more strongly to the law of Mahomet than any others".[1]

Equally absurd is the remark attributed to the Duke of Vladimir; it is, moreover, in the flattest contradiction to the rest of the report, as also to the second missionary letter, which will be discussed below.

This being so, we must look with all the greater suspicion on the friar's remarks regarding the Hungarians themselves, for here if anywhere his enthusiasm would be likely to betray him. It may, I think, be accepted that he actually reached a nation which he recognised as his brothers; but one may well ask how far his account of them is accurate, and even what nation it was.

It has been truly remarked, by the great and authoritative Hungarian scholar who has dealt most recently with this problem,[2] that neither the first, nor the second letter of the Hungarian friars identifies "Maior Hungaria" with the land of the Baškirs. Gombocz' own belief is my own, that a "first frontier of the Magyars" actually existed in the ninth century near Bolgar; and he appears to think it possible that the two groups of Magyars might have understood each other, had the separation been thus one of a few centuries only. He rejects the identification of the Magyars with the Baškirs altogether.

Other writers again believe that the nation with whom Julian spoke were not Baškirs, but Voguls, who appear still to have been living on the western or the southern slopes of the Urals in the thirteenth century.[3]

M. Németh, as I mentioned previously, identifies the Magyars with the Baškirs, adducing what seem to me to be very cogent arguments.

1 Densusianu, p. 271.

2 Professor Gombocz, "A Magyar öshaza és a nemzeta hagyomany", in the Nyelvtudományi Közkmények, XLV, 129–94; XLVI, 1–33; CLVII, 168–93. The second part is specially devoted to the "Magna Hungaria" question.

3 Cf. E. de Moór's review of Gombocz' work in the U.Ĵ. VII, Heft 3/4, pp. 442–9. Reference is made here to A. Kannisto, "Ueber die früheren Wohngebiete der Wogulen", Finnisch-Ugrische Forschungen, XVIII, 57–89.

Writing as a historian only, I venture modestly to agree with Professor Németh.

It is true that Julian's letters do not identify Magna Hungaria with Baškiria. The "gesta Hungarorum" which Julian quotes at the beginning of his little essay are undoubtedly either the chronicle of the "Anonymus", or an archetype of the latter; for Julian's whole opening paragraph is full of echoes of the Anonymus which do not recur in the other versions of the Hungarian Chronicle, as a comparison of the texts, however brief, will show. It is interesting to note, however, that the Anonymus neither mentions a "Maior Hungaria" at all, nor does he indicate by so much as a word the existence of relatives of the Magyars on the east.

For part of his information the friar must therefore have been indebted to more general works of geography (a modernised version of Orosius?), but the continued existence of Greater Hungarians he could not have learned from such works, but rather, as I pointed out above, from the Cumans, who had first come into close contact with the Magyars only a few years before he started on his mission.

There is, indeed, another possibility: the news might have come through Russian sources, and might in that case refer to the inhabitants of what the Russians called "Yugria", who seem to have been the Voguls and Ostjaks. This was certainly the origin of the later rumours to which reference will be made below; but I see strong objections to it in the present instance. Setting aside the coincidence of the journey's having been undertaken immediately after the Hungarians and Cumans had come into intimate relations, we have the quite undeniable fact that "Magna Hungaria" was identified with the country of the Baškirs immediately after the friars' journey, and on the strength of it.

Rubruquis' testimony has already been quoted; but even before Rubruquis wrote, the very first of the western emissaries to the Mongol court[1]—Plan Carpini—makes precisely the same definition. In his history of the Mongols, Plan Carpini writes of

---

[1] Plan Carpini travelled in 1245–7. On his return he composed a "history of the Mongols" and a narrative of his journey.

the Mongols (it may be remarked, inaccurately): "Inde (*sc.* ex Hungaria et Polonia) revertentes venerunt (*sc.* Tartari) in terram Morduanorum. Qui sunt pagani. Et eos bello devicerunt. Inde procedentes contra billeros id est bulgariam magnam et ipsam destruxerunt omnino. Inde procedentes aquilonem adhuc contra bosarcos[1] id est ungariam magnam et eos etiam devinxerunt".[2]

In his description of his journey he has: "Comania vero habet ad aquilonem immediate post rusciam id est magnam bulgariam bascarcos porossitos samacedos";[3] while his companion, Brother Benedict, in the corresponding passage has: "Fratres vero euntes per comaniam...in Ruscia vero antea habuerunt Morduanos a sinistriis hii sunt pagani et habent caput retro rasum pro majore parte. Postea Syleros (= Byleros) et hii sunt pagani postea Bascardos qui sunt antiqui Hungari".[4]

Similarly Ascelinus, who travelled in 1246, has: "Haec Comania ab aquilone immediate post Russiam habet Morduynos, Byleros id est magnam Bulgariam, Bastarcos, id est magnam Hungariam".[5]

All these accounts are obviously drawn from a single geographical description, which must have been compiled not later than 1247, and certainly identifies the Baškirs with "Magna Hungaria".

Again, in his list of nations conquered by the Mongols, Plan Carpini has: "Byleri, magna Bulgaria, Baschare, magna Hungaria".[6]

Finally the identification found its way into the Hungarian national Chronicle, which accepted it without further question; for Kezai's Barsacia, and the other variants in the remaining versions of the Chronicle, are indubitably due to this identification.

Next there comes the question whether the description in Julian's narrative is or is not applicable to the Baškirs.

In a general fashion—historically speaking—it certainly is so

---

1 Variae lectiones are: bosarcos, baschare, bascart, biscart, baschart, lyashyait.
2 Densusianu, p. 233; ed. Pullé, p. 83.
3 Densusianu, p. 236; Pullé, p. 111. 4 Pullé, pp. 122–3.
5 Densusianu, p. 234. 6 *Ibid.* p. 236.

applicable. We have not, as a matter of fact, any direct evidence of how the Baškirs fared in their struggle with the Mongols. Some writers of an older generation imagined themselves to have found such evidence (incidentally, thus grossly exaggerating the importance of the nation) in the references to "Madjars" found in some of the Chinese and similar sources for the Mongol campaigns. Thus the Yüan-ch'ao-pi-shi (in the biography of Subutai) includes the "Madjars" among the "eleven nations of the north" whom Ogotai ordered Subutai to subdue.[1] But this list was not composed from Ogotai's marching orders, but after the event, from the names of the countries actually conquered, and its Madjars are undoubtedly the Magyars of Hungary. In its more detailed account of the campaign in Hungary, the Yüan-ch'ao-pi-shi makes the Mongol army cross the Carpathians and attack "the k'ie-lieu or king of the Ma-dja-rh".[2] The name also appears in another Chinese source (the biography of K'u-o-li-ghi-sze) in an undoubted reference to Hungary.[3] Conversely, the mentions of Baškirs in the Arabic-Turkish accounts (Rešid-ed-din, Abulghazi, the Tarikh Dži-hankušai, etc., hence the accounts of Abulfēdā and Dimašqi) all without exception refer to the Magyars of Hungary, even where, in their confusion, they make two nations—Baškirs and Magyars—live side by side in the Hungarian plain.

We know that the Baškirs were given by the Mongols a seal and a flag, emblems of their national independence.[4] As it was by no means Mongol policy to waste time and blood subduing unprofitable corners of the world which could never supply them with anything beyond mercenaries, it seems more than reasonable to suppose that some at least of the Baškirs played a role very similar to that of the Mordvinians, submitting more or less readily to the Mongols, and fighting in their army. Julian's account is therefore perfectly reasonable. The initial occasion, on which they defeated the Mongols, was probably that of 1223, when the raiders were repulsed by the Bulgars. Afterwards, they submitted to Džuči and his successors.

---

1 Bretschneider, I, 300.   2 *Ibid.* I, 331.   3 *Ibid.* note 776.
4 Turanians and Pan-Turanianism (*British Admiralty Handbook*, 1920 ?), p. 188.

The "magnum flumen Etyl", two (or ten) days beyond which the Baškirs were living, has been identified with the Bjelaja.[1] It could, of course, also be the Kama, or any other large tributary of the Volga. I see little difficulty in imagining Baškirs to have been found close to Bolgar in the year 1036, when Batu's army was preparing for its great advance.

For these various reasons, it appears to me to be certain that Julian actually visited the country of the older "Inner Baškirt", our old friend the "first frontier of the Magyars". There is only one real difficulty, the language question. For under no circumstances can one imagine that the language of the two groups of Magyars was identical in the thirteenth century, or even that they were able to communicate easily with one another. Moreover, al-Kašgarī, as early as the eleventh century, definitely reckons Baškir among the Turkish dialects.[2] But here I revert to the fact previously pointed out: that as regards details, the writer (and it should be remarked that this was not Julian himself, but a certain "brother Richard" who told his story) was something more than imaginative. Nomads such as these will hardly have possessed "vicos et villas" (moreover, Rubruquis himself tells us that there were no cities east of Bulgar); it seems more than doubtful whether they really, as alleged, "knew from the stories of their ancients that the other Hungarians were descended from them"—more particularly as this was not the case.[3] Among primitive peoples, however, a very slight similarity between languages is counted by friendly optimists as identity. When travelling in Eastern Europe, in the more remote parts, I have myself often been asked to repeat a few words of English, and have then been informed that my language was "the same as German".

Julian's second letter,[4] although it also omits to identify, in so

1 See above, p. 52, for instances of the name Etyl being applied to *tributaries* of the Volga.

2 See above, p. 39.

3 See above, p. 78.

4 This letter has been preserved in two versions, which show considerable variations. One of them (H.) was printed by Baron J. Hormayr-Hörtenburg in the *Goldene Chronik von Hohenschwangau* (Munich, 1842), Part II, pp. 67 ff.; the other (D.) by B. Dudik in his *Iter Romanum* (Vienna, 1895), pp. 327 ff. They are both reproduced by Densusianu (no. CXIV, *a* and *b*).

many words, Baškiria with Magna Hungaria, seems to me to be equally incompatible with any other supposition. This letter, which is a far more coherent affair than the other, consists of a report sent by a certain Brother Julian of the Preaching Friars (commonly assumed, on grounds of general probability, to be identical with the hero of the former letter) to the Apostolic Legate in Hungary, the Bishop of Perugia.[1] He had been ordered to go to "Magna Hungaria", but when he reached "ad ultimos fines Bruscie" he learned that "Ungari pagani, et Bulgari, et regna plurima" had been destroyed by the Mongols.

A description of the Mongols then follows, together with an account of the opening of their campaigns in the West against the Khwārism Shah, who is here described as "Soldanus de Hornach" (D'Ornach).[2]

[1] The Bishop of Perugia was sent by Pope Gregory IX to Bulgaria and Constantinople to negotiate on the question of the Latin Empire (Densusianu, nos. cxix and cxxiii). He was also to carry out a mission in Hungary. When the negotiations with Asen of Bulgaria broke down, the Legate was charged with organising a crusade against him in Hungary (ibid. no. cxxv). This mission certainly lasted him through 1238 (ibid. nos. cxxvii, cxxxiii, cxxxiv).

[2] Plan Carpini, c. 5, calls the town Orna, and describes it as "nimium populosa" before its fall, and containing many Christians, Khazars, Alans, Ruthenes and others. He places it on "a great river" on which also Ianckint (Jangy-kent) stood, and names the "Altus Soldanus" as its ruler. It was thus quite undoubtedly a city of the Khwārism Shah. If Plan Carpini is right, and Ornach stood on the same river as Jangy-kent, which stands on the Syr Daria, then Ornach may be Otrar, as suggested by Bretschneider (Med. Geog. p. 134) and Rockhill (The Journey of William of Rubruck, London, Hakluyt Society, 1900, p. 14, note 1). It is, however, far more likely that the friar mixed up the Syr Daria and the Amu Daria, and that Ornas was Džordžan (Urghendj). Plan Carpini's description of the taking of Ornas agrees exactly with the Oriental accounts of the taking of Džordžan. Confusion has been introduced by the description of "Benedict the Pole" who accompanied Plan Carpini on his mission. This story is a mere variant of Plan Carpini's (let those who will believe that it was taken down from Benedict's "oral statement") and contains the remark (I quote from Rockhill's translation, pp. 34–6, not having the Latin by me): "While the friars were travelling through Cumania, they had on their right the country of the Saxi, whom we believe to be the Goths, and who are Christians, after them the Gazars, who are Christians. In this country is the rich city Ornarum (of Ornas) which was captured by the Tartars by means of inundations of water. After that the Circasses, etc." On the strength of this Frähn (Ibn Fozlän und Anderer Berichte, Petersburg, 1832, p. 162) believes Ornas to be "the ancient Tanais at the mouth of the Don". Rockhill properly rejects the suggestion, but might have pointed out that the whole mention is simply ignorantly brought in here in connection with the "Gazars, who are Christians" from Plan Carpini's own description of Christian Gazars (Khazars) living in Ornas. Practically the same story as Julian's is given by a Russian bishop at Lyons in 1245 (Examinatio facta de Tartaris apud Lug-

After this, we hear of wars against the Persians (this will have been in 1220/1), then against the Cumans (this is Subutai's expedition of 1221/3. "Inde reversi ad magnam Ungariam, de qua nostri Ungari originem habuerunt, et expugnaverunt eos quatuordecim annos, et in quintodecimo anno obtinuerunt eos, sicut ipsi pagani Ungari viva voce retulerunt."

Since Bolgar was first attacked in 1223, and fell in 1237, the dates are thus accurate enough. This is, indeed, a different story from that of the first letter, which makes the Baškirs submit voluntarily to the Mongols and join forces with them; but I suggest it to be equally accurate. The informants there were "Rutheni, Bulgari, Ungari" who had fled westward on the fall of Bolgar, a state with which the whole story is much concerned. It is easy to suppose that those Baškirs who were near Bulgaria, and were probably still tributary to them, as in the ninth century, had joined with their suzerains in opposing the Mongols, while the hordes roaming the steppe near to Džuči's camp had submitted to their new masters.

After this the Mongols turned west and subdued "quinque regna paganorum maxima", given in H. as "Faschiam, Meroviam, Regnum Bulgarorum et Wedint", which had two princes, one of whom submitted to the Mongols, while the other fled. D. has "Sasciam, Fulgarium, Wedint et Merowiam, Poydowiam, Mordanorum regnum", the last-named having the two princes. These names are rather obscure, particularly as one list appears to add up to four, the other to six.

I think, however, that D. is certainly nearer the true text, and that Merowiam, Poydaviam are to be taken as the two parts of the Mordvinian nation. We thus get Saqsīn, Bulgar, Wedint (a name which I cannot explain) and two nations of Mordvinians.

There follows a sketch of the situation at the time of writing, which is accurate for the autumn of 1238, and makes the letter a document of considerable historical value.

dunum per dominum papam, Pertz, *M.G.H.* S.S. xxviii, 474), and other echoes of it may be found in Matthew of Paris, *ad ann.* 1238–40. It seems, therefore, that Julian's story of the origin of the Mongol invasion of Khwārism was that current in Russia, and the name Ornach or Hornach was the Russian name of the city.

It seems hardly possible that the above description could apply to any other nation than the Baškirs, in the corner between the Mongols and Bolgar, and west of Saqsīn and the Mordvinians. I have thus no hesitation in identifying the "Ungari pagani" of this second letter also with the Baškirs.

D. ends with a paragraph, not found in H., to the effect that while the writer was still waiting "in curia Romana" he had been preceded by four other friars, who had reached the territory of "Sudal" and there had met certain "Ungari pagani" fleeing from the Mongols, whom they baptised in the Catholic faith. The "dux de Sudal", however, not wishing them to come under Rome, expelled the friars, who then "declinaverunt ad civitatem Recessue" in the hope of reaching, either "Magna Hungaria" or the "Morducani", or the Mongols themselves. Two of them stopped there; the other two went on and reached the Mordvinians, but on the very day on which their chief surrendered to the Mongols, as related previously (a remark which shows that the list in D., giving the Mordvinians the two princes, is the correct one). The other two, after waiting for some time, sent a messenger to find out what had happened to their comrades; but he was killed by the Mordvinians.

It is, I think, to Julian's second mission that the note of Albert de Trois-Fontaines refers, when he writes *ad ann.* 1237 that the rumour was current that the Mongols proposed to attack "Cumania and Hungary". "To see whether this was true, four preaching friars were sent from Hungary, who went as far as Old Hungary" (a natural mistake and exaggeration) "a hundred days' journey. Returning they announced that the Mongols had now occupied and subjected Old Hungary."

On the other hand, when a bishop of Hungary writes to a colleague in 1241 that it is impossible to get certain information about the Mongols, because their advance guard of Mordvinians kill all who approach them: "and I think they killed the Preaching and Minorite Friars and other messengers sent by the king of Hungary to explore"[1]—I believe him to be referring to the fate of the four friars mentioned in Julian's second letter,

1 Densusianu, no. CLIX.

and to have derived his information (not necessarily directly, of course) precisely from that letter.

It is interesting to note that Pope Innocent IV, in 1253, includes "Ungari Maioris Ungarie" among the pagan nations among which the Preaching Friars were authorised to work.[1] They had been absent from a similar list compiled in 1245[2] and were therefore taken under the Papal wing officially only on the occasion of the more serious attempts made by the Papal See, a few years after the invasion, to establish contact with the Mongols.[3] Pope Michael IV has a further reference to the missions of both Minorites and Dominicans among "the most remote peoples", including both the Mongols themselves and the "Ungari Maioris Ungarie". John XII in 1329 praises the incorruptible faith of the "Ungari Asiatici"; and even as late as 1369 we read of a mission to the "Scythians of Greater Hungary".[4]

It is my own view that the Magna Hungaria story ought to be disassociated altogether from the later rumours, which began to be current, a couple of hundred years later, of a Hungarian-speaking nation in the East. The first reference to these later rumours (so far as I know) appears in the works of Pope Aeneas Sylvius, who wrote in his Cosmography (which appeared in 1458) that he had spoken to a native of Verona, who had penetrated via Poland and Lithuania to the sources of the Don, and not far beyond them had found a certain race of rude idolaters speaking the same language as the Magyars. He had hoped to convert these to the Roman faith, with the help of Franciscan monks; but had been thwarted by the Prince of Moscow.[5]

---

1 Densusianu, no. CXCVIII.   2 *Ibid*. no. CLXXII.

3 The list of 1253 includes "Tartari" as well as "Christiani captivatori apud Tartaros".

4 For these quotations, see Gombocz, *op. cit.* XLVI, p. 23.

5 *Aenaeae Sylviae opera quae extant omnia*, Basiliae, 1751, p. 303: "Nos hominem allocuti sumus, qui per Poloniam ad Litanum ad fontes Tanais pervenisse se affirmavit, easque transcendisse et omnem illam barbariae borealem perscrutatum". *Ibid*. pp. 307–8: "Noster Veronensis, quem supra diximus ad ortum Tanais pervenisse, retulit populos in Asiatica Scythia, non longe a Tanai sedes habere, rudes homines et idolorum cultores, quorum eadem lingua sit cum Hungaris Pannoniam incolentibus, voluisseque cum

This information is quoted by Thuroczy[1] and by Bonfinius, who tells us that Matthias Corvinus had heard the same story from Russian merchants (a Sarmaticis quibusdam mercatoribus) and sent "legates and explorers" to find the relatives of the Magyars (cognatum gentem) and to bring them back to settle in the depopulated plains of Hungary. He does not, however, appear to have achieved his purpose, his death thwarting his intentions.

A whole series of later writers reproduce a story to much the same effect.[2] The most interesting of them is Herberstein, who, when in Moscow in the early sixteenth century, made an attempt to check the accuracy of the rumours. Having mentioned two "Domini knezi Juhorski" subject to the Grand Duke of Moscow, he goes on to say that this "Ugria" was the original home of the Huns, and its inhabitants were said still to speak the same language as the Magyars; but despite diligent search, he found no one from there with whom his servant, who knew Magyar, could converse.[3]

The chief source of these rumours seems, then, to have been reports of Russian fur-traders, who had visited "Ugria" in the pursuit of their calling, and had been struck by the similarity between the language spoken by the natives of that district, and by the Magyars.

I willingly accept the opinion of the experts that these were Voguls.[4] I cannot, however, see any connection between these

plerisque sacrarum literarum professoribus, viris religiosis, et ex ordine beati Francisci, qui linguam illam nossent, eo proficisci, et sanctum Christi evangelium praedicare; sed prohibitum a domino, quem de Mosca vocavit, qui cum esset Graeca perfidia maculatus, aegre ferebat Asiaticos Hungaros Latinae conjugi ecclesiae, et nostris imbui ritibus". On the basis of this information, Aeneas Sylvius makes up his own note: "Extat adhuc non longe ab ortu Tanais altera Hungaria, nostrae hujus de qua sermo est mater, lingue et moribus pene similis, quamvis nostra civilior est et Christi cultrix, illa ritu barbarico vivens servat idolis".

1 *Chronica*, I, 9.

2 See the quotations adduced by Gombocz, *op. cit.* CLVIII.

3 "Haec est Juharia ex qua olim Hungari progressi, Pannoniam occupaverunt, Attilaque duce multas Europe provincias debellarunt....Aiunt Juharos in hunc diem eodem cum Hungaris idiomate uti, quod an verum sit, nescio. Nam utsi diligentior inquisiveram, neminem tamen ejus regionis hominem habere potui, quocum famulus meus, linguae Hungaricae peritus, colloqui potuisset."

4 Cf. Moór, *op. cit.* p. 448. It may be pointed out that the "Ugrians" of the far north-east were from earliest times connected with the fur-trade; the Burtäs also; but not the Baškirs—at any rate, not the Baškirs of the steppe.

rumours and the earlier tale of "Magna Hungaria". Neither Aeneas Sylvius nor the very learned Thuroczy (nor any other of these writers) makes any reference to the old missions and explorations; it would appear as if the memory of them had quite died out, after leaving only in the Hungarian Chronicle the tell-tale reference to "Bascardia".

To sum up my conclusions:

Whether the whole of the Baškir nation was originally identical with that of the Magyars, as maintained by M. Németh, or not, I should not venture to say. In any case, I am convinced that a portion of the Magyar nation was living in the ninth century in the situation described in the old report. These are identical with the "Inner Baškirs" of al-Balḥi's itinerary, and with the Baškirs of Ibn Fozlān's report. The Oriental writers habitually described the Magyars as Baškirs, either because the two nations were identical, or, if the original Baškirs were not identical with these Magyars (if, in other words, there was any racial distinction between the Inner and the Outer Baškirs), because the two were closely akin, and the Magyars received the name of the more numerous and important nation. Hence the name was transferred to the Magyars of Hungary.

In the early thirteenth century the Cumans brought to Hungary news of other "Baškirs" living in the east. The Magyars, identifying themselves with the Huns, believed these to be remnants living in the country from which the Huns had come. Their missionaries sought, and one of them found, Magyar-Baškirs, descendants of the "first frontier of the Magyars", with whom he was able to make himself understood. The identity of the Baškirs with the old Hungarians was at once assumed, and the name "Magna Hungaria" was applied to the land of the Baškirs, and attempts made to Christianise it. These attempts lasted only a short time, and were presently forgotten. The Magyar-Baškirs, under Turco-Tatar admixture, lost the remainder of their Finno-Ugrian characteristics.

Two centuries later, news began to reach the Western world of Ugrians (Voguls, etc.) speaking a language akin to Magyar. These rumours, which were based on fact, and came mainly through Russian traders in furs, were unconnected with the previous story of "Magna Hungaria".

The Etymology of the Term Σάβαρτοι ἄσφαλοι

BOTH Professor Marquart[1] and Professor Darkó[2] interpret the Σάβαρτοι ἄσφαλοι as a composite Arabic term, the form Σάβαρτοι betraying the Arabic origin, as opposed to the Σεβόρτιοι of the De Ceremoniis (the Armenian form).

If the word Σάβαρτοι is an Arabic form, then ἄσφαλοι must be an Arabic form also; and Marquart explains it as a rendering of the Arabic أسْفَلُ, asfalu—lower—southernmost, by contrast with the Upper Black Ugri, i.e. the rest of the Magyar nation.

Against this, Darkó objects: firstly, when Constantine wrote, the remaining Magyars were already established in their present homes, so that we should look for a distinction, not between north and south, but between east and west. And this, indeed, is the distinction actually made by Constantine himself, at the end of c. 38 where the Magyars driven πρὸς τὸ δυτικὸν μέρος are described as corresponding with those who live πρὸς τὴν ἀνατολήν.

Secondly, according to Professor Darkó, the word asfalu could not be used to describe "lower" on the map, but only either "miserable, despicable"—a meaning which he rightly rejects—or "living at a lower altitude", in the plains; which, as he points out, is precisely what the Caucasian Magyars were not. He therefore offers for the source of "ἄσφαλοι" aswadu = black, being in this case an interpretation of the Sev, either by the Arabs in general, or by Constantine's informant in particular.

The objections which Darkó raises to Marquart's theories seem sound; but against his own theory must be put forward the fact that, whereas asfalu could be transliterated into Greek as ἄσφαλοι, aswadu could not; moreover the tautology seems unlikely.

Further, as M. Fehér[3] points out, the Arabic and Persian form required to translate the Armenian Sev- would not be

---

1 Streifzüge, pp. 39 ff.
2 Darkó, "Die auf die Ungarn bezüglichen Volksnamen der Byzantiner", B.Z. XXI (1912), pp. 422 ff.
3 Beziehungen, pp. 57 ff.

Σαβ- but Σιαβ-. Now, the forms which we actually get are the following:

Al-Balāḍurī	Sāwardiyya
Istachrī	Siyāwardiyya
Mas'ūdī	Siyāwardiyya
Dimašqi	Sāwardiyya[1]

Thus although the tenth-century writers Mas'ūdī and Istachrī seem to use the translation of *Sev-* = black, the oldest and most valuable source, Balāḍurī,[2] who is supported by the later writer Dimašqi, gives us the non-Arabic (Persian) for *Saw*.[3]

But if Σάβαρτοι is not an Arabic form, there is no reason to make ἄσφαλοι an Arabic form either; and the only reasonable explanation of the word is to regard it, in fact, as a low Greek variant of ἀσφαλεῖς—an *epitheton ornans*.

This leaves the etymology of Σάβαρτοι unexplained. There seem to be two possible explanations. The first, that of Marquart, sees in the word the Armenian adjective *Sev* (Persian *Siav*) + Ugri (Ugrians), the form showing "in comparison with the Slavonic 'Ugri' the well-known Alanic or Ossetic consonantal displacement".

The "Black Ugri" make a brief appearance in the Russian Chronicle, where it is usually assumed that the reference is to the Magyars, as opposed to the White Ugri, or Khazars.[4] The latter identification seems, however, to be more than doubtful, in view of the fact that the Khazars were almost certainly not Ugrians at all, but Turks; besides which, the Russian Chronicle was well acquainted with the Khazars, to whom it refers repeatedly by name. It is still more risky—indeed, totally unjustified—to go further and identify the Black Ugri with the "black" or inferior race of the Khazars mentioned by Ibn

---

1 Miss Smith has kindly verified these readings for me from the MS. She writes: "The readings in Balāḍurī and Dimašqi, which agree, are both fully vowelled, and therefore there can be no doubt of the transliteration. The readings in Istachrī and Mas'ūdī are not vowelled in the Arabic. Further, the sentence given in Istachrī is omitted in de Goeje's text, and given only in a note as inserted in one MS only".

2 He died A.D. 892.

3 It may be mentioned that the Abu el Kassim whom M. Fehér also quotes is an imaginary gentleman invented by d'Ohsson in the nineteenth century as a peg on which to hang his extracts from Mas'ūdī, etc. (*Les Peuples du Caucase*).

4 "Nestor", I, 10.

Fozlān; and that for two reasons. Firstly, the description given by this author lays stress on the *physical* darkness of the race in question, who are described as "almost like the Hindus", a description certainly never applicable at any time to the Magyars; and secondly because when Ibn Fozlān wrote, the Magyars had long since left the vicinity of Khazaria and were comfortably ensconced in their present homes.

On the other hand, there seems no reason why the Russian Chronicle should not have contrasted the Magyars as "Black Ugri" with the Ugri of Ugria, in the Urals, the name of whom at least was known to the early Russians, if they had no personal acquaintance with them. If we could take Σάβαρτοι as = Black Ugrians, we should have the great advantage of not finding ourselves forced to look for a totally new name for the Magyars, the name "Ugrian" or "Hungarian" being that under which, in one form or another, they are traditionally known to almost all their neighbours.

But this explanation encounters the great difficulty that we are unable to account for the prefix *Sav-* or *Sev-*. Both Constantine and the Armenian writers seem to make it quite clear that the full name was the national name applied by the Magyars to themselves. M. Fehér therefore explains the term by the alleged identity of the Magyars with the Savirs. This, again, is very difficult. Not only does the identity remain to be proved in more convincing fashion than has yet been effected, but it requires that the Magyars should describe the name as that borne by them in the ninth century and still remembered in the tenth. What, then, has happened to the national name "Magyar", which, as the oldest report proves, was already current for the whole nation in the early ninth century? This is a point which M. Fehér ignores.

As I do not propose here to follow the Magyars back into the fifth and sixth centuries, I leave the point open, merely mentioning the difficulties in each case. For my purpose it is enough to show that the attempts to prove an Arabic source for the name Σάβαρτοι ἄσφαλοι have failed. The name, whatever it is, is the Magyar national name, and the source for the whole story "B" in the *D.A.I.* C. 38 is a Magyar national source, as opposed to the Slavonic source of "A".

EXCURSUS IV

The Bulgaro-Greek War and the Magyar "Landnahme"

THE sources for the Bulgaro-Greek war are the following:
The Byzantine historians Leo Grammaticus,[1] Theophanis Continuator,[2] Georgius Monachus,[3] the author
described in the Bonn edition as Symeon Magister[4] and the
later chroniclers Cedrenus,[5] Zonaras,[6] etc.; passages in Leo
the Philosopher,[7] Constantine,[8] and the correspondence between
Symeon and Leo Magister relative to the return of prisoners;[9]
further the Old Slavonic "Miracles of St George",[10] the German
Annales Fuldenses[11] and the Arabic historian Tabarī.[12]

Hostilities were opened by Symeon who, taking as pretext
a commercial dispute, invaded Byzantine territory.[13] The regular
Byzantine troops were absent on a campaign against the
Saracens;[14] Leo was therefore only able to send the city guard,
under the Stratelat Krenates, against Symeon.[15] Symeon
easily defeated these troops, cut off in mockery the noses of the
Khazars who fell into his hands, ravaged Thrace and appeared
before Constantinople.

The Emperor made an attempt to avert the danger by
appealing to the religious sentiments of the recently converted

---

1 Ed. Bonn, pp. 266–9.　　　　　2 Ed. Bonn, pp. 357–9.

3 Ed. Bonn, pp. 853–5.

4 Ed. Bonn, pp. 701–3. This is not, however, Symeon's work, but only a late
and inaccurate copy of Theophanes.

5 Ed. Bonn, II, 254–6.　　　　　6 Ed. Bonn, III, 442–4.

7 Migne, *P.G.* CXI, p. 257.　　　　8 *D.A.I.* cc. 41, 50.

9 Published by Sakellion in the Δελτίον τῆς ἱστορικῆς καὶ ἐθνολογικῆς
ἑταιρείας τῆς Ἑλλάδος, T. Aʹ (Athens, 1883), pp. 380 ff.

10 Cit. Zlatarski, *Istoria na Blgarskata Država*, vol. I, part II (Sofia, 1927),
pp. 281 ff.

11 *Ad ann.* 894–6 (Pertz, *M.G.H.* I, 512).

12 Quoted by Marquart, *Streifzüge*, p. 531. The passage is also translated by
Abicht, "Der Angriff der Bulgaren auf Konstantinopel im Jahre 896",
Archiv für Slavische Philologie, XVII, 47 ff. (1895).

13 Georgius Mon. p. 853.　　　　14 Leo, *Tactica*, p. 281.

15 Georgius Mon. *l.c.*

Bulgars. This is explicitly stated only by Tabarī;[1] but plain allusions to this appeal to Christianity occur both in the narrative of the *Annales Fuldenses*, according to which the Bulgars afterwards fasted to expiate their attack on the Christians, and in the words of Leo the Philosopher, who says expressly that he sent for the Bulgars "in order that the Christian Greeks might not, if they could help it (ἑκόντες), be soiled with the blood of Christians".

The appeal must have had its effect; for Symeon undoubtedly retired beyond the Balkans. This is sufficiently proved by the fact that the subsequent narrative mentions no further fighting between Greek and Bulgarian troops, although the Greeks afterwards marched out against Symeon. Symeon also took with him, as the correspondence between him and Leo Magister shows, a number of important Byzantine prisoners.

The Greek narrative (Georgius Monachus, etc.) now goes on immediately to say that Nicetas Sclerus was sent to the Danube to hire the Magyars as allies. The Kavar version in the *D.A.I.*, however, says that the Magyars were "summoned", as though they had been further east (or north) when the mission arrived. An agreement was concluded with the Magyar chiefs Arpád and Cursan (one of whom was probably the supreme chief of the nation, the other the Gylas) and hostages were taken; Nicetas returned with these to Constantinople. Then the Emperor sent Eustathius back with the fleet to ferry the Magyars over, while Nicephorus Phocas, who had by now returned from Asia Minor, was sent at the head of the land forces "against the Bulgarians". The Emperor also sent delegates to Symeon to treat for peace. Symeon, however, on learning of the combined attack planned against him by sea and land, shut the delegates up in prison, as coming on a fraudulent errand.

Symeon appears to have sent troops to meet Phocas; for the chroniclers say that he was "busied"[2] with the Greek army when the Magyars arrived. The river had been fortified to prevent their crossing; but the Magyars, led by Liountinas, son

---

1 Tabarī says: "The tyrant of the Rūm sent word to the king of the Slavs: 'Our religion and yours is the same; why should we slay one another's men?'"
2 ἀσχολούμενος, Leo Grammaticus, 267.

of Arpád,[1] and guided by Imperial officers who took the lead in clearing away the barriers erected against them, crossed the Danube.[2] The first Bulgarian force sent against them was crushingly defeated; and dispersed into small groups which the Magyars slaughtered as they fled. Symeon rallied them and himself led them back against the enemy, but thinking better of it, retired into the fortress of Silistra.[3] The victorious Magyars then called upon the Emperor to ransom the Bulgarian prisoners which they had taken—in accordance, it must be assumed, with the terms of their treaty with the Empire. This ransom must have been one of the rewards which they had arranged to obtain. The Emperor duly sent delegates to conclude the traffic.

According to the Greek chroniclers, Symeon now requested the Emperor for peace, through the Drungarius Eustathius, the commander of the fleet which had ferried the Magyars across the Danube. The Emperor consented; despatched Leo Chaerosphactes to open up negotiations, and withdrew the army under Nicephorus, which had hitherto, apparently, remained altogether inactive. He also withdrew the fleet under Eustathius. "But Symeon did not deign to speak to Leo, but held him in restraint. And marching out against the Magyars, who had no backing of help from the Greeks, but were caught unawares, he slaughtered them all, increasing his truculence."[4] For this phrase, the continuer of Theophanes has the rather different wording that the Magyars "were not able to receive help from the Greeks".[5] After this victory, Symeon returned to the fortress of Mundraga or Mudagra, and having rid himself of the enemies on his flank, "found Leo in Mouldraga and said to him, 'I will not make peace unless I get all my prisoners'. So the

---

1 *D.A.I.* c. 40.   2 *Ibid.* c. 50.

3 Constantine, *D.A.I.* c. 50, makes Symeon suffer two heavy defeats; the Kavar story (c. 40) mentions only one. The *Miracles of St George* are explicit; the writer himself took part in the campaign. He describes the first defeat most graphically. Of the second occasion, when he tells us that Symeon rallied his forces in person, he says that "there was no disaster, because no blood was shed; and so I went to war, but returned, thank God, safe and sound".

4 George Monachus, p. 854, ἐκείνων ὀχύρωμα βοηθείας μὴ ἐχόντων παρὰ ῾Ρωμαίων, ἀλλ᾽ ἀπρονοήτων ἐαθέντων.

5 Theoph. Cont. p. 359, μὴ δυνηθέντες παρὰ ῾Ρωμαίοις βοήθειαν δέξασθαι.

Emperor agreed"[1] and Leo came to Constantinople with a Bulgarian plenipotentiary, and handed them over. Thereupon peace was concluded.

The *Annales Fuldenses*, in their account, make no mention of the purchase of the prisoners by the Greeks, of the recall of the Greek forces, or of the Greco-Bulgar negotiations. They simply tell us that Symeon was twice heavily defeated, and in their despair the Bulgars sent for advice to Symeon's aged father, Boris, who had first converted the nation to Christianity, and was now living in a monastery under the name of Michael. Boris ordered a national fast for three days, as a penance for the wrong done to the Christians. After this, the Bulgarians engaged the Magyars in a frightful battle and defeated them heavily, although themselves suffering severely.[2]

The important question now arises, where these events took place. Symeon, as we have seen, was in Silistra, on the Danube, where it bends northward to take in the Dobruja. It is much to be doubted whether the Imperial forces had ever penetrated beyond the Balkan passes; for, as we have seen, they seem to have taken no part in the fighting, and it is hardly likely that this would have been the case, had they forced the dangerous mountain passes. Moreover, Symeon's negotiations were opened up first with the commander of the fleet, and not of the army. It seems, therefore, probable that the Magyars had retired back across the Danube with their prisoners, before attempting to sell them to the Greeks, and had conducted this transaction, and their negotiations with the Greeks generally, through the medium of the fleet; for it would have been excessively dangerous to march the prisoners down by land through the Dobruja— which, after all, is not a large piece of country—with Symeon waiting on the flank, at Silistra. It is also reasonable to suppose that the Magyars had arranged to cover their retreat before looking on the campaign as concluded. If they needed the fleet

---

1 Leo Grammaticus, 268.

2 "Quo peracto, durum inierunt certamen, pugnantibus vero ambabus acerrime partibus, ad ultimum misericordia Dei victoria, quamvis cruenta, Christianis concessa est. Quis enim gentilium Avarorum strages tantis congressionibus enumerando possit exponere? Cum Bulgarorum, ad quos victoria concessit, numero 20 milia equitum caesa inveniuntur."

to take them over, they needed it to take them back also, particularly as on the return journey they would have their wounded.

The Kavars' version reproduced by Constantine also states definitely that the Magyars returned to their homes, and makes no mention of a defeat in Bulgaria.[1] It is this account which requires to be reconciled with the others at our disposal.

What was Symeon doing while the Magyars bartered his prisoners to the Greeks? Was he really only engaged in seeking the consolations of religion? Was a three days' national fast really sufficient to turn defeat into victory, in the way described by the pious *Annales Fuldenses*? Obviously he was too weak to take the field and try his fortunes once more against the same combination of enemies—the Magyars fighting, the Greek army and fleet in waiting—as had already defeated him so disastrously. But after the Greek army and navy had been withdrawn, he still played for time, prolonging the negotiations until he had first defeated the Magyars. But the constellation, as described by Georgius Monachus, etc. was still essentially the same as before, since the Magyars had defeated him without any important help from the Greeks. What, then, changed defeat into victory for Symeon?

Surely, the intervention of the Petchenegs. Symeon must have been a fool indeed had he neglected the existence of these formidable enemies of the Magyars. When we find him playing for time as he did, remaining inactive while the redemption of the prisoners was going on and afterwards delaying the Greek envoys, he must have been negotiating for the help of the Petchenegs. There can be no reasonable doubt that what caused him to break off the negotiations with Greece was the news that the help of the Petchenegs had been secured. It follows then that the double attack made upon the Magyars by the Bulgars and Petchenegs, described in c. 40 of the *D.A.I.*, is identical with the defeat of their army related by the Greek chroniclers and the *Annales Fuldenses*.

There are admittedly discrepancies between this story and

1 *D.A.I.* c. 40: καὶ ἐξελάσαντες μέχρι τῆς Πρεσθλάβου διῆλθον ἀποκλείσαντος αὐτὸν εἰς τὸ κάστρον τὸ λεγόμενον Μουνδράγα, καὶ εἰς ἰδίαν χώραν ὑπέστρεψαν

that of the Kavars as given in c. 40; but on any interpretation of that chapter certain inaccuracies must be faced. For this chapter makes no mention at all of any defeat of the Magyar army by Symeon, such as we know to have occurred. It simply tells us that the Magyars, on invitation from the Emperor, "made war upon Symeon, and trounced him soundly, and came as far as Preslav, and shut him up in the fortress called Mundraga, and returned home". It cannot, therefore, be interpreted otherwise than as a highly euphemistic description, coloured by national pride. And if the Kavar account seems to make the defeat of the Magyars take place after the definitive conclusion of peace between Symeon and the Empire, this, too, need not be taken too literally. The fact that negotiations had begun, and the Greek army and fleet withdrawn so that it was no longer able to help the Magyars, is quite near enough for their phrase εἰρηνεύεσθαι καὶ λαβεῖν ἄδειαν.

The definitive retreat of the Magyars into Hungary must then be placed, on our reading, at the end of the same year as their campaign with Bulgaria, and the conclusion of peace between Symeon and the Empire. Nor, indeed, is it easy to conceive of any ταξείδιον which could have taken the Magyar army away immediately after this year. Brave as the Magyars are, they must have been men of iron and brass to go campaigning in distant lands with the Petchenegs, whom they so greatly feared, on the one flank, and an irritated and revengeful Symeon who had just defeated them so crushingly on the other.

Further, the disappearance of the Magyars from the field of battle may be inferred from the events which followed; for, very shortly after the conclusion of peace, Symeon recommenced hostilities on the pretext that all the prisoners had not been handed over as agreed; and inflicted on the Greek forces a crushing defeat at Bulgarophygon.[1] There is here no suggestion that the Magyars appeared as allies of Byzantium, nor even that their aid was invoked; nor would it appear that Symeon's change of heart, if it was really responsible for his improved fortunes against the Magyars, was equally efficacious in making him keep his hands off the Greeks.

1 Georgius Monachus, p. 855, etc.

So much for the general course of the war.

The dating of it presents many difficulties. The only one of the Greek historians who commits himself to a definite date is "Symeon", who includes his account of the war in a paragraph beginning "in the third year of Leo's reign". It has, however, been shown that "Symeon" is totally unreliable in the matter of dates; and de Boor goes so far as to say that "it is pure chance if a date as given by Symeon ever happens to be right".[1]

It is in any case impossible to date the outbreak of the war before the summer or autumn of 893. Vladimir, as a passage in the *Annales Fuldenses* shows, was still king of Bulgaria in 892.[2] Moreover, the campaign is related by the Greek chroniclers as beginning after the death of the Patriarch Stephen; and Stephen died, as de Boor showed, on May 17th, 893 (or possibly 894).[3]

Zlatarski believes the real quarrel between Symeon and the Greeks to have been due to the former's ecclesiastical reforms; in which case, one must allow a certain time to elapse after Symeon's accession, and he therefore places the outbreak of the war in 894.[4] I find, however, one great difficulty here.

The correspondence between Leo Magister and Symeon is occupied with the question of the exchange of prisoners. The first letter in Sakellion's collection is from Symeon, and in its terseness it is one of the most effective documents in the history of diplomacy. It runs:

The eclipse of the sun, and its date, not only to a month, week or day, but to the hour and the second, your Emperor prophesied to us *the year before last* (προπέρυσι) in the most marvellous fashion, and he also explained how long the eclipse of the moon will last. And they say he knows many other things about the movements of heavenly bodies. If this is true, he must also know about the prisoners; and if he knows, he will have told you whether I am going to release them or keep them. So prophesy one thing or the other,

1 De Boor, *Vita Euthymii* (Berlin, 1888), p. 80.
2 *Ad ann.* 892. In that year Arnolph sent messengers to Vladimir to renew the alliance between the Empire and Bulgaria, with a view to a campaign against Moravia. They returned in 893 with presents. The campaigns were carried out in 892 and 893.
3 *Vita Euthymii*, p. 94.
4 His arguments are summed up in *Izvestia z Blgarite*, pp. 90–101.

and if you know my intentions, you shall get the prisoners as reward for your prophecy and your embassy, by God! Greetings.[1]

Zlatarski applies this letter to the later negotiations; but this involves a very grave chronological difficulty. Symeon's jeer at the Emperor's astronomical attainments, which he repeats with sardonic amusement in a second letter,[2] cannot possibly refer to anything but the famous eclipse of the sun, mentioned by all the Byzantine chroniclers, which had occurred shortly before. The date of this eclipse was August 8th, 891.[3]   Now, Symeon says most explicitly that it occurred "the year before last"—the word προπέρυσι cannot, so far as I am aware, bear any other meaning. Therefore the correspondence—the earlier part of it at least—must be dated in 893. Therefore Symeon's opening attack on the Greeks must also be dated in the summer or autumn of 893.

Moreover, closer examination of these letters will show that they must have been written after Symeon's initial attack, and before any counter-measures by the Greeks. There is in them no word of the Magyars, nor of any Bulgarian prisoners taken by the Greeks or their allies. As the fate of these Bulgarian prisoners was Symeon's principal preoccupation in the later stages of the war, it is not conceivable that he should have made no reference to them in the letters, instead of contemptuously advising the Greeks to guess what was in his mind. The whole tone of the correspondence shows that the Bulgarians held all the trumps, which was not the case after the Magyar intervention. It may be added that the letters do not, on either side, show the bitterness which must have crept into them in the later stages of a bloody war. Further, during the later stages the Greek envoy was in Bulgaria, and negotiated verbally with Symeon, while the letters show him corresponding with Symeon from a distance. Leo actually made three separate journeys to Bulgaria, as later letters show.[4]

1 Sakellion, letter 1.
2 In the third letter of Sakellion's collection (the second from Symeon) the Bulgarian refers again to ὁ σὸς βασιλεὺς καὶ μετεωρολόγος.
3 Csuday, *Geschichte der Ungarn*, I, 63.
4 Sakellion, letters 18, 22.

The negotiations must have taken some time; for couriers moved slowly, and several letters were exchanged—the tone of the Greek shows, moreover, that he was experiencing trouble and delay in getting an answer out of Symeon. It would appear, therefore, that a considerable interval elapsed between Symeon's raid and the Emperor's counter-measures. Indeed, not to assume this would, I think, in any case be to take a somewhat too cynical view of Leo's attitude towards his "fellow-Christians". It was probably really only as a last resort that the Magyars were called in. Moreover, the campaign against the Arabs could obviously not be wound up at a word.

Therefore the dating of the outbreak of the war need not necessarily be the year immediately preceding that of the Magyar intervention; particularly as Symeon's original invasion was made on a very light pretext, and does not seem to have been very much more than a raid.

The Magyars had been engaged on a campaign in Hungary in 892, probably also in 893, and certainly in 894, the Emperor (Arnulph) having undertaken the first campaign only after assuring himself of Bulgaria's friendship.[1] In 894 the Emperor Leo sent an ambassador to Regensburg "with gifts";[2] and it seems more than plausible that the purpose of this journey was to arrange that the German Empire did not support Bulgaria against the Magyars and interfere with the Byzantine plans.[3] The Western chronicler then gives a brief notice *ad ann.* 895 to the effect that "the Avars (i.e. the Magyars) invading the territory of the Bulgarians, were defeated by them and a large proportion of them killed".

In 896 the *Annales Fuldenses* give a much more detailed account of the whole story—of the Greco-Bulgar alliance and the consequent Bulgaro-Magyar war, ending with the defeat of the Magyars. The account closes with a mention of the embassy of a certain Bishop Lazarus to Ratisbon. It is not hard to see

1 The *Annales Fuldenses, ad ann.* 892, mention "a great multitude of Hungarians" helping Arnulph. The campaign was renewed in 893. The *Annales Fuldenses, ad ann.* 894, have the entry "Avari, qui dicuntur Ungari, in his temporibus ultra Danubiam peragrantes...totam Pannoniam usque ad internecionem deleverunt". Cf. also the *Ann. Sang. Maj.*

2 *Annales Fuldenses, ad ann.* 894.   3 Zlatarski, *Istoria*, 294.

that we have here an amplification of the earlier brief notice, drawn from information supplied by Lazarus. From this it would follow that the whole Magyar intervention, victory and defeat included, took place in 895.

Tabarī mentions a summer campaign of the Arabs against Byzantium in 281 H. (March 13th, 894–March 1st, 895) but none in 282 H. (March 2nd, 895–February 18th, 896). There was fighting in Sanwal of 281 H. (December 4th, 894–January 1st, 895). This would mean that the Byzantine troops did not return from Asia Minor until the spring of 895.[1]

Tabarī's account of the war is extremely interesting for more than one reason. It runs as follows:

In this year [283 H. = Feb. 19th, 896–Feb. 7th, 897] there arrived, it is said, a letter from Tarsus, telling that the Slavs made war on the Rūm with a great multitude and ravaged many villages of theirs, till they reached Constantinople and forced the Rūm to seek refuge there, and the Rūm shut the doors of their capital. Hereupon the tyrant of the Rūm sent word to the king of the Slavs: "Our religion and yours is the same, why shall we slay one another's men?" Then the king of the Slavs answered him: "This is the realm of my fathers, and I will not cease from thee until one of us has overcome his adversary". Then when the king of the Rūm saw no salvation from the ruler of the Slavs, he gathered together the Moslems who were with him and gave them weapons and begged them to help him against the Slavs. They did this, and the Slavs were put to flight. When the king of the Rūm saw this, he grew afraid of them himself. Therefore he sent to them and called them back and distributed them in the provinces for fear they might commit treachery against him.

This account does not, as Marquart imagines, contain an account of the battle of Bulgarophygon, but of the whole course of the war, somewhat misunderstood by the informant in Tarsus. The "Moslems" of the letter are in truth no Moslems at all, but heathen Τοῦρκοι = Magyars. As for the final sentence, it may well be founded on a basis of fact. It is quite conceivable that the Emperor, even at this early date, took some Magyars into his service, in which case it is very likely that he distributed them in distant provinces.

As regards dating, Tabarī shows that the war was over in time for news of it to reach Tarsus in 896. The combination of

---

1 Cf. Marquart, *Streifzüge*, 529.

Tabarī and the *Annales Fuldenses* shows that the actual fighting between the Bulgars and Magyars took place in 895.

To sum up, then: the war broke out in 893, but that year saw little fighting except Symeon's initial advance. 894 was spent by the Greeks in negotiating first with the Bulgars, afterwards with the Magyars and Germans simultaneously. In 895 the fighting took place, and towards the end of the year Symeon combined with the Petchenegs and inflicted upon the Magyars the defeat as a result of which they migrated into Hungary at the end of the same year.

The German annals mention the Magyars only in Bulgaria in 895/6; but the *Annales Fuldenses* for the latter year tell us that owing to the increasing danger, the Emperor entrusted his "dux", Brazlavo, with the defence of "Urbs Paludarum", or Moosburg, south-west of Lake Balaton.[1] It seems reasonable to think that the Emperor took these precautions in view of the arrival of the Magyars. Moreover, although the Chronicles are silent respecting the Magyars in 897 and only report their scouts on the Brenta in 898,[2] while their first big raid was in 899, they must have harassed Pannonia continuously for some years before that date. The very interesting letter written to the Pope by the Bavarian bishops in A.D. 900 complains that the Moravians, who had accused the Bavarians of making compacts with the heathen Magyars, had themselves "many years" committed precisely the same offence, sending Magyars to ravage Pannonia.[3]

1 *Annales Fuldenses, ad ann.* 896: "Stipantibus vero in partibus conflictibus, imperator Pannoniam cum urbe Paludarum tuendam Brazlavoni, duci suo, commendavit".

2 Luitprand, *Ant.* 2, 7.

3 "Epistola episcoporum Bavariensium ad Joannem P. IX scripta a. 900", printed in Ginzel, *Die Slawenapostel Cyrill und Method*, codex, pp. 68 ff. Ginzel commits the extraordinary mistake of supposing that the Hungarians shaved themselves as an outward show of Christianity! On the contrary, the "pseudochristiani" are Moravian subjects (possibly Avars) who shaved their heads in the heathen Magyar fashion (cf. Regino, *ad ann.* 889 of the Magyars: "capillos usque ad cutem tondunt, etc.").

The extract from the bishop's letter runs: "Quod nos praefati Sclavi criminabantur, cum Ungaris fidem catholicam violasse, et per canem seu lupum aliasque nefandissimas et ethnicas res sacramenta et pacem egisse, atque ut in Italiam transirent pecuniam dedisse...innocentia nostra probaretur. Quia enim Christianis nostris longe a nobis positis semper imminebant et perse-

The only reason for putting the *Landnahme* at a later date is a desire to adhere literally to the Kavar story in the *D.A.I.*, but this story is, as I have shown, in any case inaccurate. Professor Marczali[1] gives 895 on another line of reasoning. Sviatopolk of Moravia died in 894.[2] Constantine tells us that after his death his sons "lived in peace one year (ἕνα χρόνον), but with war and dissension arising among them, and they making fratricidal war against one another, the Magyars came and destroyed them altogether and conquered their country in which [the Magyars] also live today".[3] Bury, in view of the fact that Moravia did not actually disappear till about 906, argues that Constantine's story "condenses the history of Moravia after the death of the great Duke" and can therefore give no date for the *Landnahme*.[4] This is just enough; but the outbreak of civil war is placed quite definitely one year after Sviatopolk's death, i.e. 895, and no better occasion can be imagined for the Magyars to enter Hungary, either to take advantage of Moravia's weakness, or to help one party against another.

The Magyars, then, entered Hungary late in the year 895.

cutione nimia affligebant, donavimus illis nullius pretiosae pecuniam sub-stantiae, sed tantum nostra linea vestimenta; quatenus aliquatenus eorum feritatem molliremus et ab eorum persecutione quiesceremus....Ipsi enim (i.e. the Moravians) crimen quod nobis falso semel factum imposuerunt, multis annis peregerunt. Ipsi Ungarorum non modicam multitudinem ad se sumpserunt, et more eorum capita suorum pseudochristianorum penitus detonderunt et super nos Christianos immiserunt...ita ut in tota Pannonia, nostra maxima provincia, tantum una non appareat ecclesia, etc."

1 *A Magyar Honfoglalás kútfoi*, p. 98.

2 Regino, *ad ann.* 894.　　　　　3 *D.A.I.* c. 41.

4 Bury, *op. cit.* p. 566.

APPENDIX

THE OLDEST REPORT ON THE COUNTRIES OF THE NORTH

The Petchenegs

Al-Bekrī

The road to the country of the Bajanākiyya from Jurjaniyya traverses a distance of 10 parasangs to a mountain called Khārasm on the summit of which is a minaret. At the foot of the mountain are the dwellings of a people of Jurjaniyya, who have cultivated lands there. They are a nomadic people who seek for places where there is rain and abundant herbage.

The length of their country is a 30 days' journey and likewise its breadth. To the north of them the land is Jaf-jakh also called Qaf-jaq, and to the south is the country of the Khazars, and to the west the land of the Saqlāb.—All these people are adjacent to the Bajanākiyya and make a tax on them. They are wealthy and possess beasts of burden and herds; also utensils of gold and silver and weapons.

They have ornamental belts and standards and trumpets instead of kettledrums.

Gardēzī

The road to Bajnāk comes out from Kar-Kanj by the mountain of Khārazm and from this mountain it goes towards Bajnāk and passes in front of the lake of Khārazm, which it passes on the right hand, and it goes on from there and reaches a dry country and waterless and continues for nine days, and every day or second day it reaches a well into which [travellers] lower a rope and give water to the animals. On the tenth day, the road reaches springs and water, and there is game. Every kind of bird and deer is to be found, and there is a small amount of dry herbage. The road leads · among these for sixteen days, and on the seventeenth day reaches the tents of the Bajnākiyah.

The territory of the Bajnāks is a three days' journey, and they have neighbours on every side. On the north is the country of Khafjakh and on the south-west Khazar and on the west Saqlāb and all these people are raiders and make raids on the Bajnāks and take them prisoner and sell them.

These Bajnāks are wealthy and have many animals and sheep and vessels of gold and silver.

They have weapons in plenty and belts of silver, and standards and short spears which they take into battle and they have trumpets well shaped on the outside which they sound in warfare.

The roads to Bajnāk are difficult and unpleasant. Whoever wishes to go in any direction from these needs to buy horses, since it is impossible to

Al-Bekrī

Gardēzī

go in any direction except riding owing to the badness and —— of the roads to it as traders who go there travel by a route without a road because the whole of the road to it is overgrown with trees, and that route they know by the guidance of the stars.

The country of the Bajanākiyya is all flat, without any mountains, and they possess no stronghold in which to take refuge.

Some of the Moslems who have been captive in Constantinople relate that the Bajanākiyya used to be of the religion of the Magians, but after 400 H. there came to them a Moslem captive who was versed in juris-prudence and a learned man; and he expounded Islam to a number of them and they became Moslems.

Their conversion was sincere and the call to Islam was proclaimed widely among them.

These were reproved for it by the others who had not Islamised and the matter resulted in war; God gave the victory to the Moslems over the rest, they being about 12,000 and the infidels about double that number, and the Moslems slew them and the remainder embraced Islam. Now they are all Moslems and they have learned men and jurists and readers of the Koran. Nowadays they give the name of Khawalis to those who come to them from among the captives of the Emperor of Constantinople and others, and these are given the choice of remaining with them on condition of being regarded as one of themselves and intermarrying with them at choice, or alternatively they [the Bajnāks] will take them safely to their own abode.

The Alans

Ibn Rusta

Passing out from the country of the Sarīr, you travel through mountains and meadows for a three days' journey. Then you reach the country of the Alans, and the king of the Alans himself is a Christian, but the majority of the people of his kingdom are pagans, worshipping idols. Then you travel for a ten days' journey among rivers and trees until at last you arrive at a fortress called "The Gate of the Alans", and it is on the top of a mountain, and the lower part of the mountain is a road, and around it are lofty mountains, and each day the wall of this fortress is guarded by a thousand men of its people, who are at their post night and day. And the Alans consist of four tribes; the nobles and the king belong to a tribe called Duhsās and the king is called Baghāyar [which is] the name of each one of their kings. The city of al-Bāb and al-Abwāb stretches from the top of the mountain of Qabaq to the sea of al-Khazar and projects into the sea for three miles.

Gardēzī

You travel three days from the land of the Sarīr through mountains and meadows and come to the Alans.

The king of the Alans is a Christian; all his subjects are pagans.

From the frontiers of his country to his fortress you must travel for ten days through blooming meadows and woods. The fortress is called "The Gate of the Alans". It is on the top of the mountain, and at the foot of the mountain the road goes, and all around it are lofty mountains. A thousand men guard the fortress night and day.

The Volga Bulgars

Ibn Rusta

Bulkar is adjacent to the country of the Burtās and its people dwell on the banks of the river which flows into the sea of Khazar which is called Itil, and they are between the Khazars and Saqālibs,

and their king is called Almuš and he is an adherent of Islam.

Their lands are swamps and tangled forests, and they live in them.

They are of three classes, one class is called Barsūl and another Asghal and the third Bulkār, and they all live in one place,

and the Khazars trade with them and buy and sell to them and also the Russians come to them with their merchandise, and all of them on the two sides of the river have different kinds of merchandise, such as sable and ermine and grey squirrel, etc.

Al-Bekrī

The country of the Bulkar is adjacent to the country of the Furdas, and between the country of the Bulkar and that of the Furdas is three days' journey. Their dwellings are on the banks of the river Itil and they are between the Furdas and the Saqlab: they are few in number, about 500, possessed of houses (or tents) (householders) and their king is called Almir, and he professes the Moslem religion.

The Khazars trade with them, and likewise the Rus.

Gardēzī

Bulkar is adjacent to the outlying districts of Burtās and the people of Bulkar live on the banks of the Džaihūn the water of which falls into the sea of Khazar, and they say this Džaihūn is from the river Itil and it is between Khazar and Saqlāb. They call their king Amlān and he professes the faith of Islam.

These people number about 500,000 families; all their country is forest and tangled brushwood, and they wander about in it from place to place. And there are these three classes among them, the first they call Bursul and the second Aškal and the third Bulkar, and all three live in one place,

and the Khazars trade with them and bring merchandise, and the Russians likewise.

Their merchandise is all sable and ermine and grey squirrel.

Ibn Rusta

They are a people engaged in cultivation and tillage, they sow all [kinds of] grains, wheat and barley and millet and others besides.

Most of them have adopted the faith of Islam and in their settlements are mosques and boys' schools; they have muezzins and imams. The infidels among them worship anyone whom they meet from among their friends.

Between Burtās and these Bulkariyya is a journey of three days, they raid them [the people of Burtās] and are hostile to them and take them captive.

They possess beasts of burden and coats of mail and pointed weapons, and they contribute to their king beasts of burden and other things, and when any man among them marries, the king takes from him an animal or two; when the ships of Moslem traders come to them, they take from them the tenth part.

Their dress resembles the dress of the Moslems, and they have burial-grounds like those of the Moslems.

Al-Bekri

Gardēzī

They are a people who live on the water-side and they have sown fields and goats [or seeds] and they use all kinds of grain such as wheat and barley, and have leeks [or gourds] and lentils and mash [= a kind of pea] and all kinds of things beside.

The majority of them are Moslems, and in their country are found mosques and schools and muezzins and imams. When the infidels see a friend of theirs from among the Moslems they bow down and worship him.

Between Bulkar and Burdas is a three days' journey, and they continually go on raids and they attack the people of Burdas and seize them.

They have many weapons and they all have cattle and good horses, and when the king wishes for an animal a wife, the give it him. When a man marries a wife, the king takes a horse from each one. When a boat of merchandise arrives, the king seizes one-tenth.

Their dress is like the dress of the Moslems, and their burying-grounds like those of the Moslems.

Ibn Rusta

Most of their wealth consists of the weasel and they have no silver or gold, their only money is the weasel, one weasel is current for two dirhems and a half, and the round white dirhems are obtained by them only from the Islamic peoples, they trade in it from them.

Al-Bekri

Gardēzi

Most of their wealth is from the stoat. They have no gold and silver [coin] and in place of silver they give the skin of the stoat, one for two dirhems. From the Islamic countries a dirhem is brought to them, white and round, and this dirhem they send [and obtain] from them everything [they require] and also they give that dirhem to the Russians and the Slavs, because these people will not sell to others except for solid dirhems.

Burtās

Ibn Rusta

The country of Burdas is between al-Khazar and Bulkar, and between them and the Khazars is a distance of 15 days' journey, and they are in allegiance to the king of the Khazars and he takes as tribute from them 10,000 horsemen, and they have no chief [or king] to rule over them, whose authority is accepted among them. In every district [or halting-place] of theirs there is a Shaykh or two to whom they bring their cases for judgment, when there is dissension between them, only, in the first place,

Al-Bekri

The country of Furdas lies between that of the Khazars and Balkar and between it and the country of the Khazars is a 15 days' journey.

Gardēzi

Burdas is between Khazar and Bulkar and between Burdas and Khazar is a 15 days' journey, and its people are subject to the king of Khazar, who takes from Burdas 10,000 horsemen. They have no leader to rule them, except that in every encampment [or district] there are one or two old men who decide questions between them in any dispute or affair which befalls them.

Ibn Rusta

they owe allegiance to the king of the Khazars.

Their territory is extensive, and they [live] in forests, and they are at enmity with Bulkar and the Bajanākiyya. They are robust and energetic and their religion resembles that of the Ghuzziyya. They are reflective and observant and of large physique, and if any one of them takes advantage of another or is oppressive or wounds him or pierces him, there is no reconciliation between them, nor will they meet in peace until the wounded man has taken his revenge.

When a maiden among them reaches maturity she ceases to accept her father's authority and chooses for herself whom she pleases from among the men [for a husband] and he comes to her father, seeking her in marriage and the father betroths her to him, and marries her to him, if she desires him.

These people possess camels and cattle and honey and most of their wealth is from the weasel [or stoat].

They are of two classes: one class among them burns the dead and the other buries them.

Al-Bekri

The Furdas are hostile to the Bulkar and Bajanākiyya, and their religion resembles that of the Ghuzziyya. They have an extensive territory which is flat, and one in which there is much commerce: it represents a journey of a month and a half, in length and breadth, and their numbers reach about 10,000 horsemen.

The tree which grows most plentifully is the *khalnaj*, and the greater part of their wealth consists in honey and the fur of the weasel [?], and they have large herds of cows and sheep and extensive cultivated lands.

Gardēzī

Burdas is an extensive district and every year there are hostilities between them and the Bulkars and the Bajnaks. These men of Burdas are all active and brave and their religion resembles [that of] the Ghuzziyya. They are all handsome and white skinned; if one acts treacherously towards another, or if anyone oppresses or wounds another, there can be no reconciliation between them until a fitting recompense is made.

When a maiden reaches maturity, she ceases to be under her father's authority, and she chooses whomsoever she will to be her husband. Then that man comes and asks her in marriage from her father and makes her his wife.

They have abundance of camels and cows and honey without measure. The greater part of their wealth is from the fitchet [or stoat, or weasel]. They have two classes, one of which burns the dead and the other makes graves for them.

Ibn Rusta

They live on low ground [or a plain], and most of their trees are the *khalnaj*, and they have cultivated lands, and most of their wealth is in honey, and the weasel and furs [or goats]. The extent of their country is a 17 days' journey in length and breadth.

Al-Bekri

Gardēzi

Their settlements are in the plain [or steppes] and most of their trees are the *khalnaj*. They have cultivated land and their wealth is derived from honey. Their fur garments they make from the skin of the stoat. Their country is a 17 days' journey in length and breadth,

and from their country to Khazar is all desert [steppes] but there is a way passing through cultivated land—with springs and trees and water, and some when they go from Burdas to Khazar go by way of the river Itil by boat and some by a road which is closed up and straight.

They have two javelins, and bow and arrow; they do not possess cuirass or armour. None of them has a horse, except, it may be, someone who is a headman and possessed of wealth.

They wear ear-rings [?] and an over-coat. Within their country there is no fruit, and their wine is made from honey. They have the kulah [tall Persian cap] with a turban twisted round it.

The Khazars

Ibn Rusta

Between the Bajanākiyya and the Khazars is ten days' journey through waterless steppes and forests and there is no well-marked road between the two. They journey through forests and swamps until they reach the country of the Khazars. The land of the Khazars is an extensive tract, extending on one of its sides to a great mountain, and that is the mountain which slopes down as far as Tūlas and Lūghir, and this mountain extends as far as the country of Tiflis.

They have a king called Ayshā [or Ishā] and the chief king is Khazar Khagan,

Al-Bekri

The distance from the country of Bajanākiyya to the country of the Khazars is a ten days' journey through forests and deserts, without any well-defined road, to the country of the Khazars.

It is an extensive country, and there is a great mountain adjoining one of its frontiers [extending] thence to the country of Tiflis, which is at the extreme edge of Armenia.

(Their flocks bring forth young twice in the year.

Khazar is the name of the region; their chief city is [divided] into two parts, to the east and to the west of the river Itil, which is a river flowing in their direction from Russia, and it discharges into the sea of Khazar.)[1]

Gardēzī

Between the Bajanākiyya and the Khazars is a ten days' journey through deserts and trees and wild uncultivated country until it reaches Khazar.

The country of Khazar is extensive and every side of it is a great mountain and that mountain extends as far as Tiflis.

They have a king called Abshād, who is a great king and they call their great

1 Ibn Fozlān: "Al-Khazar is the name of a district of a region called Itil, and Itil is the name of the river which flows to al-Khazar from Russia and Bulghar…Itil is a city…it is divided into two parts, one part on the west of this river which is the longer of the two and one part on the east of it".

Ibn Rusta

and he receives no allegiance from the Khazars except the name, and the [real] control of affairs devolves upon Ayshā, when he is in command of the army and the soldiers are in the position of paying no heed to anyone above him. Their great king is of the Jewish faith and likewise Ayshā, and his followers among the leaders and great men, and the rest of them are of a religion resembling that of the Turks.

Their capital is Sar'Ishan, and beside it is another city called Habnal'a.

In winter the people live in these two cities, and when spring comes they go out into the desert and remain there until the coming of winter.

Al-Bekri

One of these two cities is called Ar'ish and the other Hathkugh, and the one to the west is the larger of the two.

(Both these cities are surrounded by a wall and they have four gates: they contain baths and mosques and imams and muezzins and the mass of the Khazars are Moslems and Christians, but there are idolaters among them, and the people of a section among them, and their king, are of the Jewish faith; his palace is at a distance from the river.)[1]

Gardēzī

king Khazar Khagan, and Khazar Khagan has the name and that is all, but the chief minister for the work of the country and the officials is Abshad. No person is greater than Abshad and no one has more authority. Abshad is a Jew, so [is also] everyone who follows him, and amongst the leaders and great men there are also Jews, and the rest are of a religion which resembles the religion of the Turks of Ghuz. They have two cities, the larger of which is called Sārghash and the other Khila.

These people live in winter in these two cities and when spring comes they go out towards the plain, and they do not come into the city again until the winter.

1 Ibn Fozlān: "The king lives in the western part... This western section is enclosed by a wall... They have markets and baths, and among them are many Moslems, who are said to exceed 10,000 in number, and they possess about thirty mosques. The king's palace is at a distance from the bank of the river... this wall has four gates.... The king is a Jew and the Khazars are Moslems and Christians and some are idolaters".

Ibn Rusta

In these two cities, those who are Moslems have mosques and imams and muezzins and boys' schools.

Their king Ayshā has imposed taxes upon the people of capacity and wealth among them, [a quota] of horsemen according to the amount of their wealth and the easiness of their condition in life, and they make raids on the Bajanā-kiyya every year.

This Ayshā has control of the taxes vested in himself and he goes on raids with his soldiers and they have camels for riding [or camels in plenty] and when they go forth for any purpose, they go with weapons complete and furbished and standards and spears and strong coats of mail.
He rides out with 10,000 horsemen of those to whom he grants payment, and [also] among them are those imposed as a tribute upon the rich.

When he goes out for any purpose,

Al-Bekri

Gardēzī

In these two cities there are Moslem people; and they have mosques and imams and muezzins and writing schools.

Every year the Khazars take by force from these Moslems something of considerable value,

also they make war every year on the country of the Bajnāks and from some they bring wealth and prisoners of war.

This [booty] Abshad takes as tribute for himself and distributes to the soldiers.
In raiding the Burdas they [have] also standards and short spears and strong cuirasses and good armour.

When the king of the Khazars rides out, 2000 horsemen ride with him. Some are experienced men and some are provided by the wealthy, who go with the king with their own apparatus and tools.

When the army turns aside in any direction and goes on its way, a number of soldiers come into the house [?] in

Ibn Rusta

there is taken with him something like a small metallic disc made like a tambourine, carried by a horseman who travels with it. As he travels, his soldiers behind him see the light of that metallic disc.

When they take any plunder, they bring all these spoils into the camp, then Ayshā chooses what he likes for himself, and leaves them the rest of the spoils to divide among themselves.

Al-Bekri

Gardēzī

order to guard the family and the furniture, and they have a vanguard which goes before the army and carries candles and torches made of wax before the king, so that by that illumination he goes forward with the army.

When they find plunder, they collect it all in the camp, then their leader takes for himself what he wishes from that plunder and the rest is divided among the soldiers.

Their leader orders every man in the army to make a tent-pole [or peg] as thick as three ropes, with a sharp point, and take it with him, and then when the army halts, they fix those poles around about the army and on every pole they hang a shield, so that the camp is secured as with a wall, and if an enemy attempts a night attack he can do nothing, because on account of these poles, the camp is like a fortress.

There are cultivated lands in the country of the Khazars and many orchards. They have much wealth and abundance of honey and good wax is brought from there.

Ibn Rusta

Al-Bekrī

Gardēzī

(The reason why the king of the Khazars became a Jew[1] [for he had been a Magian] was: he became a Christian but he saw the corruption with which Christianity was affected, and concerning what grieved him therein, he consulted with one of his satraps, and this man said to him: "O king, the people who possess the books [= Scriptures] are of three classes, send for them and enquire into their doctrine and follow that one among them which is possessed of the truth". So he sent to the Christians for a bishop and the king had with him a man of the Jews, skilled in debate. This man engaged in discussion with the bishop, and said to him: "What have you to say of Moses, son of 'Amram and the Law which was sent down to him?" He said to him, "Moses was a prophet and the law is true". Then the Jew said to the king: "He has acknowledged the truth of what I said to him: ask him concerning his own faith". So the king questioned him, and the bishop said to him: "I declare that the Christ, Jesus the Son of Mary, is the Word, and that He is the revealer

---

[1] Mas'ūdī (*Meadows of Gold*, p. 407): "As we cannot insert in this book the history of the conversion of the king of the Khazars to Judaism, we refer the reader to our former works".

Ibn Rusta   *Al-Bekrī*   *Gardēzī*

of mysteries, sent from God, to whom belong glory and power".

Then the Jew said to the king of the Khazars: "He has put forward a claim which I do not recognise, and he has acknowledged the truth of what I told", and the bishop was not strong in argument.

Then the king sent to the Moslems, and they sent to him a learned man, wise and skilled in controversy, but the Jews sent someone secretly against him to poison him on the road, and he died. So the Jew won the king over to his faith, and he became a Jew.)

(The tongue of the Khazars is distinct from the tongue of the Turks and the Persians and it is a language in which no other tongue has any share.

The king has seven judges taken from among the Jews, the Christians, the Moslems and the idolaters.)[1]

---

1 Ibn Fozlān: "The tongue of the Khazars differs from that of the Turks and the Persians and has no affinity with any other language.... The king has nine judges (chosen) from among the Jews, Christians, Moslems and idolaters".

As-Sariri

Ibn Rusta

You travel from al-Khazar to As-Sariri a twelve days' journey in the steppes, then you ascend a high mountain and valleys and you travel for three days until you reach the king's fortress. It is situated on the top of a mountain and is four parasangs by four and it is surrounded by a stone wall.

The king has a throne of gold and a throne of silver.

The people of the fortress are usually Christians but the rest of the people of the kingdom are all infidels.

Under his rule are 20,000 valleys [or tribes], and these include different races of people, and they possess villages and hamlets and all of them worship a withered head.

When one of them dies, they place him on a bier, and take him out to the open field, and leave him three days on the

Al-Bekri

The country of As-Sariri is a journey of 12 parasangs from the country of the Khazars, in the steppes, until you reach a high mountain. You ascend it and travel on for three days, until you reach the fortress of the king of As-Sariri, which is surrounded by a wall.

The king has a throne of gold which used to belong to the kings of Fars [= Persia].

They are Christians, but in general the people under his rule are idolaters.

Their king rules over 20,000 valleys [or nations],

in which are races of men who worship a withered head.

When one of them dies, they place him on a bier, and carry him out into a field and leave him there three days, and a

Gardēzi

From Khazar to the country of Sarir is twelve parasangs. At first [the road] is through a plain, then it passes in front of a high mountain and you go on, and it continues for three days until it reaches the king's fortress, and this fortress is on the top of a mountain; it is four parasangs square and its walls are made of stone.

The king possesses two thrones, one of gold and the other of silver, and he sits on the golden throne and the silver one is for his companions.

Most of the people of that castle are Christians, and the rest of the people of his kingdom are infidels.

The kingdom contains 20,000 families and different seats [?] and they have towns and villages.
They worship a lion.

When one of them dies, they place him on a bier and carry him out into a field and leave him there three days, and a

Ibn Rusta

bier; they then ride out from the city in coats of mail and armour and come to the edge of the field and [pretend to] charge the dead man who is on the bier with their spears; they go round about the bier and point at him with their spears, but do not pierce him.

[He said] "I asked them about their actions, and they said, 'There was a man who died and was buried, and after the space of three days he cried out from his tomb, so we leave the corpse for three days, and when the fourth day comes, we make threatening gestures over him with our weapons, so that if his spirit had remained in him it would return to his body' and this had been their custom for about three hundred years."

Their king is called Awār.
From the right of the fortress a road leads out between lofty mountains and many swamps, a journey of twelve stages, until it approaches a city which is called Khāyzan.

Al-Bekri

Gardēzi

friend is placed by the bier. Then, after three days, they return, bringing their weapons, wearing coats of mail and armour and bringing other arms. They stand in a corner of the field and poise their javelins and fit their arrows to the bow and draw their swords and they pretend to attack that corpse, but they do not pierce it.

They say that the cause of this [custom] was that a certain man died and they placed him in a grave, and when the third day came, he came out from the grave and when they questioned him, he said: "My soul had departed from me, you placed me in the grave, then my soul returned to me in the grave and I arose and came forth". Now when any of them dies, they do not dig the grave for three days, then they frighten him with javelin, arrows and sword: if he is alive, he will rise up and if not, this custom still prevails.

They call their king Awāz.
To the right of Sarīr is a district which they call Jandān,

Ibn Rusta

They have a king who is called Adhranasi, who adheres to three religions. On Friday he is used to pray with the Moslems, on Saturday with the Jews and on Sunday with the Christians, and to everyone who comes to him he asserts that "every sect of these religions urges the claim of his faith, and declares that he has the truth and that everything except his religion is vain; therefore I adhere to all, so that I may know the truth of [these] religions".

At a distance of ten parasangs from this city is a city called Ranhas [?] and in it is a great tree which bears no fruit, and the people of the city gather round it every Wednesday and hang different kinds of fruit on it, and worship it and offer gifts [or sacrifices].

Al-Bekrı

(On the left of the fortress of the king of As-Sariri is a road by which the traveller journeys amongst mountains and meadows, until after three days he reaches the country of the king of Al-Lan.)[1]

1 From the description of the Alans by Ibn Rusta and Gardēzī (see p. 191).

Gardēzī

and these people of Jandān have three religions: when it is Friday, they come with the Moslems to the mosque on Friday and say the Friday prayers, and then separate, and when Saturday night comes, they go into the church and worship also in the manner of the Christians. Someone asked them why they acted thus and they said: "These three sects are different one from another and each person says 'The truth is with me', therefore we conform ourselves to all three sects, thinking perchance we shall find the truth among them".

At ten parasangs from 'Amrair is a tree which bears nothing; and every Wednesday the people of this city come and bring every kind of fruit and hang it on that tree, then they worship it and offer a sacrifice there.

The Magyars

Ibn Rusta
"A"

Between the country of the Bajanākiyya and the country of the Aškal, who belong to the Balkariyya, is the first of the Magyar boundaries.

The Magyars are a race of Turks and their king rides with horsemen to the number of 10,000 and this king is called Kanda (and this name denotes their king, for the name of the man who is [actually] king over them is Jula and all the Magyars accept the orders of their king Jula in the matter of war and defence and the like).

"B"

They possess leather tents and they travel in search of herbage and abundant pasturage. Their country is extensive and one frontier extends to the sea of Rūm,

and two rivers flow into that sea, one of them greater than Džaihūn, and their dwellings are between these two rivers and in the winter they go to whichever

Al-Bekrī
"A"

The Muhaffiyya are between the country of the Bajanākiyya and the country of the Aškal, who also belong to the Balkariyya.

The Muhaffiyya are idolaters, and the name of their king is Kanda.

"B"

They are a people who live in tents and they go in search of the places where there is pasturage. The extent of their country is 100 parasangs in breadth. One boundary of their country adjoins the region of Rūm,

Gardēzī
"A"

Between the country of Bulkar and the country of Aškal which is also part of Bulkar is the boundary of the Magariyāns,

and these Magyars are a race of Turks and their leader rides out with 20,000 horsemen and they call this chief Kanda, and this is the name of their greater king, and that chief, that superintends their affairs they call Jula and the Magyars do whatever Jula commands.

"B"

They have a plain, which is all dry herbage and a wide territory and their country has an extent of 100 parasangs by 100, and it adjoins the sea of Rūm,

since the river Džaihūn flows into that sea.

They dwell between that river, and when winter comes, any person who is

207

Ibn Rusta

river is nearest to them and settle there for the winter. They catch fish from it, and their abode for the winter is reserved to them there.

Al-Bekri

and at the other boundary where it touches the desert, is a mountain, and the people who dwell there are called Ayin—

They have horses, and flocks and cultivated lands.[1]

(Below this mountain on the shore of the sea are a people called Awghūna, and they are Christians, and adjoin the country of those Moslems connected with the country of Tiflis, and it is the beginning of the boundary of Armenia.

This mountain extends as far as the land of Bāb-el-Abwāb and adjoins the country of the Khazars.)[2]

1 Cf. Mas'ūdī, *Meadows of Gold*, p. 436.

Gardēzī

far from the Džaihūn comes near it again and in winter remains there, and they catch fish and subsist thereby. That is the Džaihūn which is on their left side. Beside Saqlāb are a people of Rūm who are all Christians and they are called Nandar, and they are more numerous than the Magyars, but they are weaker. They call these two Džaihūns the one Itil and the other Dūbā. When the Magyars are on the bank of the river they see these Nandarin there.

Above the bank of the river is a great mountain and water flows out on to the side of the mountain,

and behind that mountain are a people of the Christians whom they call Mirdāt; between them and the Nandar is a 10 days' journey.

They are a numerous people and their dress resembles that of the Arabs

2 Cf. *ibid.* p. 452.

Ibn Rusta

Al-Bekri

Gardēzī

[consisting] of turban and skirt and overcoat. They have cultivated lands and seeds and vineyards, for with them the water runs over the surface of the land and has no canals for irrigation. They state that their number is greater than that of the Rūm and that they are a separate nation. The greater part of their trade is with Arabia. That river which is to the right of the Magyars goes to Saqlāb and from there dwindles away in the district of Khazar and that river is greater than these two rivers.

"C"

The land of the Magyars is all trees and standing water, and its ground is moist. They have completely subjugated the Slavs and they always order them to provide food for them and consider them as their slaves.

The Magyars are fire worshippers.

They go out to raid Saqlāb and Rūs and carry off [the people] and sell them.

"C"

"C"

The country of the Magyars contains many trees and much water and their ground is moist and they have many fields.

They exercise dominion over all of the Saqlāb [Slavs], who are adjacent to them and they put upon them heavy burdens, and they are in their hands in the position of captives.

The Magyars worship the sun and the moon.

They are hostile to the Saqlāb and they bring them as captives by the seacoast until they come to the ascent of the country of the Greeks called Karākh,

and it is said that Al-Khazar in former days was surrounded by a ditch as a

Ibn Rusta

defence against the Magyars and other nations adjacent to their country.

When the Magyars go with the captives to Karākh, the Greeks come out to them and they trade there and deliver over to them the slaves and take Grecian brocades and carpets and other Greek goods.

Al-Bekri

They constantly plunder the Slavs and from the Magyars to the Slavs is a ten days' journey. To the...of Saqlab is a city which they call Wāntīt.

It is a custom when marrying that when a woman is sought in marriage a dowry is appointed in accordance with the wealth in cattle less or more belonging to that man.

When they sit down to appoint that dowry, the father of the maiden brings the father of the son-in-law to his own house and whatever he has in the way of sable and ermine and grey squirrel and stoat and the belly of the fox with...and brocade, he collects all these skins together to the quantity of ten fur garments and folds them inside a carpet and fastens them on the horse of his son-in-law's father and speeds him to his house. Then whatever is necessary for the maiden's dowry which they have agreed upon such as animals and money and goods is all sent to him and at that time they bring the woman to the house.

Gardēzī

These Magyars are a handsome people and of [good] appearance and their clothes are of silk brocade and their weapons are of silver and two are encrusted with gold.

The Slavs

(N.B. Al-Bekrī substitutes, for this section of Džaihānī's report, that of Ibrahim Ibn Jaq'ūb, with excerpts from Mas'ūdī.)

Ibn Rusta	*Gardēzī*
Between the country of the Bajanā-kiyya and the country of the Saqlāb-iyya is a ten days' journey, and near the frontier of Saqlāba is a city called Wāyīt [or Wāyīb].	Between the Bajnāks and Saqlāb is a ten days' journey,
You travel to it through deserts and two tracts without any well-defined road and [with] springs of water and tangled trees until you come to their country. The country of Saqlāba is a flat country and full of trees and they dwell there and they have no vines nor fields. They have a kind of large jar made of wood used as nests for their bees and their honey and they call them Uliyshaj and there comes from one jar as much as the contents of two jugs.	and this journey is without road, but the route is by way of springs and trees. Saqlāb is an extensive region, and possessed of abundance of trees, and most of its people live among the trees. They have no vineyards nor cultivated land: they have jars made out of wood and abundance of honey and from one hive as much as 50 or 60 or 100 *mans* of honey [400, 480, 800 lb.] may be taken. They feed pigs and have herds of them and they have...sheep.
They are a people who herd pigs like sheep.	
When one of them dies, they burn him with fire, and the women, when someone belonging to them dies, cut their hands and faces with knives.— When that corpse has been burnt, they come to it on the morrow and take the ashes from that place and put them in a small earthenware vessel and place it on a hill. Then a year after the death, they take 20 large jars of honey, and the relations of the dead assemble and they eat and drink there and then go away.	When anyone dies among them, they burn him; if their women die, they cut off the hand of that woman and cut her face with a knife. When they burn a corpse, they come the next day and take the ashes from that place and put them into bags and place them on the top of a hillock. When a year has passed after the death, they bring a great deal of honey, and the people of the dead man's family assemble and they go to the top of the hillock and eat from the honey and return.
If the dead man had three wives and one of them wishes to show her love to him, in the presence of her dead [husband] she takes two pieces of wood and sets them upon the surface of the earth then she puts another piece of wood across the tops of them and suspends from the middle of it a rope with one end secured to her neck, she being mounted on a chair, and when she has done that, the chair is taken from under her and she remains hanging	

Ibn Rusta

until she is strangled and dies and when she is dead she is cast into the fire and burnt.

All of them are worshippers of bulls.

Most of their crops are millet, and when the time of harvest comes, they take a handful of the millet grain; then throw it up to the heavens and say: "O Lord, Thou art he who hast provided our sustenance, complete thy favour towards us".

They play on the seven-chorded lute and the mandoline and flute, and the length of their flute is two cubits and on their lute are eight strings.

Their wine is made of honey.

They make music [or are cheerful] at the burning of the dead, with the intent of rejoicing at God's mercy towards him.
They possess but few animals and none has a horse [or beast of burden] except the distinguished man.

Their weapons are javelins and shields and spears and they have no others.

Their king is Sūbanj to whom they give their allegiance and from whom they take orders, and his dwelling is in the middle of the country [or town] and the most distinguished man known to them is one who is called king of the kings [or chief of the chiefs] whom they name Suwāy-yāt Balk and he is more important than Sūbanj and Sūbanj is his deputy and this king has riding animals. He does not eat any food except milk taken from the curd. He has excellent coats of mail strong and precious and the city in which he lives is called Jarwāb. There they have a market three days a month and there they trade.

Gardēzī

They worship a [or the] cow.

Most of their crops are millet [or vetch] and when the time of harvest is come, they put that millet grain into a sieve, and then they throw it up to the heavens and say: "O Lord, Thou hast made this new day for us, give us therein what we desire".

They have different kinds of music [stringed instruments] and tambourines and reed-pipes and their reed-pipes are of the length of two spans and their harp [or lute] has eight strings and is broad.
Their wine is made of honey.

They play their lutes at the time of burning of the dead, and they say: "We are rejoicing, because mercy has been shown towards him". They have few horses and their dress is a shirt and they have boots [or stockings] and their shoes are like those of Tabaristan which are worn by the women of Tabaristan.

Their life is hard and one of scarcity. The weapons with which they fight are javelins and shields and spears.

Their king [or chief] wears a crown and they are all obedient and submissive to him and the greater king they call Suwiyyat Malik and his deputy is called Suwih.

They call the city in which the king lives Jarāwāt. Three days in every month in that city they have a market day and they go there for everything and sell everything there.

Ibn Rusta	*Gardēzī*
In this country the cold is very severe, and it reaches such severity that a man there digs himself in like a wild animal under the earth and then makes himself a roof of wood like that of a church. Then he heaps earth on to it, and the man enters it with his family and brings some firewood and stones, and kindles a fire there until it gets warm and becomes red, and when it becomes very hot, he sprinkles water on it, so that the vapour rises in that place and the house is warmed, and they remain in that house until the spring.	They have a custom of making a fortress: everybody comes together and they make a fortress, because the Magyars constantly come and raid and plunder them. When the Magyars come, the Slavs go into that fortress which they have made and most of their dwellings in winter are castles and fortresses, and in summer among the trees.
Their king collects taxes from them every year. If a man among them has a daughter, the king takes from her clothes a robe once in the year, and if a man has a son, the king takes from his garments a robe, a second time in the year. If a man has neither son nor daughter, the king takes a garment from the clothing of his wife or a slave-girl.	
	They have many prisoners of war.
If a thief is caught in his kingdom, he orders him to be hanged or puts him to work at the frontiers of his country.	When they catch a thief, they seize all his property and they send him to the outskirts of their country and there punish him.
	Among them adultery does not exist, and if a woman has a man as lover, she goes to him, and when she puts her hand in his, if she is a virgin, he marries her, and if not he sends her away and says: "If you have connived, you shall have marriage". If a married woman commits adultery, they kill her and accept no excuse.
	They have wine and honey in abundance, and a man among them may have 100 jars of wine of honey.

The Russians

(N.B. Al-Bekrī omits this report.)

Ibn Rusta

Russia is an island around which is a lake, and the island in which they dwell is a three days' journey through forests and swamps covered with trees and it is a damp morass such that when a man puts his foot on the ground it quakes owing to the moisture.

They have a king who is called Khāqān Rūs,

and they make raids against Saqlāba, sailing in ships in order to go out to them, and they take them prisoner and carry them off to Khazar and Bulkar and trade with them there.

They have no cultivated lands; they eat only what they carry off from the land of the Saqalāba.

When a child is born to any man among them, he takes a drawn sword to the new-born child and places it between his hands and says to him: "I shall bequeath to thee no wealth and thou wilt have naught except what thou dost gain for thyself by this sword of thine".

They have no landed property nor villages nor cultivated land; their only occupation is trading in sables and grey squirrel and other furs, and in these they trade and they take as the price gold and silver and secure it in their belts [or saddle-bags].

They are cleanly in regard to their clothing, and the men wear bracelets of gold: they are kind to their slaves and clothe them well for they engage in trade.

The Russians have many cities and they expend much money on themselves.

Gardēzī

Russia is an island, which is placed in a sea, and this island is three days' journey in length and breadth and it is all trees and thickets, and its ground is very moist, so much that if you put your foot on the moisture, the ground quakes from its dampness.

They have a king whom they call the Khāqān of Rūs.

In this island there are men to the number of 100,000, and these men constantly go out to raid the Slavs in boats, and they seize the Slavs and take them prisoner and they go to the Khazars and Bulkar and sell them [there].

They have no cultivated land nor seed, and their seed is usually [or is plunder] from the Slavs.

When a child is born to them, they place a drawn sword in front of him and his father says: "I have neither gold nor silver, nor wealth which I can bequeath to thee, this is thine inheritance, [with it] secure prosperity for thyself and eat thine own food".

Their merchandise consists of sable and grey squirrel and they have good slaves.

They are a people cleanly in their dress and they have good slaves.

Ibn Rusta　　　　　　　　　*Gardēzī*

They honour their guests and are kind to strangers who seek shelter with them, and everyone who is in misfortune among them. They do not allow anyone among them to tyrannise over them, and whoever among them does wrong or is oppressive, they find out such a one and expel him from among them.

They do not hold it lawful that anyone should oppress a stranger, and if [such a one] is oppressed, they secure justice for him from that man [who oppresses him].

They have Sulaymani swords, and when there is any call to war, they go out all together, and do not scatter, but are as one hand against their foes until they have conquered them.

The clothing of the people of Rūs and Saqlāb is of linen and their men have gold bracelets on their hands. In the island is great cities [*sic*], and within it is an abundance of Sulaymani swords. When they make war, they are all of one mind, and do not have disputes, especially when in sight of the enemy.

If one of them has a complaint against another, he summons him before their king and they plead their case against each other, and if he settles their differences it will be as he wishes, but if they disagree with his opinion, he orders them to settle it with their swords, and whichever sword is the sharper will be victorious, and the two sets of kindred go out, and they two take up their weapons, and the dispute is adjudged in favour of the one who gets the better of his friend.

If one has a complaint against another they go before the Khāqān [to see] whether by his decision that dispute can be settled, and if not he orders them to fight a duel with swords, and whoever effects a thrust, the owner of that sword is [considered] less at fault.

They have doctors who act as judges, whose judgment is esteemed above that of the king, who are like lords [*or* gods] to them. These men order them to come forward with what they desire to their Creator, of women and men and horses, and when the doctors have decreed a thing there is no escape from fulfilling their behest, and the doctor takes the man and the beast from them and casts a rope about his neck and hangs him from a beam, until his soul has departed, and the doctor says that this is an offering to God.

They have doctors and their decision is accepted even by their kings. If a doctor seizes a man or woman and hangs a rope about his neck and suspends him from a pedestal until he dies, and says "this is the king's order", no one says anything to him, they simply acquiesce in that.

These people are vigorous and courageous and when they descend on open ground, none can escape

Ibn Rusta   *Gardēzī*

from them without being destroyed
and their women taken possession of,
and themselves taken into slavery.
The Russians are strong and observant, and their raids are not made
riding, but their raids and fights are
only in ships.

Their king seizes a tithe from the
merchants. Constantly 100 or 200 of
them come to Saqlāb and by force
seize from them maintenance while
they are there. From Saqlāb many
men go and serve the Russians in
order that through their service they
may be safe.

When they put on their trousers
of 100 spans, they draw them to the
knee and then fasten them.

As regards their clothes, they have
a kaftan and they wear tall caps,

Not one of them goes to satisfy a
natural need alone, but he is accompanied by three of his companions
who guard him between them, and
each one of them has his sword
because of the lack of security and
the treachery among them, for if a
man has even a little wealth, his own
brother and his friend who is with
him covet it and seek to kill and
despoil him.

but they are all untrustworthy, so
much so that if one goes out to
satisfy a need, two or three persons
with weapons go with him to guard
him, since if they find one alone, they
kill him.

When a great man among them dies,
they erect for him a tomb like a
spacious house, they place him in it
and with him his body-clothes and
the gold bracelets which he used to
wear, and abundance of food and
jars of wine and money also, and they
place with him in the tomb his wife
whom he loved, while she is still
alive, and the door of the tomb is
sealed upon her and she dies there.

When a great man is slain, they make
a grave for him in the earth, wide and
large, as spacious as a house, and
they place with him all his body-
clothes and a handful of rice and a
jug of... and wine and food and
money, and they place his wife, still
alive, with him, and seal the top of
his grave, so that his wife dies.

H

EXTRACTS FROM *L'ABRÉGÉ DES MERVEILLES*

The Slavs. They form several nations; some are Christians, others follow the religion of the Magians and adore the sun. They have a sweet sea which begins in the northern regions and advances southward, and another sea which stretches from the east to the west, in a point where it communicates with a third sea which comes from the region of the Bulgars. They have several rivers; they inhabit all the countries of the north; they have no salt sea; their country being distant from the sun, the sea in it is sweet; it is when it draws near the sun that it becomes salt. The countries which border on them to the north are uninhabited, on account of the cold reigning there and the frequency of earthquakes. The majority of their tribes practise the Magian religion; they adore fire and allow themselves to be burnt by it. Their cities are numerous; they have churches with spires which are struck as one strikes clappers.

There is a nation between the Slavs and the Franks which follows the religion of the Sabeans, viz. it worships the planets. This is a very intelligent people and skilled in the arts of war. It makes war on the Slavs, the Burğān and the Turks. It has 7 feasts in the year, according to the name of the 7 planets, and that of the sun is the most splendid.

The Greeks. [Yunan.] The Greeks are the old Rūmī, descendants of Yunan, son of Japhet, son of Noah. They are the most learned of peoples. [There follows a description exclusively of ancient Greece.]

The Ankīradah.[1] These are the descendants of Amir, son of Japhet, and occupy a vast kingdom between the Rūmīs and the Franks. Their king is powerful; they have many cities. Most of them are Christians today, but some of them have no religion. They have to fight against the Franks and the Slavs who surround and repulse them. Their dress is the same as that of the Rūmīs.

The Franks. They are also descended from Japhet. Their kingdom is extensive and important. They have several kingdoms, governed by only one king. Their capital is called Darīwah. They are also Christians. They are today divided into branches and behind them dwell other races. Their principal enemies are the Slavs; but on account of the extent of their kingdom, they have also to do battle with the Rūmīs and the Ankīradah. Commerce is very highly developed among them. There are among them Christians, Magians, Manichees; there are some which burn themselves.

Spain. The kingdom of Spain comprises 24 cities placed under the authority of one single king [they were formerly Manicheans but became Christians]. There was in the capital of Spain a house, the

1 The MS readings are: el Ihtāradah, and el Ankīradah, Dimašqi has el Ankāradah, Mas'ūdī Nūkoberd and Nūkoberda.

door of which each king shut with a padlock on attaining to the power. This practice continued till the days of king Lodrik (Roderick) ...[Roderick refused to lock it, and in the same year the country was invaded by Arabs].

The Burğān.[1] These are descendants of Yunan, son of Japhet. Their kingdom is important and extensive. They make war against the Rūm, the Slavs, the Khazars and the Turks; their most formidable enemies are the Rūm. From Constantinople to the land of the Burğān is 15 days' journey; their kingdom measures 30 days' journey by 20. Every strong place, with the Burğān, is surrounded by a fence fringed and surmounted by a sort of network of wood, which constitutes a defence similar to that of a wall raised behind a ditch. The Burğān are of the religion of the Magians and they have no books [i.e. no revealed religion]. The horses which they use in battle are always free in the fields, and none may mount on them except in time of war. If they find that a man has mounted on one of those animals at any other time, they kill him. When they make ready for battle, they form up in lines. They place the men in front, and behind they collect their women and children. The Burğān know neither dinars nor dirhems; all their transactions, as also their marriage contracts, are made by means of oxen and sheep. When peace is concluded between them and the Rūm, they send to the Rūm young slaves of both sexes, Slavs, or of a similar race. When a chief among them dies, they collect the servants of the dead man and the men of his following and having made their recommendations, they burn them with the dead man; they say: "We burn them in this world, but they will not burn in the other". Or else they dig a great cave into which they lower the dead; they make enter with him his wife and the men of his suite and leave them there until they are dead. It is customary among them, when a slave has committed a fault for which his master wishes to punish him, that he throws himself on the ground before his master who beats him at his will; and if the slave rises before recovering permission, he may be slain. It is also their custom to give larger portions of their heritages to girls than to boys.

---

1 *Al-Bekrī:* "As for the Burğān, they are descendants of Yunan b. Jafath and they are Magians. Their kingdom is extensive, and they make war against the Rūm and the Saqlāb and the Khazars and the Turks. The Greeks are the most vigorous against them, because of their proximity for between Constantinople and the frontier of the kingdom of Burğān is only a 15 days' journey. The kingdom of Burğān is 20 days' journey by 30 days. They do not ride horses except in warfare. When the Greeks made peace with them, they sent to the Greeks the tribute of maidens and youths which they had taken from the Saqlāb. When a man dies, their custom is to place him in a deep sepulchral vault; he is lowered into it with his wife and servants and they remain there until they die, but some of them are burned with the dead man".

The Turks. They are the descendants of Japhet, son of Noah, and are divided into several races. They have cities and fortresses. There is one tribe of Turks which lives on the top of mountains and in deserts, under tents of felt; their only occupation is the chase. Those who catch nothing, cut the jugular veins of their mounts, catch the animal's blood and roast it. These Turks eat vultures, crows and other creatures. They have no religion. There are others which follow the Magian religion. There are also some who have embraced Judaism. Their great king is called Khakhan. He has a throne of gold, a mitre of gold, a belt of gold and raiment of silk. It is said that the great king of the Turks cannot show himself, and that if he did, no one could support the sight of him. [There follows an account of divination by fire.]

The Rūmīs. They are the sons of Esau; Rūmī is their nickname. When Constantine attained to the power, he professed Christianity; he assembled the bishops in council and was baptised. The Christians formed after him a hierarchy consisting of patriarchs, bishops, priests, deacons, Magians, domestics, leaders of troops.... [There follows an account of their meals and religion.] Their king is called the Merciful king (el Malik en-Rahim), he is equitable and just; he wears the diadem. [The statement is also made that the king of the Rūmīs wears the red sandals.]

EXTRACTS FROM *THE BOOK OF LANDS* OF AL-ISTACHRĪ

(Translated from the German version of A. D. Mordtmann published in the *Schriften* of the Akademie von Hamburg, vol. I, part II (1845).)

Pp. 1, 2. The lands of Islam border in the east on India; in the west on Asia Minor, the land of the Alans, Aran, Serir, the land of the Khazars, Rūs, Bulgars and Slavs, and a part of the land of the Turks....

The land of the Guz lies between the lands of the Khazars, the Kimāk, the Kharlukh and the Bulgar. Dilem lies between Džordžan as far as Barab and Esbidšab; the land of the Kimāk lies beyond the Kharlukh in the north; the Kharlukh between the Guz, the Khyrghyz and the Slavs (?). The land of the Khyrghyz lies between the Toguz-Guz, the Kimāk, the Ocean and the Kharlukh. Baarai lies between Tübet, the Kharlukh, the Khyrghyz and Čin. Čin lies between the sea, the Toguz-Guz, Tübet and the Slavs, and is two months' journey in extent. The Rūs live between the Bulgars and the Slavs. One Turkish people has separated from the rest, and gone to dwell between the Khazars and the Rūm; they are called Bedžnāk (Petche-negs); they did not dwell here originally, but have attacked these countries and ended by conquering them....

Khazar is the name of a people and not of a country; the latter is called Atel after the river which runs through it and flows into the Sea of Khazar; it lies between the Sea of Khazar, the Rūs, the Guz and Serir.

P. 87. It is said that on the mountain, at the foot of which Bāb-el-Abwāb lies, more than 70 tongues are spoken, so that no tribe understands the other, on account of the differences of tongues.

P. 88. Armenia borders on Asia Minor, Berdaa, the Khazars and Azerbaidžan.

P. 90. The inhabitants of Berdaa and Šamkur are of Armenian origin and are called Siyāwardiyya, Ahl el Abalt (a mixed people), good-for-nothings and bandits.

Pp. 103 ff. Khazar is the name of a land, the capital of which is called Atel; also the river which flows out of the land of the Rūs and the Bulgars is called Atel. The city of Atel consists of two parts, one of which lies on the west side of the river Atel; this is the larger part; the other part lies on the east side.

The king lives in the western part, and is called in their speech Balk, also Bak (= Beg). The length of this portion is about one parasang, and it has walls; the dwelling-places are scattered about and are of felt, only a few are of clay. The city has markets and baths, and many Mahomedans dwell here; there are said to be more than 10,000 of them, and they have some 30 mosques. The palace of the king lies far from the bank of the river, and is built of bricks; there is no other building of brick except this, because the king does not allow anyone to have one. In the walls are four gates which lead to the river and the plain. The king is a Jew; his body-guard is said to amount to some 4000 foot. The Khazars are Mahomedans, Christians, Jews and idolaters; the Jews are the least, the Mahomedans and Christians the most numerous. Only the king and his court are Jews; the common people consist mostly of idolaters, who worship various gods. Their judges follow old laws which are different from those of the Mahomedan, Christian and Jewish religions. The king has an army of 12,000 men. When a soldier dies, another is put in his place. Their pay is but small. The revenues of the king are drawn from customs and tithes on the wares which by their law are levied on all roads to the sea and on the rivers, and on everything consumed by the inhabitants. The king has nine judges among the Jews, Christians, Mahomedans and idolaters; the people apply to these judges, and not to the king, when they go to law. When the judges sit in judgment, a messenger plies between them and the king. The food of the inhabitants consists mainly of rice and fish. The eastern part of the city of the Khazars is inhabited mainly by merchants. The Moslems, the merchants and the villages are independent of the king and have their own armies, troops, etc. The tongue of the Khazars is like no other.

The river Atel rises near the Khyrghyz and flows between the Kimāk and the Guz and forms the frontier between them. Then it turns west to the Bulgars, but again turns east to near the Rūs, flows past the Bulgars, then past Burtās, until it falls into the Sea of Khazar, where it is said to split into more than 70 mouths. The main stream of the river flows through the land of the Khazars, till it falls into the sea. It is said that the water of this river would be greater than the Džaihūn, if it were all united in one channel. The water is so large and strong that it flows out two days' journey into the sea and pushes away the sea water, and being sweet, it freezes in winter. The colour of the sea water is different, too, from that of the river.

In the land of the Khazars is a city called Semender, between Atel and Bāb-el-Abwāb. Here there are some 4000 vineyards. Here many Mahomedans dwell, but their king is a Jew, a relative of the Khazars; they are 2 parasangs distant from the frontier of Serir, and between the two nations is peace. The inhabitants of Serir are Christians. It is said that this Serir [throne] belonged to a king of the Persians, and was of gold, and took many years to make. The inhabitants of Serir and the Mahomedans keep peace with one another, because they fear one another. I know of no other place in the land of the Khazars where men gather together, except Semender.

Burtās is a people bordering immediately on the Khazars; they live in valleys along the Atel, and live scattered. Burtās, Khazar and Serir are names at once of the country and of the prince.

The Khazars are not like the Turks, they have black hair and are of two races; the one are called Karadžuk (black eyes) and are of so dark a brown that they are almost like Indians; the other class are fair of complexion, beautiful and noble. The slaves of the Khazars are idolaters, who sell their children and make slaves of them.

As for their constitution, the greatest among them is called Khazar Khagan, who stands over the king, but is appointed by him. When they want to appoint a Khagan, they go to him and bind his neck with a silken cord; when he is near dying, they ask him: "How long wilt thou be like this king?" He answers "So and so long". If he outlives this time, they kill him. The office of Khagan can only be given to a man of noble family. He can neither command nor forbid, but he is honoured and revered when any comes to him. No magnate can approach him except the king or a man of the royal house, and he only when he has to speak with him. Then the king throws himself on the ground before him, reveres him, and remains far from him until allowed to approach. The Khagan is informed of all important events. Of the Turks and their relatives among the unbelievers none may see him, unless he is converted; no one is like him for majesty and nobility. When he dies and is buried no one may pass his grave without dismounting and doing him honour, and one may only remount when some distance from the grave. Obedience to the king is so absolute that if he wishes to have a noble killed, and does not wish the execution to be public, he orders him to kill himself, whereupon the man goes to his home and kills himself. The nobles who are qualified for the post of Khagan have no power or authority, but when one of them attains the rank, they do homage to him and do not consider his earlier circumstances; but none is raised to this rank who does not hold the Jewish faith. The golden throne and the golden tent belong to the Khagan alone; his family is above that of the king, and his dwellings in the land are taller than those of the king.

Burtās is the name of a district; its inhabitants have wooden houses and live dispersed. They are divided into two tribes; the one lives on the extreme frontier of the Guz, near the Bulgars; they are said to number about 2000 males; no one can take their habitations; they are subject to the Bulgars. The other tribe is next to the Bedžnāk; they and the Bedžnāk are Turks, and neighbours of Rūm. The tongue of the Bulgars is similar to that of the Khazars. The Burtās and Bulgars are Mahomedans. The days among them are said to be so short that one cannot journey there more than half a parasang [a day].

The Rūs are divided into three tribes; the one lives near the Bulgars; their king lives in the city Kuthāba, which is greater than Bulgar. The second tribe is called Saqlāb, the third Uthanie, and their king lives in Artha. Merchants only come to Kuthāba; to Artha none goes, because the inhabitants kill every stranger and throw him into the water. Therefore no one reports on their affairs, and they have no connection with anyone. From Artha black fox furs and lead are exported. The Rūs burn their dead with their belongings, for the good of their souls. They wear short kaftans. Artha lies between the land of the Khazars and Great Bulgaria which borders on Rūm on its north side. These Bulgars are very numerous, and so powerful that they lay tribute on the Rūm who are their neighbours. The Inner Bulgars are Christians....

P. 106. From Atel to Semender 8 days; from Semender to Bāb-el-Abwāb 4 days. From Atel to the first frontier of Burtās 20 days; from one end of Burtās to the other about 15 days. From the first frontier of Burtās to the Bedžnāk 10 stations; from Atel to Bedžnāk 1 month. From Atel to Bulgar through the steppe about 1 month; by water about 2 months up stream and 20 days down. From Bulgar to the first frontier of Rūm about 10 stations; from Bulgar to Kuthāba about 20 stations; from Baǧgīrd to the Inner Bulgars 25 stations.

P. 127. Khwārism is the name of a land....To the north and
west of it live the Guz....In the south of it is a great city called
Džordžania, the greatest city in Khwārism after the capital. It is the
trading depot of the Guz, and from here the caravans go to Khorasan,
to the land of the Khazars and to Džordžan.

IDRĪSĪ ON THE BAŠKIRS[1]

The Seventh Section of the Sixth Climate

This section comprises a part of the Caspian Sea, divers depen-
dencies of the country of Inner Basdjirt, of Outer Basdjirt, and of
what belongs to the country of Asconia, in the north. Most of these
places are composed of continuous deserts and barren wastes. The
villages in them are very few in number, sparse, most miserable, and
communications difficult and dangerous, on account of the constant
quarrels of the inhabitants.

We have already indicated, in the fifth Climate, the limits of Inner
Basdjirt.[2] The population lives on its own resources, and its trade and
industry suffice its needs. These peoples continually attack one
another and raid the surrounding countries for the objects necessary
to them. The country is fertile, the pastures abundant, the herds
numerous. The Basdjirts are divided into two tribes, which inhabit
the extremities of the country of the Guz, not far from that of the
Bulgars. They muster about 2000 soldiers. [They take refuge in
inaccessible mountains and are as brave as they are enterprising.][3]
Their last boundaries touch the country of the Petchenegs, people
which like them are of Turkish race, neighbours of the Rum and for
the most of the time at truce with it.

From Outer Basdjirt to Namdjan, eastward, 10 days' journey....
This city is situated...near a chain of mountains where copper is
mined and exported to Khwārism and the Guz...also furs...which
are sent by water to the Caspian...as are salted fish and hence, along
the sea-shore, to Ītīl....From Namdjan to Ghourdjan, on the
northern Volga, a city belonging to Asconia of the Turks, 8 days....

1 Idrīsī, ed. Jaubert, p. 406.

2 Idrīsī's description of Hungary is given under the sixth Climate, the country
being referred to under that name. In the fifth Climate the "Eastern branch
of the Volga" is described as rising "among the Basdjirt", and a river
named Morgha, north of the Aral Sea, as separating the country of the Basdjirt
and that of the Guz.

3 This sentence is repeated in the author's report on the Petchenegs, but
comparison with Istachrī shows that it is in its proper place here.

From Ghourdjan to Caroukia, down the river, 8 days, or by land, westward, 10 days.

Caroukia is a city composed of wooden houses and felt tents. It is continually exposed to the attacks of the Bulgars, who live 10 days' journey from it and make incessant war on it.

From Caroukia to Outer Basdjirt, 10 days through precipitous mountains, and by narrow and difficult roads.

From Caroukia to Inner Basdjirt, 12 days.

Basdjirt is a country in which the inhabitants are extremely sparse. From the centre of the country called Inner to the centre of the Outer is 11 days.

The habits of the Baškirs are the same as those of the Turkish Bulgars, and like them they wear long kaftans.

IBN FOZLĀN ON THE BAŠKIRS

...We reached the land of a certain Turkish people called Baš-gurd. We went in great fear of them, for they are the worst of the Turks, the most powerful and the boldest in giving battle. If one of them attacks an enemy, he cuts off his head and takes it with him, leaving the body. They shave their beards, and eat lice; they are wont to search among the seams of their tunics most diligently and then to crush the lice between their teeth when they have caught them. There was with us one of them who, having been a Mahomedan, acted as a servant. I saw him once, after squashing with his nail a louse which he had taken from his tunic, pop it into his mouth and roll it on the tip of his tongue. Catching my eye, he exclaimed: "What a delicious morsel!"

Each of them cuts a figure for himself from wood like a phallus and fashions it. Before going on a journey or to meet an enemy, he kisses it and adores it, saying: "O my Lord, grant me this or that". I told the interpreter to ask why they do this, and why they worship it like a god. "From something like this", he answered, "did I issue and I know nothing else which produced me, but this."

There are some among them which think they have twelve lords [= gods] and some think that winter, summer, night, day, death, life and the earth are each ruled by his god; but the god which is in heaven is above them all. So he takes council of them and acts on their advice, and each approves what the other has done. O execrable impiety—may God avert it!

We also saw some among them that worshipped serpents; others fish, others cranes. As regards these, they told me that once they had been put to flight by an enemy, but that he had been attacked in the rear by cranes and forced to flee. Therefore they must pay cranes divine honours, because they put their enemies to flight.

IBN FOZLĀN ON THE VOLGA BULGARS

(From Jāqūt's *Geographical Dictionary*.)

Bulghār with Dumma and Ghayn, the capital city of the Saqālib [Slavs], is situated in the North and is very cold and the snow does not clear away from the ground either in summer or winter and its people seldom see the earth dry. Their houses are built only of wood, and their method is to place one plank [*or* lathe] upon another and to fasten them together by strong pegs also of wood. Fruit and pleasant things are not produced in their land.

Between Itil, the capital city of the Khazars, and the Bulghār by way of the desert (steppes) is about a month's journey and the journey to it by the river Itil takes about two months, and coming down (i.e. down stream) about twenty days. From Bulghār to the boundary of ar-Rum is about ten stages and from it to Kuyaba, the capital of the Russians, is 20 days' journey and from Bulghar to Bashjird is 20 days. The king of Bulghār and his subjects had Islamised in the days of Muqtadir b'Illah, and they sent a messenger to Baghdad to inform Muqtadir of that and ask him to send someone to teach them the prayers and the sacred law of Islam, but I have no information as to the reason why they embraced Islam, and I have read a letter written by Ahmed b. Fudlan, in which he said: "There arrived the letter from Almus b. Shilki Blatawar, king of the Slavs, to the Commander of the Faithful, Muqtadir b'Illah, in which he asked him to send him someone who would instruct him in the faith and teach him the sacred law of Islam, and build a mosque for him and erect a pulpit for him, that from it the call to religion might be proclaimed throughout his country and all regions of his kingdom. He asked him for a builder [who could build him] a fortress in which he could fortify himself against hostile kings. He [Muqtadir] agreed to that, and his ambassador was Nuthayr al-Hazmi.

"I read the letter from the beginning to him and began to deliver the directions contained in it and to introduce the jurists and teachers. The messenger from the Sultan was Susan ar-Rassy, freedman of Nuthayr al-Hazmi. [He said,] Then we journeyed from the City of Peace [i.e. Baghdad] until the 11th night of the month Safar in the year 309.

[Then he said,] "When we were at a distance of a day and a night's journey from the king of the Saqālib, to whom we were going, he sent to meet us the four kings who were under him, and his brothers and his children, and they came to meet us, bringing bread and meat and millet and they travelled with us and when we were a distance of two parasangs from him, he himself came to meet us and when he saw us, he alighted and saluted us, bowing and thanking God. There was money in his sleeve, and he scattered it upon us and erected tents for us and we alighted there. We reached him on Sunday the 12th night of Muharram in the year 310, and the journey from Jūrjāniyya, the capital of Khārizm was seven [? seventy] days, and we remained until Wednesday in the tents which were pitched for us, until the kings of his land and his notables had assembled to listen to the reading of the letter. On Thursday we spread out the two pieces of cloth [or coverings] that were with us and we saddled the horse with a fine saddle and covered it with black and put a turban on it, and I took out the Khalifa's letter and read it, and the king remained standing. Then I read the letter of the Vezir Hamid b. al-Abbas, and he remained standing, though he was a stout man, and his companions scattered dirhems upon us. We brought out gifts and presented them to him, then we bestowed a robe of honour on his wife, who was seated beside him, this being their custom and habit. Then he came to us and we went to his tent, and with him were the kings on his right hand, and he ordered us to sit at his left side, and his children were seated before him and he was alone [or apart] on a throne covered with Grecian brocade. He called for a table of food, and it was brought to him and upon it was roast meat, and the king began, and took a knife and cut a morsel and ate it, and a second and a third; then he cut off a piece and gave it to Susan the envoy, and when he had received it, a small table was brought and placed before him. It is their custom that no one stretches out a hand to the food until the king has given it to him, and when he has received it, a table is brought to him. Then the king cut off a piece and offered it to the kinglet on his right hand and a table was brought to him: Then he gave it to the second kinglet and a table brought to him and so on until there was a table before everyone who was present and each one of us ate from a table which was not shared with anyone, and no one received [or took] anything from anyone else's table. When the meal was finished, everyone of us took what remained on his table to his own dwelling, and when he had finished, he called for wine [or a drink] made of honey, which they call as-Sajū, and he drank and we drank.

"Before our coming he had been prayed for[1] thus: 'O God, bless the king, Blatawar, king of Bulghār" and I said to him, 'God [alone]

---

1 In the prayer before the Friday sermon in the mosque.

is king, and it is not fitting that anyone [else] should be given this
title, especially from the pulpit. Your master, the Commander of the
Faithful, has appointed this to be said for himself in the pulpits in
East and West, "O God, bless Thy bond-servant, and Thy Khalifa
Ja'far, the Imam Muqtadir b'Illah, the Commander of the Faithful"'.

"The king said, 'How ought it to be expressed?' I said, 'Your
name and your father's name should be mentioned'.

"Then he said, 'My father was an unbeliever, and I also do not
like my name to be mentioned, since it is that which was given to me
as an unbeliever, but what is the name of my master the Commander
of the Faithful?' and I said, 'Ja'far'. He said, 'Is it allowable then
that I should be called by his name?' I said, 'Yes'. He said [then],
'I have made my name Ja'far, and the name of my father 'Abd Allah',
and he gave instructions to the preacher to that effect and [from that
time] he used to say in the prayer, 'O God, bless Thy servant Ja'far
b. 'Abd Allah, the Amir of Bulghar, follower [or client] of the
Commander of the Faithful'.

[He said,] "I saw in his country so many wonderful things that
they were beyond count and amongst them, that the first night we
spent in his country, an hour before sunset, I saw the horizon become
deep-red and I heard high-pitched sounds in the firmament and a
roaring noise, and I raised my head and there was a cloud red as fire
close to me and, behold, that roaring noise and the sounds were from
it and within it were [beings] like men and horses, and in the hands
of these phantoms were bows and spears and swords and I saw it
clearly and [? or] imagined it and there appeared another fragment
[of cloud] like it, and I saw in this also, men and weapons and horses
and this fragment set upon the first, as one squadron attacks another.
We were terrified of this and began to humble ourselves before God
and to offer prayers, and the people of the country laughed at us and
were astonished at what we did. We went on looking at the fragment
[of cloud] attacking the other and they were joined together for an
hour, then they separated and the matter continued thus until night
had come, then they vanished. We asked the king about it and he
asserted that his ancestors used to say that these were the believers
among the djinns and the unbelievers who fought with one another
every evening, and that they never failed to do so each night.

"I went into my tent with the king's tailor, who was a Baghdadi,
to talk, and we talked of all the affairs of mankind, for half an hour
and we were expecting the call to evening prayer. When the call
sounded, we went out of the tent and, behold, the dawn had appeared
and I said to the Muezzin, 'To which prayer did you call?' and he
said, 'The dawn', and I said, '[What of] last evening's prayer?' He
said, 'We pray that together with the sunset prayer'. Then I asked
about the night prayer, 'As you see', he said, 'and it [the night] has

been shorter than this and now it has begun to lengthen', and he said that for a month he had not slept at night for fear lest he should miss the early morning prayer. It is the case that if a man puts the pot on the fire at sunset, before it has had time to cook, he prays the morning prayer.[1]

[He said,] "I myself have seen how long the days are with them and how for a period of the year with them, the day is long and the night short, then the night is long and the day is short. The second night after my arrival I saw very few stars, I supposed [something] over 15 scattered about, and the red glow which preceded the sunset had not disappeared at all and the night was so light that one man could recognise another at more than a distance of a bowshot. The moon appears [= rises] in the horizon only for an hour, then dawn breaks and the moon disappears.

[He said,] "The king told me that a distance of three months' journey beyond his country, were a people called Wisu, and the night with them is less than an hour.

[He said,] "I saw, when the sun rose, that all their land was covered with a red glow, everything in it, the ground and the mountains and everything which a man could see, at sunrise, as if it were a great cloud, and the red glow did not cease until it reached the zenith. The people of the land informed me that in winter the night returns to the length of the day and the day returns to the shortness of the night, so that if a man goes out to the river called Itil, which is less than a parasang's distance from us, at daybreak, he does not reach it before night has come and the stars have all risen in the heavens".

I noted that they considered the howling of dogs a lucky omen, and they say that it brings them a fruitful year and blessing and peace. I saw that they had so many snakes that as many as ten, or even more, would be coiled about the branches of a tree, and they do not kill them, nor are they injured by them.

They have apples which are very green and sour and the slave-girls eat them and are poisoned; nothing grows more plentiful than the hazel-nut, and I have seen a grove of them 40 parasangs in breadth. I saw among them a tree of great height, its trunk bare of leaves and its top like the top of a palm-tree, and leaves slender, but [bunched] together. At a certain place in the trunk which they know, they bore a hole, under which they place a vessel and from that hole there flows into it water sweeter than honey and if a man drinks too much of it, it intoxicates him like wine. Their chief food is a kind of millet and horse-flesh, although wheat and barley are plentiful in their country. Whoever sows anything, takes it for himself, the king has no right

1 Between daybreak and sunrise.

over it, except that they owe him from every house an ox-hide and if he orders a troop to raid some country, he shares with them [i.e. in the plunder]. They have no oil except fish-oil, and they use this in the place of olive-oil and sesame-oil and for that reason they were greasy: all of them wear caps [or hats]. When the king rides out, he rides alone without a servant, and no one with him, and when he passes through the market, everyone rises up and takes his hat from his head, and puts it under his arm-pit, and when he has passed them, they put their hats on their heads again. So also does everyone who enters into the king's presence, both small and great, even his own children, and his brothers who, the moment they see him, take off their hats and put them under their arm-pits. Then they make a sign with their heads towards him and sit down, then they stand [again] until he orders them to sit, and everyone who "sits" in his presence settles himself down kneeling and he does not take out his hat, nor let it appear until he goes out from the king's presence and then he puts it on.

Thunderbolts are very frequent in their country, and when a thunderbolt falls into the house of one of them, they do not go near it and they leave it until time extinguishes it and they say that this place is the object of God's anger.

When they see a man who is quick [of perception] and with a knowledge of things, they say, "This man's duty is to serve our Lord", and they take him and put a rope round his neck and hang him on a tree until [his body] falls to pieces.

When they are travelling and one of them wishes to satisfy a natural want, and he does so with his weapon on him, they plunder him and take his weapon and all that is with him, but whoever [in this situation] lays aside his spear and places it at a distance, they do not interfere with him and this is their custom.

Men and women go into the river to wash themselves naked, and do not cover themselves from one another, [yet] they do not commit fornication in any way nor [is this] a cause for it.

If anyone among them commits adultery, whoever it may be, they set up four pegs and fasten his hands and feet to them and cut him in pieces[1] from neck to thigh with an axe, and they do likewise with the woman; then they hang up each portion of him and of her on a tree.

[He said,] "I strove to make the women veil [or cover] themselves from the men, when swimming, but I did not succeed". They put the thief to death as they do the adulterer.

There is much [more] to say of them, [but] we have confined ourselves to this.

1 Or split him.

EXTRACTS FROM cc. 37–40 OF THE
DE ADMINISTRANDO IMPERIO

c. 37: *About the race of the Patzinaks.*

(You must know) that Patzinaks had their habitation in the beginning on the river Atel[1] and likewise on the river Geech,[2] having as their neighbours the Mazars and the so-called Uz.[3] But fifty years ago the said Uz agreeing with the Khazars, and allying themselves in war against the Patzinaks, prevailed, and drove them away from their own country, and the said Uz hold it to this day. But the Patzinaks fleeing, went round seeking a place for their home; and coming on the country over which they rule today and finding the Magyars[4] inhabiting it, conquering them in the turn of battle and driving them out, they chased them away and settled in it, and have been ruling that land, as we said, for 55 years up to today.…

You must know that the Patzinaks are called Kagkar,[5] but not all of them, but the people of the three hordes of Iabdierti and of Kouartzitzur and of Chabouxingula, as being more manly and more noble than the rest; for this is what the surname Kagkar[6] means.

c. 38: *Concerning the genealogy of the race of the Magyars and whence they spring.*

(You must know) that the race of the Magyars had their homes in old times next to Khazaria in the place called Levedia after the surname of their first voivode, which voivode was called Levedias as his own name, but the name of his rank, as also the others under him was called voivode. In this place—the aforesaid Levedia—there is a river, the stream Chidmas, which is also called Chingulous.[7] But they were not known as "Turks" at that time, but for some reason were called Savartoi asphaloi. And the Magyars consisted of seven hordes, but at that time they had no ruler, either native or foreign, but there were certain voivodes among them, of which the principal voivode was the above-mentioned Levedias. And they lived in community with the Khazars[8] for three years, fighting as allies of the Khazars in all their wars. But the Khagan, the ruler of Khazaria, on account of their valour and military assistance, gave the first

---

1 Ἀτήλ, the Volga.　　　　　2 Γεήχ, the Ural.

3 ἔχοντες τούς τε Μαζάρους συνοροῦντας καὶ τοὺς ἐπονομαζομένους Οὔζ.

4 Τούρκους.　　　　　5 Κάγκαρ.

6 ὡς ἀνδρειότεροι καὶ εὐγενέστεροι τῶν λοιπῶν· τοῦτο γὰρ δηλοῖ ἡ τοῦ Κάγκαρ προσηγορία.

7 ποταμός ἐστι ῥέων Χιδμάς, ὁ καὶ Χιγγυλοὺς ἐπονομαζόμενος.

8 συνῴκησαν δὲ μετὰ τῶν Χαζάρων ἐνιαυτοὺς τρεῖς.

voivode of the Magyars, the man called Levedias, a woman as wife,
a noble Khazar, because of the fame of his valour and the lustre of his
race, that he might beget children of her; but that Levedias, by some
chance, had no family of the same Khazar woman. But the Patzinaks
who were formerly called Kangar (for this Kangar-name was used
among them meaning nobility and valour),[1] well, they, taking up
arms against the Khazars and being defeated, were forced to leave
their own country and to inhabit the land of the Magyars. And war
breaking out between the Magyars and the Patzinaks who at that
time were known as Kangar,[2] the army of the Magyars was conquered and divided into two parts; and the one part migrated
eastwards into the parts of Persia, who even now are still called by
the old name of Magyars, Savartoi asphaloi; but the other part
emigrated westward, together with their voivode and commander[3]
Levedias, into the district called Atelkuzu,[4] in which district the
nation of Patzinaks is living today. But after a little time had
passed, that Khagan, the ruler of Khazaria, told the Magyars to send
them by boat[5] their first voivode. So Levedias, coming to the
Khagan of Khazaria, asked him the reason why he had sent for him
to come. But the Khagan said to him, that: we have sent for you for
this reason, that since you are well-born and sage and manful and
the first of the Magyars, that we may promote you to be the ruler[6]
of your race, and that you may be subject to our laws and orders.
But he, answering the Khagan, replied, that I am truly grateful for
your relations and policy towards me, and I express my becoming
thanks, but rather there is another voivode of mine called Almutzes,[7]
and he has got a son called Arpades; it is better that one of these,
either Almutzes or Arpades, should become ruler and be under your
suzerainty. So the Khagan, pleased at this speech, sent his men with
him to the Magyars, who, after conferring about this with the
Magyars,.the Magyars chose Arpád to be their ruler rather than his
father Almutzes, as being more worthy and distinguished in wisdom
and counsel and valour and suitable for such a rule; whom they also
made ruler after the custom and usage[8] of the Khazars, raising him
on their shields. But before this Arpád the Magyars never had any
other ruler; wherefore the ruler of Hungary is drawn from his race

1 οἱ Πατζινακῖται οἱ πρότερον Κάγγαρ ἐπονομαζόμενοι (τοῦτο γὰρ τὸ Κάγγαρ
ὄνομα ἐπ᾽ εὐγενείᾳ καὶ ἀνδρείᾳ ἐλέγετο παρ᾽ αὐτοῖς).
2 τῶν Πατζινακίτων τῶν τηκιναῦτα Κάγγαρ ἐπονομαζομένων.
3 ἀρχηγῷ.   4 Ἀτελκούζου.
5 χελάνδια.   6 ἄρχοντα.
7 The name in the Hungarian Chronicles is Almus; and Professor Moravcsik
tells me that it is probable that Ἀλμούτζης is the correct MS reading in the
Greek, not Σαλμούτζης as hitherto read.
8 ζακάνον.

up to today. But after some time the Patzinaks, falling upon them, chased them away with their ruler Arpád. So the Magyars, turning and seeking a land to live in, came and chased away the inhabitants of Great Moravia, and settled in their land, in which the Magyars are living to this day; and since that time the Magyars have made no war with the Patzinaks....

And up to today the aforesaid Magyars living in the West send their agents to the above-mentioned race of Magyars which settled in the parts of Persia, and have regard to them, and often carry back answers from them to themselves.

(You must know) that the place of the Patzinaks, in which the Magyars were living at that time, is called by the name of the rivers that are there. And the rivers are these: first river that called Varuch [Βαρούχ]; second river that called Kubu [Κουβοῦ]; third river that called Trullos [Τροῦλλος]; fourth river that called Pruth [Βροῦτος]; fifth river that called Sereth [Σέρετος].

c. 39: *About the race of the Kavars* (Καβάρων).

You must know that the so-called Kavars are of the race of the Khazars; and indeed there was a concerted rising against their rule and civil war breaking out, their original Government prevailed; and some of them were slaughtered, and some fled, and came out and settled with the Magyars in the land of the Patzinaks, and they made friends with one another and were called certain Kavars. Whence too they taught the tongue of the Khazars to the Magyars themselves, and up to today they have the same dialect; but they have also the other language of the Magyars. But because they showed themselves more efficient in wars and more manly of the eight hordes [*sic*], and leaders of war, they were elected the first hordes; and there is one leader among them, that is, in the three hordes of Kavars, who exists up to today.

c. 40: *About the hordes of Kavars and Magyars.*

First is that which broke off from the Khazars, this above-mentioned horde of the Kavars, second of Neke [Νέκη], third of Megere [Μεγέρη], fourth of Kourtugermatos [Κουρτυγερμάτου], fifth of Tarianos [Ταριάνου], sixth Genach [Γενάχ], seventh Kare [Καρή], eighth Kase [Κασή]. And so combining with one another, the Kavars with the Magyars settled in the land of the Patzinaks. But after this being summoned by Leo the Christ-loving and respectable Emperor, they crossed and making war on Symeon they trounced him soundly, and driving him before them as far as Preslav they advanced, shutting him up in the fortress called Mundraga, and returned to their own land; and at that time they had Liountinas [*or* Liountis] son of Arpád as their ruler. But after Symeon had again made peace with the Emperor of the Greeks, and got security, he sent to the Patzinaks, and made an agreement with them to make war on and annihilate the Magyars. And when the Magyars went away on a campaign [ταξείδιον] the Patzinaks with Symeon came against the Magyars, and completely annihilated their families, and chased away miserably the Magyars left to guard their land. But the Magyars returning, and finding their country thus desolate and ruined, moved into the country occupied by them today, that which is called, as said above, after the name of the rivers. But the place in which the Magyars formerly lived is called after the name of the river which flows through it, Etel, and Kuzu,¹ in which the Patzinaks are now living, but the Magyars, pursued by the Patzinaks, came and settled in the country in which they are now living. But in that same place there are some old monuments; and first is the bridge of the Emperor Trajan at the beginning of Hungary; and then also Belgrade, three days from the same bridge, in which also is the tower of the great and holy Emperor Constantine; and again towards the issue of the river is that place called Sirmium, being two days' journey from Belgrade; and from there Great Moravia, the Unbaptised, which the Magyars also destroyed, over which Sviatopolk formerly ruled. These are the monuments and names along the Danube; but what is above this, where is the whole settlement of the Magyars,² they now call after the names of the rivers flowing there: first river the Temes [Τιμήσης]; second river Tut [? Τούτης]; third river the Mures [Μορήσης]; fourth the Körös [Κρίσος]; and again another river the Theiss [Τίτζα]. And neighbours of the Magyars are on the east the Bulgars, where also the Danube separates them; and to the north the Patzinaks; and to the west the Franks; and to the south the Croats. But these eight hordes of the Magyars do not obey their own separate princes, but they hold councils of war on the rivers, to which part war calls on them to fight together with all wisdom and zeal. But they have as their first head [κεφαλήν] the ruler from the house of Arpád in succession, and two others, the Gylas [Γυλᾶς] and the Karchas [Καρχᾶς] who have the office of judge; and each horde has a ruler.

You must know that the Gylas and the Karchas are not proper names, but offices.

You must know that Arpád the great ruler of Hungary had four sons, first Tarkatzus [Ταρκατζοῦν], second Ielech ['Ιελέχ], third Iutotzas ['Ιουτοτζάν], fourth Zaltan [Ζαλτάν].

You must know that Tarkatzus, the first son of Arpád, had a son

---

1 ὀνομάζεται κατὰ τὴν ἐπωνυμίαν τοῦ ἐκεῖσε διερχομένου ποταμοῦ Ἐτὲλ, καὶ Κουζοῦ.

2 τὰ δὲ ἀνώτερα τούτων, ἐν ᾧ ἐστὶν ἡ πᾶσα τῆς Τουρκίας κατασκήνωσις.

Teveles [Τεβέλη]; and the second son Ielech had a son Iezelech [Ἰεζελέχ]; and the third son Iutotzas had a son Phalitzis [Φαλίτζιν], the present ruler; and the fourth son Zaltan has a son Taxis [Τάξιν].

You must know that all the sons of Arpád are dead; but their sons Phales [Φαλῆς] and Tases [Τασῆς] and their cousin Taxis are alive. You must know that Teveles is dead, and a son of his is Termatzus [Τερματζοῦς], who recently came on an embassy with Bultzus [Βουλτζοῦ], the third ruler and Karchas of Hungary.

You must know that Bultzus the Karchas is the son of Kale [Καλή] the Karchas; and that Kale is a proper name, but Karchas is a title, like Gylas, which is greater than Karchas.

INDEX OF SOURCES

References to the Appendix are printed in italics.

INDEX OF NAMES, PLACES
AND SUBJECTS

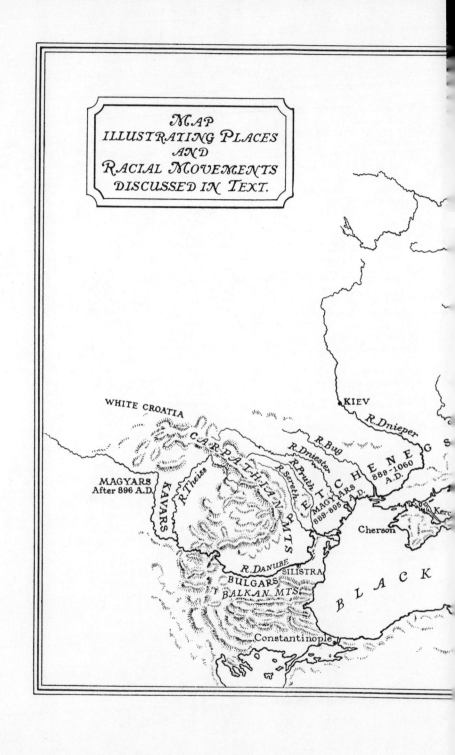

MAP
ILLUSTRATING PLACES
AND
RACIAL MOVEMENTS
DISCUSSED IN TEXT.